BOARD AND TABLE GAMES

Tile from Sumerian gaming board *c*. 3000 B.C.

BOARD AND TABLE GAMES

FROM MANY CIVILIZATIONS

R. C. BELL, M.B., F.R.C.S.

Drawings by Rosalind H. Leadley
Photographs by Kenneth Watson
Diagrams by the author

LONDON
OXFORD UNIVERSITY PRESS
NEW YORK TORONTO
1960

OXFORD UNIVERSITY PRESS

AMEN HOUSE, LONDON E.C.4

*Glasgow New York Toronto Melbourne
Wellington Bombay Calcutta Madras
Karachi Kuala Lumpur Cape Town
Ibadan Nairobi Accra*

PRINTED IN GREAT BRITAIN

INTRODUCTION

This book has been written to introduce some of the best board and table games from the world's treasury to the reader. They have been arranged in six chapters:

RACE GAMES
WAR GAMES
POSITIONAL GAMES
MANCALA GAMES
DICE GAMES
DOMINO GAMES

Chapter 7 describes methods of making boards and pieces, and the Appendix contains ten biographies.

The games starred (*) in the table of contents have not been described in English before. Most of the remaining material is only to be found in reports of museums and learned societies, foreign articles and books long out of print. A short glossary of technical terms is given on p. vii; and to save space the bibliography also serves as a table of contents. Whenever possible the games have been described under English titles. The reader is advised to omit the lists of rules on a first reading; later any game that interests him can be studied in more detail.

Boards used for one game were sometimes taken for another; the chequered chess board was used for draughts (both war games), shaturanga (a war game) was played on the ashtapada board (a race game), and the board for fox and geese (a war game) was used for solitaire (a game of position). Such adaptations make game-reconstructions from antique fragments of doubtful value: because the x people of Upper Ruritania used a board for a particular game, it does not follow that the y people of lower Ruritania used the same board for the same game; nevertheless it is reasonable to assume that they may have done so until contrary evidence appears.

Books on card games are readily available and, therefore, they have not been included; international chess has been omitted for the same reason. Ninety-one games are described and the oldest was played some 5,000 years ago. May every reader find pleasure in these pages!

A companion volume is planned, and games or information from readers will be most welcome and should be sent to the author, c/o the Oxford University Press. The source of any material included will be fully acknowledged.

ACKNOWLEDGEMENTS

The author is indebted to the writers of all the publications in the bibliography, but there is an especial debt to the works of H. J. R. Murray, Stewart Culin and Willard Fiske. It is a pleasure to thank Dr. W. S. Mitchell, the Librarian of King's College Library, Newcastle-upon-Tyne, and his staff, for their unstinting help in procuring books and articles; Mr. Raymond S. Dawson for obtaining material during a recent visit to Peking and for help with Chinese writings; Mr. M. Caturani for help with Italian and Spanish; Miss Agnes Kramer for help with German; Miss K. Kasbekar for her account of Tablan; Mr. S. Afoakwa for help with Wari; Mr. A. P. Mohideen for Chinese Games; and Professor Eric Thompson for assistance with Mayan and Aztec games.

Prof. F. E. Hopper and Prof. H. D. Dickinson read the manuscript at an early stage and made valuable suggestions; Mrs. Norma Trelease prepared the typescript; the staff of the Oxford University Press have been most painstaking and helpful throughout the stages of publication; and last but not least, I wish to thank my wife who has shared her house for several years with numerous boards and pieces.

GLOSSARY

COLUMN	See diagram below.
CROWNHEAD	Spaces on which a piece becomes promoted to a king.
CUSTODIAN CAPTURE	Capture by trapping an enemy piece between two of one's own.
DIAGONAL MOVE	The piece moves diagonally across the board.
DIE	The singular of dice.
EN PRISE	A piece is en prise when it is liable to capture at the opponent's next move.
FILE	See diagram below.
HUFF	Confiscation of a piece which has infringed a rule.
LONG DIE	A four-sided die.
LONG LEAP	A jump by a piece over another piece to land beyond, but vacant squares may intervene on either side of the captured piece.
ORTHOGONAL MOVES	The piece moves along a rank or file.
RANK	See diagram below.
REPLACEMENT	A capture made by a piece moving on to a space occupied by an enemy piece and removing it from the board.
ROW	See diagram below.
SHORT LEAP	A capture made by a piece jumping over an enemy piece on an adjacent space to land on the space immediately beyond.

CONTENTS AND BIBLIOGRAPHY

PAGE

INTRODUCTION   v

ACKNOWLEDGEMENTS   vi

GLOSSARY   vii

ILLUSTRATIONS   xx

GAME   REFERENCES

Chapter One: RACE GAMES

1. CROSS AND CIRCLE RACE GAMES

NYOUT   Culin, S. *Korean Games.* Philadelphia   1
1895, pp. 66–73.
Ruiz, Alberto. *Anales del Instituto Nacional de Antropologia e Historia.* Mexico 1952, Vol. 5, p. 27.
Ruppert, K. *The Mercado Chichen Itza.* Yucatan. Carnegie Inst. Washington Pub. 546, Contribution No. 43, 1943, fig. 4c.
Thompson, Eric. Personal communication 1956. I am indebted to him for drawing my attention to the last two articles and also for the estimation of the age of the board at Palenque.

ZOHN AHL   Culin, S. *Chess and Playing Cards.*   4
Washington 1898, p. 686.

PATOLLI   Taylor, E. B. 'On the Game of Patolli   6
in Ancient Mexico, and its probable Asiatic Origin.' *Anthropology,* London 1881, p. 116.

PACHISI   Falkener, E. *Games Ancient and Orien-*   9
tal. London 1892, p. 257.
Culin, S. *Chess and Playing Cards.* Washington 1898, p. 851.

LUDO   12

2. SPIRAL RACE GAMES

THE HYENA GAME   Davies, R. 'Some Arab Games and   12
Riddles.' *Sudan Notes and Records* viii, 1925, p. 145.

THE ROYAL GAME OF GOOSE   Strutt, J. *The Sports and Pastimes of*   14
the People of England. 3rd edn. 1845, p. 336.

GAME	REFERENCES	PAGE
THE ROYAL GAME OF GOOSE (*cont.*)	Whitehouse, F. R. B. *Table Games of Georgian and Victorian Days.* 1951, p. 57.	

3. SQUARE BOARD RACE GAMES

*THAAYAM	Dr. Thillai-nayagam. Personal communication 1956.	17

4. PEG SCORING BOARDS

THE PALM TREE GAME	Lord Carnarvon and Carter, H. *Five Years' Excavation at Thebes* quoted by Peet, T. E. *Universal History of the World*, ed. Hammerton, p. 562. Gadd, C. J. 'An Egyptian game in Assyria.' *Iraq* 1. 1934, p. viiib and p. 46. *Illustrated London News*, 23 October 1937, p. 709.	20

5. THE BACKGAMMON GROUP

THE SUMERIAN GAME	Woolley, Sir Leonard. *Ur, The First Phase*, London (Penguin) 1946.	23
THE GAME OF THIRTY SQUARES	Ridgeway, W. *Journal of Hellenic Studies.* 1896, Vol. XVI, p. 288. Towry-White, E. 'Types of Ancient Egyptian Draughtsmen.' *Proceedings of the Society of Biblical Archaeology*, Vol. XXIV. 1902, p. 261. Nash, W. I. 'Ancient Egyptian Draughtsboards and Draughtsmen.' *Proceedings of the Society of Biblical Archaeology*, Vol. XXIV. 1902, p. 341. Murray, H. J. R. *History of Board Games other than Chess.* Oxford 1952, p. 12.	26
LUDUS DUODECIM SCRIPTORUM	Austin, R. G. 'Roman Board Games. I' in *Greece and Rome*, Vol. IV (1934), p. 30.	30
TABULA	Emery, Walter B. *Nubian Treasure.* London 1948, p. 46 and Pl. 32. Austin, R. G. 'Roman Board Games. II' in *Greece and Rome* IV (1934–5), p. 76. Austin, R. G. 'Zeno's Game of Table.' *Journal of Hellenic Studies* 1934. Vol. LIV, p. 202.	34

GAME	REFERENCES	PAGE
TABULA (*cont.*)	Austin, R. G. *Archaeologia Cambrensis.* 1938, p. 250. Lanciani, R. 'Gambling and Cheating in Ancient Rome.' *North American Review.* 1892, pp. 97–105. Gusman, P. *Pompei. The City, Its Life and Art.* London 1900, p. 220. Murray, H. J. R. *History of Board Games other than Chess.* Oxford 1952, p. 29.	
CHASING THE GIRLS	Fiske, W. *Chess in Iceland.* Florence 1905, pp. 89, 353.	37
TOURNE–CASE	Fiske, W. *Chess in Iceland.* Florence 1905, p. 183.	38
SIXE–ACE	Fiske, W. *Chess in Iceland.* Florence 1905, pp. 88, 356. Cotton, C. 'The Compleat Gamester' (p. 78) in *Games and Gamesters of the Reformation.* London 1930.	39
FAYLES	Fiske, W. *Chess in Iceland.* Florence 1905, pp. 167, 295.	41
BACKGAMMON	Fiske, W. *Chess in Iceland.* Florence 1905, pp. 173–294. Richard, W. L. *Complete Backgammon.* 1st Eng. edn. London 1938. Murray, H. J. R. *History of Chess.* Oxford 1913, footnote p. 120.	42

Chapter Two: WAR GAMES

1. THE ALQUERQUE GROUP

ALQUERQUE	Parker, H. *Ancient Ceylon.* London 1909, pp. 579, 644. Fiske, W. *Chess in Iceland.* Footnote p. 255.	48
THE STONE WARRIORS	Culin, S. *Games of the North American Indians.* Washington 1907, p. 799.	48
FIGHTING SERPENTS	Culin, S. *Games of the North American Indians.* Washington 1907, p. 801.	50
THE SIXTEEN SOLDIERS	Parker, H. *Ancient Ceylon.* London 1909, p. 583.	51

2. THE CHESS GROUP

SHATURANGA	Forbes, D. *History of Chess.* 1860. Murray, H. J. R. *History of Chess.* Oxford 1913, pp. 55–77.	51

GAME	REFERENCES	PAGE
SHATRANJ	Murray, H. J. R. *History of Chess.* Oxford 1913, pp. 220–338.	57
CIRCULAR OR BYZANTINE CHESS	Strutt, J. *Sports and Pastimes of the People of England.* 1845 ed. p. 311. Murray, H. J. R. *History of Chess.* Oxford 1913, pp. 177 and 342.	62
THE COURIER GAME	Murray, H. J. R. *History of Chess.* Oxford 1913, p. 482. McBride, H. A. 'Masterpieces on Tour.' *National Geographical Magazine.* December 1948.	62
MODERN INTERNATIONAL CHESS	. . . . .	65
THE MAHARAJAH AND THE SEPOYS	Falkener, E. *Games Ancient and Oriental.* 1892, pp. 217–24.	65
CHINESE CHESS	Hyde, T. *Historia Shahiludii.* Oxford 1694, p. 158. Culin, S. *Korean Games.* Philadelphia 1895, p. 82. Murray, H. J. R. *History of Chess.* 1913, p. 119.	66
*THE JUNGLE GAME	I am indebted to Mr. A. P. Mohideen who sent this game to me from Hong Kong, and to Mr. R. Dawson, Department of Oriental Studies, Durham University, for the translation of the Chinese instruction sheet.	68
TIBETAN CHESS	. . . .	70
3. DRAUGHTS		
ENGLISH DRAUGHTS	Murray, H. J. R. *History of Board Games other than Chess.* Oxford 1952, p. 72. La Roux, M. *The Complete Draughts Player.* London 1955, pp. 7–16.	71
THE LOSING GAME	. . . . .	72
DIAGONAL DRAUGHTS	. . . . .	73
ITALIAN DRAUGHTS	Murray, H. J. R. *History of Board Games other than Chess.* Oxford 1952, p. 78, quoting Mallet, P. *Le Jeu des Dames.* Paris 1668.	73
TURKISH DRAUGHTS	Falkener, E. *Games Ancient and Oriental.* 1892, p. 237.	73

GAME	REFERENCES	PAGE
REVERSI	*Hoyle's Games Modernised.* London 1923, p. 447.	74
CONTINENTAL OR POLISH DRAUGHTS	*Hoyle's Games.* London 1853, pp. 404–421.	75

4. THE TAFL GROUP

FOX AND GEESE	Fiske, W. *Chess in Iceland.* Florence 1905, p. 146. Redstone, V. B. 'England among the Wars of the Roses' in *Trans. R. Hist. Soc.* n.s. XXI. 1902, p. 195.	76
TABLUT	Linneus, C. *Lachesis Lapponica.* London 1811, ii. 55.	77
SAXON HNEFATAFL	Armitage, R. J. *Time of St. Dunstan.* Oxford 1923, p. 69. Murray, H. J. R. *History of Board Games other than Chess.* Oxford 1952, pp. 55–64.	79
COWS AND LEOPARDS	Parker, H. *Ancient Ceylon.* London 1909, p. 581.	81

5. THE LATRUNCULORUM GROUP

SEEGA	Lane, E. W. *Modern Egyptians.* 1890, p. 320. Petrie, F. *Objects of Daily Use.* British School of Archaeology in Egypt, 1927, p. 56.	82
HIGH JUMP	Marin, G. 'Somali Games.' *Journal of the Royal Anthropological Institute*, LXI. 1931, p. 506.	84
LUDUS LATRUNCULORUM	Varro, M. T. *De Lingula Latina*, vii. 52. Ovid, P. O. N. *Ars Amatoria*, ii. 208; iii. 358. Bassus, S. *Laus Pisonis* in the first part of the fourth volume of Wernsdorf's *Poetae Latinae Minores*, p. 236, v. 192. (These three authors are quoted by Austin, R. G. 'Roman Board Games', *Greece and Rome* IV (1934–5), p. 24.)	84

6. RUNNING-FIGHT GAMES

*TABLAN	Dr. K. V. Kasbekar. Personal communication. The board in fig. 143 has belonged to her family for at least fifty years and is probably much older than this.	87

GAME	REFERENCES	PAGE
*PULUC	Sapper, von K. *Boas Anniversary Vol.*, article 190, p. 238. (I am indebted to Professor E. Thompson for drawing my attention to this article and to Miss Kramer for her translation.)	89

Chapter Three: GAMES OF POSITION

1. MORRIS GAMES

GAME	REFERENCES	PAGE
NOUGHTS AND CROSSES	White, A. B. *British Chess Mag.* 1919, p. 217.	91
THREE MEN'S MORRIS	Ovid, P. O. N. *Ars Amatoria*, iii. 365–6. Hyde, T. *De Historia Nerdiludii.* Oxford 1694, p. 211. Fiske, W. *Chess in Iceland.* 1905, pp. 122–38. Murray, H. J. R. *History of Board Games other than Chess.* 1952, p. 37.	91
SIX MEN'S MORRIS	Murray, H. J. R. *History of Board Games other than Chess.* 1952, p. 43.	92
NINE MEN'S MORRIS	Parker, H. *Ancient Ceylon.* 1909, p. 507. Macalister, R. A. S. *Archaeology of Ireland.* 1928, p. 123. Sjovold, T. *The Viking Ships.* Oslo 1954, p. 7. Fiske, W. *Chess in Iceland.* 1905, p. 105.	93

2. THREE-IN-A-ROW GAMES

GAME	REFERENCES	PAGE
DARA	Fitzgerald, R. T. D. 'The Dakarkari People of Sokito Province, Nigeria. Notes on their material Culture.' *Man*, XLII. 1942, p. 26.	95

3. FIVE-IN-A-ROW GAMES

GAME	REFERENCES	PAGE
GO-BANG	Volpicelli, Z. 'Wei-Chi.' *Journal of China Branch, Royal Asiatic Society.* n.s. 26. 1894, p. 80.	96
HASAMI SHOGI	Harbin, E. O. *Games of Many Nations.* Abingdon Press, New York, Nashville 1955, p. 107.	97

4. REPLACEMENT GAMES

GAME	REFERENCES	PAGE
FIVE FIELD KONO	Culin, S. *Korean Games.* Philadelphia 1895, p. 102.	98
HALMA	Hedges, S. G. *The Home Entertainer.* Odhams Press (undated), p. 76.	98

GAME	REFERENCES	PAGE

5. TERRITORIAL POSSESSION

WEI-CH'I   Volpicelli, Z. 'Wei-chi.' *Journal of*   99
China Branch, Royal Asiatic Society.
n.s. 26. 1894, p. 80.
Culin, S. *Korean Games.* Philadelphia
1895, p. 91.
Falkener, E. *Games Ancient and*
Oriental. 1892, p. 239.
Pecorini, D. and Tong Shu. *The*
Game of Wei-chi. Longmans 1929.
Cheshire, F. *Goh or Wei-chi.* Hastings
1911.

6. PATIENCE GAMES

SOLITAIRE   Hedges, S. G. *The Home Enter-*   109
tainer. Odhams (undated), p. 79.

Chapter Four: MANCALA GAMES

1. TWO-RANK MANCALA

MANKALA'H   Lane, E. W. *An Account of the Manners*   111
and Customs of the Modern Egyptians.
Reprint from the 3rd edition of 1842.
Minerva Library 1890, p. 315.
Petrie, F. *Objects of Daily Use*, British
School of Archaeology in Egypt,
1927, p. 55.
Parker, H. *Ancient Ceylon.* London
1909, pp. 224, 594.

PALLANGULI   Mohandas, S. Personal communica-   113
tion 1957.
Durai, H. G. 'Pallanguli', *Man*, November 1928, p. 185.

WARI   Afoakwa, S. Personal communica-   114
tion 1957.
Bennett, G. T. in *Religion and Art*
in Ashanti by R. S. Rattray. Oxford
1927, pp. 382–98.
Jobson, R. *The Golden Trade.* 1623,
reprint 1904, p. 48.
Herskovits, M. J. 'Wari in the New
World.' *Journal of the Royal Anthro-*
pological Institute. Vol. XLII. 1923,
pp. 23–37.

GAME   REFERENCES   PAGE
2. FOUR-RANK MANCALA
CHISOLO   Smith, E. W. and Dale, A. M. *The*   121
                 Ila-speaking Peoples of Northern
                 Rhodesia. London 1920, Vol. 2, pp.
                 232–37.
                 Chaplin, J. H. 'A note on Mancala
                 Games in Northern Rhodesia.' *Man*,
                 Vol. LVI. 1956, p. 168.

            Chapter Five: DICE GAMES

DICE   Culin, S. *Chinese Games with Dice and*   123
                 Dominoes. Washington 1895, p. 535.
                 Tacitus, C. *Germania A.D. 99.* Cap.
                 XXIV.
                 Fiske, D. W. *Chess in Iceland.* 1905,
                 footnote p. 249.
                 Sturluson, S. *Heimskringla*, translated
                 by S. Laing. 2nd edn. London 1889,
                 iii. pp. 1–2. (Quoted by D. W. Fiske.)
                 Wright, T. *History of Domestic Manners*
                 and Sentiments in England during
                 the Middle Ages. London 1862.
                 Lanciani, R. 'Gambling and Cheating
                 in Ancient Rome.' *North American*
                 Review. 1892, p. 97.

      1. GAMES WITH TWO-SIDED DICE
HEADS AND TAILS Strutt, J. *Sports and Pastimes of the*   125
                 People of England. London 1845
                 ed., p. 337.

THE BOWL GAME   Brown, Mrs. N. W. 'Some Indoor   125
                 and Outdoor Games of the Wabanak
                 Indians.' *Trans. Roy. Soc. Canada.*
                 Sec. II. 1883, p. 41. (Quoted by S.
                 Culin, *Chess and Playing Cards.*
                 Report Nat. Museum. 1896, p. 707.)

      2. GAMES WITH SIX-SIDED DICE
THIRTY-SIX   Scarne, J. *Scarne on Dice.* 1946, p. 381.   127
PIG   Scarne, J. *Scarne on Dice.* 1946, p. 178.   128
ACES IN THE POT Wood and Goddard. *The Complete*   128
                 Book of Games. 1940, p. 351.
BARBUDI   Scarne, J. *Scarne on Dice.* 1946, p. 367.   128
HAZARD   Hoyle, E. *Hoyle's Games Improved.*   130
                 Edited by C. Jones. 1786, pp. 252–
                 255.

GAME	REFERENCES	PAGE
HAZARD (*cont.*)	Cotton, C. *Compleat Gamester.* 1674. Reprinted in the English Library 1930 as *Games and Gamesters of the Restoration*, p. 82. Ashton, J. *The History of Gambling in England.* London 1898. Quinn, J. P. *Fools of Fortune.* 1890.	
BUCK DICE	Scarne, J. *Scarne on Dice.* 1946, p. 371.	134
MARTINETTI	Scarne, J. *Scarne on Dice.* 1946, p. 388.	134
DROP DEAD	Scarne, J. *Scarne on Dice.* 1946, p. 374.	135
INDIAN DICE	Scarne, J. *Scarne on Dice.* 1946, p. 369.	135
SHIP, CAPTAIN, MATE AND CREW	Scarne, J. *Scarne on Dice.* 1946, p. 390.	136
SEQUENCES	Wood and Goddard. *The Complete Book of Games.* 1940, p. 363.	136
TWENTY-SIX	Scarne, J. *Scarne on Dice.* 1946, p. 356.	137
ACES	Scarne, J. *Scarne on Dice.* 1946, p. 384.	137

3. GAMES WITH SPECIAL DICE

BELL AND HAMMER	Card of Instructions in a Bell and Hammer Set in the author's possession, *c.* 1850, maker unknown. Rogers, A. Personal communication 1958.	138
CROWN AND ANCHOR	King, T. *Twenty-one Games of Chance.* Foulsham, London (undated), p. 54.	140
LIAR DICE	(A form played at Oxford University) Ogbourn, Miss L. A. Personal communication.	141

4. CHINESE DICE GAMES

STRUNG FLOWERS	Culin, S. *Chinese Games with Dice and Dominoes.* Washington 1895, p. 493.	143
THROWING HEAVEN AND NINE	Culin, S, *Chinese Games with Dice and Dominoes.* Washington 1895, p. 494.	144
PUT AND TAKE	Traditional form (Durham miners).	146

Chapter Six: DOMINO GAMES

FISHING	Culin, S. *Chinese Games with Dice and Dominoes.* Washington 1895, pp. 508–18.	148
DISPUTING TENS	Culin, S. *Korean Games.* Philadelphia 1895, p. 117.	149

b

GAME	REFERENCES	PAGE
COLLECTING TENS	Culin, S. *Korean Games.* Philadelphia 1895, p. 118.	150
MA-JONG	Culin, S. *Chinese Games with Dice and Dominoes.* Washington 1895, pp. 518–21. 'East Wind'. *Mah Jongg.* London 1923. Harr, L. L. *How to Play Pung Chow.* New York 1923. Bray, J. *How to Play Mah Jong.* New York 1923. Racster, O. *Mah-jongg.* London 1924. Anonymous. *The Standard Rules of Mah-jongg.* Chad Valley Co. 1924. Reeve, E. G. *Advanced Mah Jongg.* London 1924. Ranger, L. *Directions for playing Ma jong.* Shanghai (undated). Higginson, C. M. W. *Mah Jongg, How to play and score* (undated).	151
EUROPEAN DOMINOES	Strutt, J. *Sports and Pastimes of the People of England.* 3rd edn., 1845, p. 322.	160
THE BLOCK GAME	Hedges, S. G. *The Home Entertainer.* Odhams (undated), p. 87.	161
THE BERGEN GAME	Dawson, L. H. *Hoyle's Games Modernised.* 1923, p. 469.	162
FORTY-TWO	Morehead, A. H. *The Modern Hoyle.* Winston 1944, p. 255. Harbin, E. O. *The Fun Encyclopaedia.* 1940, p. 36.	163
BINGO	Dawson, L. H. *Hoyle's Games Modernised.* 1923, p. 470.	163
DOMINO CRIB	As played in the Officers' Mess, R.C.A.F. Station, Topcliffe, Yorks., 1945.	165
THE MATADOR GAME	Dawson, L. H. *Hoyle's Games Modernised.* 1923, p. 467.	168
CYPRUS	Anonymous Pamphlet published by the Embossing Co., Albany, New York, U.S.A. (undated).	169
TIDDLE-A-WINK	Anonymous Pamphlet published by the Embossing Co., Albany, New York, U.S.A. (undated).	170

PAGE

Chapter Seven: MAKING BOARDS AND PIECES 171

Appendix: BIOGRAPHIES

AUTHOR	REFERENCES	
AS–SULI	Murray, H. J. R. *History of Chess.* Oxford 1913, p. 199.	177
CHARLES COTTON	*Dictionary of National Biography.* Vol. IV, p. 1223. Beresford, J. *Poems of Charles Cotton 1630–1687.* London 1923, Preface. Walton, I. and Cotton, C. *The Complete Angler.* London 1823 edn.	179
THOMAS HYDE	*Dictionary of National Biography.* London 1908, Vol. X, p. 403.	182
EDMOND HOYLE	*Dictionary of National Biography.* London 1908, Vol. X, p. 133. Pole, W. *The Evolution of Whist.* 1895, pp. 35–69.	185
JOSEPH STRUTT	*Dictionary of National Biography.* 1909, Vol. XIX, p. 65.	187
DUNCAN FORBES	*Dictionary of National Biography.* 1908, Vol. VII, p. 386.	189
EDWARD FALKENER	*Dictionary of National Biography.* Supplement Vol. XXII, p. 624.	191
STEWART CULIN	*Who Was Who in America 1847–1942.* Marquis, Chicago. Dorsey, G. A., *The American Magazine.* June 1913. Wechsler, M. Dept. Primitive Art, Brooklyn Museum, New York. Personal communication.	192
WILLARD FISKE	*Dictionary of American Biography.* Vol. VI, p. 417. White, H. S. *Willard Fiske, Life and Correspondence.* 3 vols. Oxford 1925. Fiske, W. *Chess in Iceland.* Florence 1905.	194
H. J. R. MURRAY	Obituary in *British Chess Magazine,* August 1955. Miss K. M. E. Murray, Personal communication	196
CONCLUSION		199
INDEX		201

LIST OF ILLUSTRATIONS

Tile from Sumerian gaming board   *Frontispiece*
Diagram of row and column   vii

Chapter One: RACE GAMES

Figure   1. Nyout   1
  2. Nyout ring and pam-nyout   1
  3. Mayan game from Palenque   3
  4. Mayan game from Chichen Itza   3
  5. Zohn Ahl   4
  6. Dicing sticks for Zohn Ahl   5
  7. Patolli cross, counters and beans   6
  8. Pachisi cloth   10
  9. Pachisi pieces, dice and shells   10
 10. Ludo   12
 11. Hyena   13
Plate I. Royal and pleasant game of Goose   *facing p.* 14
  IIa. Shaturanga   *facing p.* 15
  IIb. Indian chess   *facing p.* 15
Figure 12. Thaayam   17
 13. Board from Thebes   20
 14. Board from Megiddo   20
 15. Board from Ur   22
 16. Cribbage   22
 17. Board from Royal Tombs of Ur   23
 18. Diagram of Movement in Sumerian game   24
 19. Senat   25
 20. Game of Thirty Squares   26
 21. Board from Ak-hor   27
 22. Wall drawing from Benihassan   27
 23. Board from Qustul   29
 24. Fritillus   29
 25. Silver mirror-back   30
 26. Ludus Duodecim Scriptorum board from Holt   31
 27. Ludus Duodecim Scriptorum boards from Italy   32
 28. Wall-painting of gamblers with dice (Pompeii)   33
 29. Wall-painting of a fight (Pompeii)   33
 30. Zeno's game of Tabula   34

31. Chasing the Girls   37
32. Tourne-case   39
33. Sixe-Ace (two players)   40
34. Sixe-Ace (four players)   40
35. Fayles   41
36. Medieval Tables   42
37. Backgammon   44
Tailpiece: Antique Chinese Tableman in filigree ivory   46

Chapter Two: WAR GAMES

38. Alquerque board (Ancient Egypt)   47
39. Alquerque   47
40. Stone Warriors   49
41. Fighting Serpents   50
42. Sixteen Soldiers   50
43. Ashtapada board   51
44. Moves in Shaturanga   52
45. Shaturanga   53
46. Concourse of shipping   55
47. Muslim chessmen   58
48. Shatranj   59
49. Circular or Byzantine chess   61
50. Courier chessmen   62
51. Courier chess positions   62
Plate III.   'The Chess Players' (Van Leyden)   *facing p.* 64
Pl.IV,Fig.52. Blind player's chess set   *facing p.* 65
Figure 53.   Maharajah and the Sepoys   65
54. Chinese chess board   66
55. Chinese chess pieces   67
56. Jungle game   69
57. English draughts   72
58. Draughtsmen   72
59. Diagonal draughts   73
60. Turkish draughts   74
61. Polish draughts   74
62. Fox and thirteen Geese   76
63. Fox and seventeen Geese   76
64. Tablut   77
65. Tablut pieces and custodian capture   78
66. Board from Wimose   79
67. Hnefatafl pieces   80
68. Hnefatafl   80
Plate V.   Hnefatafl in a tenth-century manuscript *facing p.* 80
Plate VI.   Two consecutive pages from *De Ludis*
              Orientalibus   *facing p.* 81

Figure 69. Cows and Leopards   81
        70. Seega   82
        71. Multiple custodian capture   83
        72. High Jump   83
        73. Stone Ludus Latrunculorum board   85
        74. Tablan   88
        75. Puluc   89
Tailpiece: Green king of a Tibetan chess set   90

Chapter Three: GAMES OF POSITION

        76. Noughts and Crosses   91
        77. Three Men's Morris   92
        78. Three Men's Morris (another form)   92
        79. Six Men's Morris   93
        80. Nine Men's Morris   93
        81. Board from the Gokstad ship   94
        82. Dara   95
        83. Go-bang   96
        84. Hasami Shogi   97
        85. Custodian capture in Hasami Shogi   97
        86. Five Field Kono   98
        87. Halma   99
        88. Wei-ch'i board   100
        89. Wei-ch'i: Notation   101
        90. Wei-ch'i: Single captures   101
        91. Wei-ch'i: Multiple captures   101
        92. Wei-ch'i: Safe formation   102
        93. Wei-ch'i: Safe formation   102
        94. Wei-ch'i: Unsafe formation   102
        95. Wei-ch'i: Unsafe formation   102
        96. Wei-ch'i: Safe formation   103
        97. Wei-ch'i: Safe formation   103
        98. Wei-ch'i: Impasse   104
        99. Wei-ch'i: Perpetual attack   104
       100. Wei-ch'i: Fences   106
       101. Wei-ch'i: End position   107
       102. Wei-ch'i: Handicaps   108
       103. Solitaire   109
Tailpiece: Wooden Wei-ch'i bowl filled with tze   110

Chapter Four: MANCALA GAMES

       104. Mankala'h   111

105. Mancala, Ancient Egypt　　　　111
106. Wari　　　　115
107. Awari　　　　120
108. Chisolo　　　　121
Tailpiece: Antique Pallanguli board (redrawn from Durai)　　　　122

Chapter Five: DICE GAMES

109. Etruscan dice　　　　123
110. Grotesque dice　　　　124
111. All-tes teg-enuk bowl　　　　126
112. All-tes teg-enuk tallies and dice　　　　126
113. Martinetti　　　　134
114. Bell and Hammer cards　　　　138
115. Crown and Anchor dice　　　　140
116. Exploded Crown and Anchor die　　　　140
117. Crown and Anchor board　　　　140
118. Poker dice　　　　141
119. Exploded Poker die　　　　141
120. Strung Flowers: Six Triple Throws　　　　143
121. Strung Flowers: Sequence　　　　143
122. Strung Flowers: Two Alike　　　　144
123. Strung Flowers: Dancing Dragon　　　　144
124. Throwing Heaven and Nine　　　　145
125. Put and Take　　　　146
Tailpiece: Antique Chinese dicing cup of ivory　　　　146

Chapter Six: DOMINO GAMES

126. Chinese Dominoes　　　　147
127. Domino wood-pile　　　　148
128. Wood-pile for Collecting Tens　　　　150
Plate VII. Ma-jong tiles and counters　　　　*facing p.* 152
Plate VIII. Lorry drivers playing Chinese chess　　　　*facing p.* 153
Figure 129. Ma-jong: Wind discs and Tong　　　　153
130. Ma-jong: Dead Wall　　　　154
131. Ma-jong: Change of direction　　　　157
132. Development of Dominoes　　　　160
133. The Block game　　　　161
134. Domino Crib　　　　167
135. Matador　　　　168
136. Cyprus　　　　169
Tailpiece: Ma-jong Flower tile　　　　170

Chapter Seven: MAKING BOARDS AND PIECES

Tailpiece: Bell and Hammer mallet, dice and cup   176

137. *Poker work*. Fighting Serpents
138. *Wood carving*. Wari
139. Diagram of hollowing out a cup
140. *Chip-carving*. Ludus Latrunculorum
141. *Inlaying*. Medieval Tables
142. *Marquetry*. Continental Draughts
143. *Paint work on white wood*. Tablan
144. *Paint on matting*. Patolli
145. *Formica on plywood*. Cows and Leopards
146. *Pottery*. Ancient board (Palenque)
147. *Gilt on rexine*. Nine Men's Morris
148. *Beadwork on leather*. Zohn-ahl
149. *Embroidery*. Pachisi
150. *Paper*. Chinese chess
151. *Paper on linen*. Game of Goose
152. *Metalwork*. Pallanguli
153. *Perspex inlay*. Senat
154. *Ivory*: Shatranj pieces
155. *Bone*. Hnefatafl pieces
156. *Bone*. Tibetan chessmen
157. Dominoes
158. *Pottery*. Pieces for Game of Thirty Squares
159. Gambling sticks
160. *Ivory billiard balls*. Sundry dice
161. *Wood-turning*. All-tes teg-enuk
162. Cypher of Charles Cotton
163. Signature of Charles Cotton
164. Signature of Edmond Hoyle

*Plates
IX–XXIV
between
pp.176–7*

Tailpiece: Rajah from Indian chess set (From Hyde's *De Ludis Orientalibus*)   198

Afterpiece: Pompeian wall-painting   199

CHAPTER ONE

Race Games

1. CROSS AND CIRCLE RACE GAMES

In 1949 North Korea invaded South Korea across the Thirty-ninth parallel and the war that followed made this obscure country a household word throughout the western world. The Kingdom of Korea was founded in 1122 B.C. and before the Christian era the Koreans were highly civilized. One of their games, Nyout, is an example of a Cross and Circle game that has survived unchanged down countless centuries.

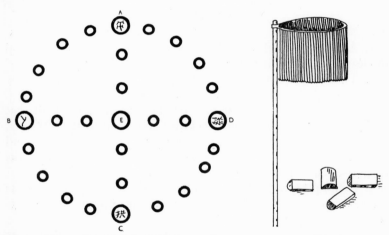

FIG. 1. Nyout board (after Culin, *Korean Games*)

FIG. 2. Nyout ring and four pam-nyout (after Culin, *Korean Games*)

NYOUT

The Nyout board consists of twenty-nine marks which are often drawn on a piece of paper. Those in the centre and at the four quarters are larger than the others. The mark at the top is CH'UT—Exit.

The pieces are called MAL or horses, and are made of wood, stone or paper and are moved according to the throws of four dice known as PAM-NYOUT. These are about 1 in. in length, white, and flat on one side, convex and blackened by charring on the other. They are usually made of the wood of a thick bushy tree like the prunus. Ebony makes an excellent substitute. To prevent cheating the dice are thrown through a ring of straw about 2 in. in diameter, which is fastened to the end of a stick a foot long which is stuck in the ground.

Scores

4 black sides up	..	5 ⎱ and the player
4 white sides up	..	4 ⎰ has another turn
3 white sides up	..	3
2 white sides up	..	2
1 white side up	..	1

If a block falls in an upright position it counts as though it fell with the black side up.

Rules of Play

1. All the players throw the blocks in turn, the highest becoming the leader and the others follow in the order of their throws.

2. Throwing a five or a four allows the player another throw which is made before moving his piece.

3. The players enter their men on the mark to the left of that marked EXIT, and move anti-clockwise according to their throws. The object of the game is to get an agreed number of horses around the circle and out at A. If a horse lands on one of the cardinal marks it short-circuits along a limb of the cross.

4. If two play, each player has four horses; if three play each has three horses; and if four play the players sitting opposite are partners and have two horses each.

5. If a player's horse catches up with another of his own, he may double them up as a team and then move them around as one piece.

6. If a player's horse moves on to a mark occupied by an opponent's piece the latter is caught and must go back to the beginning and start again. When a player makes a capture he has an extra turn.

7. When a player throws a 5 or a 4 and has a second throw he may divide the throws between two horses.

8. A player may move his partner's horses instead of his own.

9. When a horse is about to enter the board a throw of 5 takes it

to the spot marked B (fig. 1), and it may move towards the exit by the radius BE. If the throw is less than 5 but the next throw brings it to B it may travel along the radius BE and EA, otherwise it must continue on to C. If it lands on C it can travel along CE and EA, otherwise it must continue on towards A, the exit.

Nyout is popular among the Korean lower classes and is played as a gambling game for money in the public houses. There are records of a game similar to Nyout being played in Korea in the third century A.D.

There is considerable evidence that North America was populated from North-east Asia and this theory is supported by Amerindian games. Fig. 3 shows a drawing of a flagstone found by the Mexican archaeologist Alberto Ruiz in the temple of the Inscriptions at Palenque, a Mayan city in Central America which was inhabited about A.D. 800.

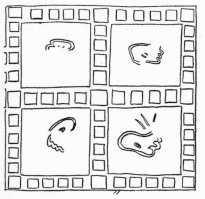

FIG. 3. Mayan game cut into a flagstone at Palenque, *c*. A.D. 800 (after Alberto Ruiz)

FIG. 4. Mayan game found at Chichen Itza, Yucatan (after Ruppert)

Fig. 4 shows a tracing one-tenth actual size of a board cut into the stucco top of a bench in a gallery at the south-eastern corner of the market place in the ruins of Chichen Itza, Yucatan. The building is thought to have been used as a barracks or as a club house for the young warriors belonging to the military orders of the Jaguars and Eagles. The board is placed conveniently for the players to sit facing each other. The stucco is damaged in places but enough remains to indicate the likeness of this board to a contemporary one for Nyout.

The Cross and Circle schema may be modified by omitting the cross. Many North American Indian games consist of a circle (often with vestigial remains of a cross) scratched on the ground, and the progress of the pieces is controlled by the throws of marked sticks. Zohn Ahl, played by the women and girls of the Kiowa Indians, Oklahoma, may be taken as representative.

ZOHN AHL

The board is marked out on the ground with forty small stones, the points being the intervals between the stones. In the centre is a flat stone, known as the AHL stone, on to which the dicing sticks are thrown. The wide gap at the North represents a river in flood, while those at the East and West are dry streams (figs. 5 and 148 on Plate XIV).

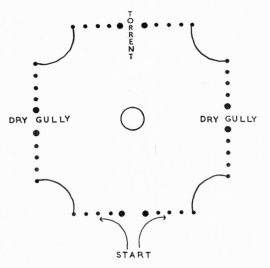

FIG. 5. Zohn Ahl track (after Culin, *Chess and Playing Cards*)

Runners. Each team has one runner and the moves of the runners are controlled by the throw of four dice sticks, the runners moving in opposite directions round the track.

Dice Sticks. These are flat on one side and round on the other. They are about 7 in. long, $\frac{3}{8}$ in. wide, and $\frac{3}{10}$ in. thick. Three of the sticks have a red stripe running down the middle of the flat side, while the fourth, known as the SAHE, has a blue stripe, and its convex side is marked with a star (figs. 6 and 159 on Plate XXI).

Scoring

One flat side up .. 1 and if this is the blue, another turn
Two flat sides up .. 2
Three flat sides up .. 3 and if the blue is included, another
Four flat sides up .. 6 [turn
Four convex sides up .. 10

Counters. Each team starts with four pebbles, shells, or white sticks which are used as counters.

RED STICKS   BLUE STICK

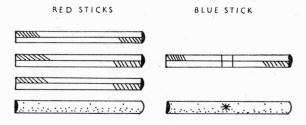

FIG. 6. Dicing sticks for Zohn Ahl (after Culin, *Chess and Playing Cards*)

Method of Play

1. The players are divided into two teams and a player from each team throws the sticks alternately, each player in a team throwing in turn and advancing her side's runner with her throw.

2. If a runner lands in the torrent at the North she must return to the start and her team must pay their opponents one counter. If a runner falls into the dry river bed at East or West the team loses one throw.

3. If the two runners meet on the same point the last to arrive sends her opponent back to the beginning and her side wins a counter.

4. When the first runner arrives back at the start the opponents have to pay a counter and the first lap is over. If the throw is big enough to take the runner beyond the start she moves the surplus number of points along the second lap. The runner winning each lap gains a counter.

5. The game ends when one side holds all the counters or, if a time limit has been set, the side holding most at that moment is the winner.

PATOLLI

The Cross and Circle can also be modified by omitting the circle. This happened in Patolli, the favourite gambling game of the Aztecs. Unfortunately, the Christian priests with misplaced zeal destroyed the native records and manuscripts and no Aztec description of the game has survived. The earliest Spanish account is Gomara's (1552), written thirty-one years after the conquest in 1521 but unfortunately it is very short. He mentions that the Emperor Montezuma sometimes watched his nobles playing at Court.

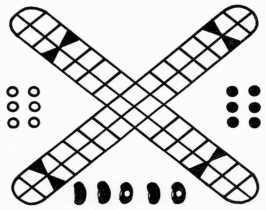

FIG. 7. Patolli cross, counters and beans (after Duran)

Duran describes these Mexican gamesters walking about with a patolliztli mat rolled up under an arm and carrying a little basket containing coloured stones used as markers. Before a game they called for a bowl of fire and threw incense into it, or sacrificed offerings of food to their dice and then they would gamble with all the confidence in the world. The nobility played for high stakes in precious stones, gold beads and very fine turquoises.

The Mexican God of Sport and Gambling was Macuilxochitl, the God of Five Flowers, and as they played the gamblers invoked his aid by rubbing the five beans between their hands, and then, as they threw them on the mat, they shouted 'Macuilxochitl!' and clapped their hands together, craning forward to see their score.

The following description is based on four early works: Sahagun (c. 1545), Gomara (1553), Duran (c. 1560) and Torquemada (1615). Father Sahagun prepared his *Historia universal de Nueva-Espana* about 1545, but it was suppressed by the ecclesiastical authorities for nearly 300 years, finally being published in 1829 by Bustamente in Mexico. Father Diego Duran (1538–1588) wrote his history *Antiguallas e Historia de los mejicanos* about 1560. It was first published under the title *Historia de las Indias de Nueva-Espana & Islas de Tierra Firme* in Mexico (1867–1880).

The board was a thin mat and painted on it in liquid rubber was a great diagonal cross reaching to the corners. Each limb was divided into sixteen compartments. Some mats were decorated with the figure of fortune as a lucky device or with its symbol, two clubs.

Twelve small stones were used as pieces, six red and six blue, and if two played each took six. (This remark suggests that more than two could play, but it is not recorded if the players formed partnerships or were independent, and if they shared the twelve pieces or increased the total number.)

Five large black beans, called patolli, each with a hole drilled in one side to act as a white pip, were rubbed between the player's hands and then thrown on to the mat to make the cast.

Scoring (Duran)

1 pip up ..	1
2 pips up ..	2
3 pips up ..	3
4 pips up ..	4
5 pips up ..	10

The stones were moved along the divisions according to the throws. Little more is known about patolli and this is not enough to play the game. By comparison with other North American games it is probable that the marked squares were penalty areas and the player was penalized for trespassing on them—possibly a turn was lost, or a forfeit paid (figs. 7 and 144 on Plate XII).

Suggested Additional Rules (for two players)

1. The players put an agreed sum into a pool and decide on the size of the forfeits.
2. One player takes six red pieces, the other six blue.
3. Each player casts the patolli in turn and the higher scorer starts the game by casting again.
4. The opening player introduces a piece on to his nearest

central square and then moves it the indicated number of compartments in either direction round the board, but whichever way his first piece moves the others must do likewise. His opponent at his opening throw also has a free choice of direction but having once chosen, the remaining pieces must travel the same way. The opposing forces may, therefore, be moving in the same or opposite directions.

5. After the entry of the first piece the others must enter the board on the player's nearest central square with a throw of 1.

6. No piece may move on to a compartment occupied by any other piece.

7. If two or more of a player's pieces can be moved to satisfy a particular throw, the player has free choice which it shall be, but if only one piece can move, the move must be made even if it is to the player's disadvantage.

8. If a player cannot move any piece he pays a forfeit into the pool.

9. A player landing on a compartment which has been reduced in size by the markings pays two forfeits to his opponent.

10. A player moving a piece on to one of the rounded compartments at the end of the limbs of the cross is awarded another turn.

11. Pieces travel round the cross and are borne off on the side of the fourth limb nearest the player with exact throws, as in backgammon. The four central squares, which have been traversed in the circuit of the piece, are excluded in the bearing off.

12. As each of the player's pieces leaves the cross his opponent pays him one forfeit.

13. The player removing all his pieces from the cross first wins the stake in the pool.

14. For three players it is suggested that each player should have five counters of his own colour making 15 counters in all. The rules remain unchanged.

15. For four players each player should have four counters, of his own colour, and the players may decide to play ALL AGAINST ALL, or that the players sitting opposite each other shall be partners and share the profits or losses of each hand. Cowrie shells, beads, dried peas, etc., can be used as forfeits.

In Asia the Cross and Circle game became variously modified as it spread westwards. The circle was invaginated against the side of the cross to form a bigger cross of three rows of squares. This increased the length of the track and removed the short cuts along the cardinals.

PACHISI

Pachisi, or Twenty-five, is the national game of India, and is found in palaces, zennas, and cafés alike. The Emperor Akbar played in a truly regal fashion on courts made of inlaid marble. In the centre of the court was a dais four feet high on which he and his courtiers sat, while sixteen young slaves from the harem, wearing appropriate colours, moved about the red and white squares as directed by the throws of cowrie shells. Traces of these royal boards are still visible at Agra and Allahabad.

Modern boards are usually made of cloth, cut into the shape of a cross, and then divided into squares by embroidery (figs. 8 and 149 on Plate XV). The marked squares represent castles in which the pieces are free from capture. A castle occupied by a player's piece is open to his partner's pieces, but closed to the enemy.

Each player has four bee-hive shaped wooden pieces marked with his own colours (fig. 9). Six cowrie shells are used as dice.

Scoring

2 cowries with mouths up	..	2
3 cowries with mouths up	..	3
4 cowries with mouths up	..	4
5 cowries with mouths up	..	5
6 cowries with mouths up	..	6 and another throw
1 cowrie with mouth up	..	10 and another throw
0 cowries with mouth up	..	25 and another throw

The game is played by four players each having four pieces. The players sitting opposite each other are partners, and yellow and black play against red and green. Each piece enters the game from the central space known in Hindustani as the Char-koni, and travels down the middle of his own limb and then round the board, returning up the centre of his own limb back to the Char-koni. On arriving back at the middle row of their own limb the pieces are turned on their sides to show that they have completed the circuit. They can only reach home by an exact throw. The moves are controlled by six cowries.

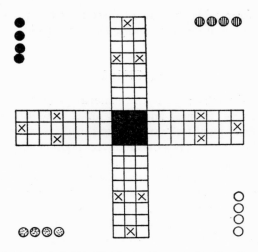

FIG. 8. Pachisi cloth and pieces (from author's collection)

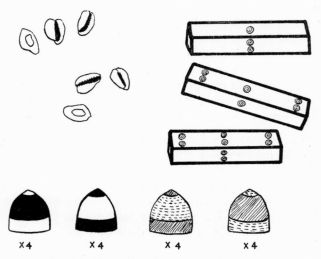

×4   ×4   ×4   ×4

FIG. 9. Pachisi pieces, three long dice and six cowrie shells
(from author's collection)

Rules

1. The cowries are thrown from the hands. When 6, 10, or 25 is thrown the player has an extra turn and he continues until he throws a 2, 3, 4, or 5; when his turn of play ends. On finishing a turn the player moves his pieces before the next player begins his turn. Each throw allows the player to move a piece the indicated number of squares and if he throws more than once in a turn, the different throws may be used to move different pieces; but a single throw cannot be split, i.e. on a throw of 4, a piece moves four squares, the player is not allowed to move two pieces two squares each.

2. A capture is made by a player moving a piece on to a square other than a castle square, occupied by an enemy piece. The latter is removed from the board and must re-enter the game at the Charkoni, with a throw of 6, 10, or 25. A player making a capture has another throw.

3. At the beginning of a game a player's first piece may enter the board whatever the throw, but the other pieces can only be entered on throwing a 6, 10, or 25.

4. The pieces move anti-clockwise.

5. A player may refuse to play when it comes to his turn, or he may throw and then refuse to make use of it. He may do this to avoid the risk of capture or to help his partner. On reaching the castle at the end of the fourth limb, he may wait there in safety until he throws a 'twenty-five' and then move out in one throw.

6. Pieces may double up on any square, but doubled men can be sent back to start again if they are hit by an equal or larger number of men belonging to the enemy, unless they are resting on a castle square.

Tactics

If a player's partner is behind in the game it may be wise to keep pieces back to help him by blocking the way to opposing pieces, or by capturing them if they threaten him. Both partners win or lose together and if one of them rushes ahead and out of the game the opponents have two throws to the remaining partner's one, and they can keep just behind him and then send him back to the beginning again with a capturing throw. Sometimes when a leading player reaches his own limb he will continue on a second circuit to help his partner instead of turning his piece over and moving up the centre.

The cowries may be replaced by three long dice (fig. 9) marked 1 and 6, and 2 and 5, on the opposing faces. If dice are used the game is called Chausar.

LUDO

About 1896 Pachisi was modified and introduced into England as Ludo, patent 14636, a cubic die being used (fig. 10). The boards and rules are available in any games shop.

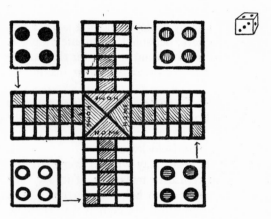

FIG. 10. Modern Ludo board and cubic die

2. SPIRAL RACE GAMES

THE HYENA GAME

Li'b el Merafib or the Hyena game is played by the Baggara Arabs of the Sudan. The board is made by tracing a spiral groove in the sand and making a random number of holes along its course. Each hole represents a day's journey. A larger hole at the centre is a well and the beginning of the track is a village. Each player has a marker which represents his mother.

The dice consists of three pieces of split stick, each about six inches long, on which the bark has been left, so that each stick has one rounded green surface and one flat white one. They are tossed up into the air.

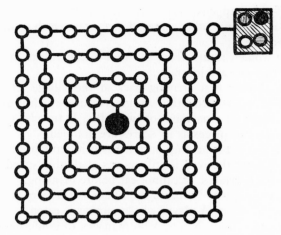

FIG. 11. The Hyena Game (after Hillelson, *Week-end Caravan*)

Scores

One white side up	..	a taba
Two white sides up	..	2 and the turn ends
Three white sides up	..	3
Three green sides up	..	6

Rules

1. The players throw the sticks in turn, each player continuing his turn until he throws a 2; when he passes the sticks to the next player.

2. A player must throw a taba before his mother can leave the village.

3. After throwing a taba the player's mother moves along the spiral two, three, or six days as indicated by the next throw. She does not move for a taba but tabas are marked down on the sand to her credit to be used later.

4. Two mothers can share the same day (hole).

5. A mother must reach the well exactly. If she is short, however, she may make up the missing days by paying the equivalent number of tabas from her son's store.

6. At the well she requires two tabas to wash her clothes, and two to start the return journey. If the player hasn't the required tabas to his credit his mother has to wait until he has collected them

for her. If this happens, however, the player is allowed to mark down for later use any other scores of 2, 3, or 6, which he may throw in the meantime.

7. The women return from the well to the village in the same way as on the outward journey.

8. The mother first arriving back at the village lets a hyena loose and her son controls this savage creature which is allowed to leave the village on a payment of two tabas. It travels at twice the speed of the other pieces as its scores are doubled.

9. At the well it is held up until it has paid ten tabas for a drink.

10. On leaving the well it still moves at double speed and eats any women it overtakes. It cannot eat before drinking.

11. The player who becomes the hyena is the winner but there are degrees of defeat. A player whose mother is eaten by the hyena is ribbed unmercifully by one who manages to guide his maternal parent home safely.

This amusing game can be made up quite simply in wood using coloured marbles for the mothers.

Flinders Petrie, the archaeologist, described in his book *Objects of Daily Life in Ancient Egypt* a spiral board which figured in the tomb of Hesy, with 545 divisions between the tail and the centre which represented a serpent's head. A similar serpent in limestone with seventy-two divisions between the head and tail was found in a tomb of the early dynasties. These may have been used for similar games.

THE ROYAL GAME OF GOOSE

In the eighteenth century A.D. Spiral Games again became popular. One of the first was the ROYAL GAME OF GOOSE and this served as a prototype for numerous similar games. It was imported into England from the continent. Plate 1 (opposite) shows an uncoloured copy which was engraved on hand-woven paper with a water-mark of vertical lines and a coat of arms. It was found in 1958 in a Northumberland farmhouse between the pages of a large atlas, published by F. Senex in 1720.

The game is undated but the portrait in the upper right-hand corner, 'JACK SHEPHERD drawn from life', shows him in handcuffs. He was born in Stepney in December 1702 and was brought up in the Bishopsgate workhouse. He was apprenticed to a carpenter, but

I

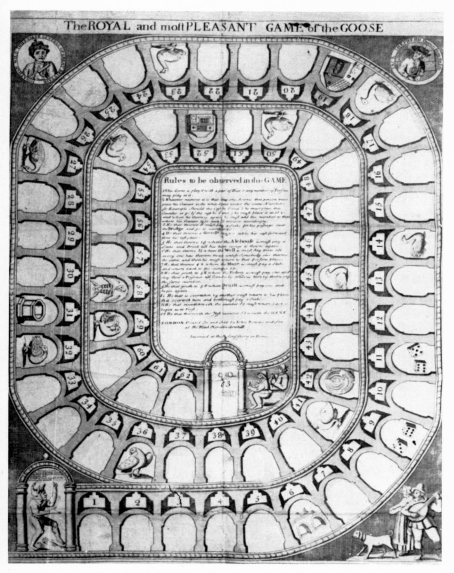

Uncoloured copper-plate engraving, *c.* A.D. 1725

(*a*) Shaturanga pieces found in London by Falkener, on a modern board
(From his *Games Ancient and Oriental*)

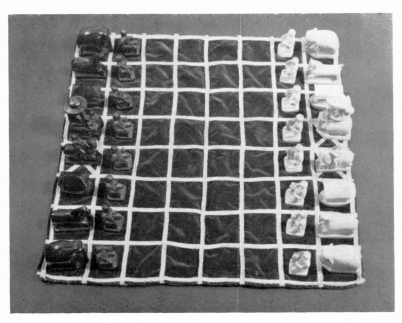

(*b*) Indian chess cloth and carved wooden pieces found
by the author in Edinburgh

ran away in 1723 and took to crime. He escaped from jail twice in the first half of 1724, and towards the end of that time was responsible for almost daily robberies in the London area. He was captured, tried, and condemned to death in July, but escaped and returned to his old haunts. In September he was re-arrested and imprisoned in the strongest part of Newgate, being chained to the floor of his cell, but escaped through the chimney to the roof of the prison and then climbed on to a neighbouring house. A few days later he was recaptured, hopelessly drunk, in a Clare Market tavern and on 16 November 1724 was hanged at Tyburn shortly before his twenty-second birthday.

The upper left-hand corner has an illustration of 'JONATHAN WILD, Thief-taker General of Great Britain'. Wild was born about 1682 in Wolverhampton and became a receiver of stolen goods. He also arranged robberies and then claimed a reward for recovery. Any property which could not be restored to the owners with profit was taken abroad in his own sloop. He betrayed Shepherd and numerous other thieves who would not work for him and in return his activities were overlooked for a time by the authorities, but he was eventually arrested for receiving a piece of stolen lace, tried at the Old Bailey, and hanged at Tyburn on 24 May 1725.

This copy of the game was apparently printed after the capture and death of Shepherd in 1724, but while Wild was still enjoying popularity as a thief-taker; and before he fell from grace and perished at Tyburn in 1725. If these deductions are correct this copy is some twenty years earlier than the suggested date of the game's importation into England from Rome given in Whitehouse's book, and it may be the oldest English copy still in existence.

The rules are given in quaint English in the central panel beneath which is written:

LONDON. Printed for and sold by John Bowles and Son at the Black Horse in Cornhill. Invented at the Consistory in Rome.

RULES

1. *This game is played with a pair of dice and any number of players may play at it.*

2. *Whatever number it is that anyone throws, that person must place his counter in the white space under the same number: for example, should the cast be 6 and 3 he must place the counter at 9: If the cast be 6 and 5 he must place it at 11: and when he throws again he must add the number to that where his counter lies and so remove accordingly.*

3. *He that throws 6 must pay a stake for his passage over the bridge and go to number 12.*

4. *He that throws a goose must double his cast forward from his last place.*

5. *He that throws 19 where the* ALE HOUSE *is must pay a stake and drink till his turn comes to throw again.*

6. *He that throws 31 where the* WELL *is, must stay there until every one has thrown twice, unless somebody else throws the same and then he must return to 'That Persons' place.*

7. *He that throws 42 where the* MAZE *is must pay a stake and return back to the number 29.*

8. *He that goeth to 52 where the* PRISON *is must pay one and stay there a Prisoner till somebody relieves him by throwing the same number.*

9. *He that goeth to 58 where* DEATH *is, must pay one and begin again.*

10. *He that is overtaken by another must return to his place that overtook him and both must pay a stake.*

11. *He that overthroweth the number 63 must return back and begin as at the first.*

12. *He that throweth the just number 63 wineth the* GAME.

Each player started with twelve counters and paid his debts into a pool which became the winner's property.

In his poem *The Deserted Village* published in 1770 Oliver Goldsmith wrote:

> The pictures place'd for ornament and use,
> The Twelve good rules, the Royal Game of Goose.

The games of pure amusement were soon followed by a host of others based on the same principles and designed for educational purposes, teaching the children history, geography, architecture, botany, and astronomy. Occasional copies may still be found in old book or antique shops: delightful hand-coloured sections mounted on canvas and contained in slip cases or between boards, similar to modern road maps on cloth.

3. SQUARE BOARD RACE GAMES

THAAYAM

When the rice is nearly ripe women and girls in Southern India spend days in the paddy frightening away the birds, and to pass the time they play several games, the most popular being Thaayam. The board (fig. 12) is marked out on the ground and little sticks are used for pieces. The dice are made from tamarind seeds which are chocolate brown in colour and cubical in shape, each of the surfaces being slightly convex. They are used in making curries. When one side of a seed is rubbed on a stone the outer husk can be rasped away leaving the white kernel exposed. Four prepared seeds, with three sides white and three left dark, are used.

Scoring   1 white side up   ..   1
                 2 white sides up   ..   2 and turn ceases
                 3 white sides up   ..   3 and turn ceases
                 4 white sides up   ..   4
                 0 white sides up   ..   8

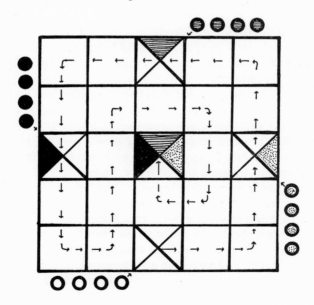

FIG. 12. Thaayam board and markers

C

If four cowries are used instead of seeds the mouth side up is the equivalent of white and the convex side up of black.

The middle squares of each side of the board are marked and represent a player's palace, while the central square is a keep or castle. Each player has four pieces which start the game off the board.

Rules

1. Each player in turn throws the dice and the highest scorer begins the game. Tying players rethrow. When a player's turn is finished the dice are passed to the player on his right who begins his turn.

2. A player continues to throw the dice until he scores a 2, or a 3, and then the turn ceases and the dice are passed to the next player.

3. A player must move a piece by the indicated amount of each throw unless it is impossible to do so. He may use the throws in any order.

4. A player can only enter a piece on to the board with a throw of 1, and the piece is placed in the player's palace. No score counts until he throws a 1, but after a 1 is thrown the piece is moved as indicated by the dice, e.g. if a player's four pieces were all off the board and he threw 8, 4, 1, 4, 2, he would introduce a piece into his palace with the throw of 1, and then with the 4, and the 2, he would move it on six squares.

5. Any throw may be shared between a player's pieces: e.g. if he threw 1, 4, 1, 4, 1, 3, the 1's could be used to introduce pieces into his palace, or to move pieces on their journey, while the 4, 4, 3, could be used to move on one piece 4 plus 4 plus 3 = 11 squares; or two or three pieces by any desired combination of the throws. A turn can be split between two or more pieces.

6. The pieces move anti-clockwise round the board until they reach the square contiguous with their palace when they turn into the inner path and travel clockwise until they again reach the square contiguous with their palace when they turn to enter the centre; and when all a player's pieces have assembled in the keep the final bearing off begins; and with each 1 thrown a piece is removed from the board. The first player to remove all his pieces from the board wins the game.

7. A player may have any number of his pieces on one square.

8. If a piece lands on a square occupied by a hostile piece the latter is hurt in battle and is removed from the board, and can only enter again via his own palace on a throw of 1, and begins his journey all over again.

9. If a player moves a piece on to a square occupied by two or more enemy pieces—except a TWIN—the latter are sent home in the same way that a single piece would have been.

10. If a player's piece hits an enemy piece the player has another turn.

11. Rule 8 does not apply to pieces resting on the marked squares which are havens of safety. This symbolizes the sanctity of a guest in a house—even if he is an enemy he is free from harm while under the host's roof. Any number of pieces of any colour may thus congregate on a palace square, and all are safe from attack. The central keep is also a common sanctuary.

12. If a player has two pieces on the palace square immediately opposite his own palace he has the option of declaring them a TWIN, or playing on in the ordinary way. A twin resting on an ordinary square can only be attacked and sent home by another twin; a single enemy piece may move on to the same square with it, or a twin may move on to a square occupied by a single enemy piece, but does not harm it. Twins are neither attacked by nor can attack, single pieces; twins can only attack or be attacked by each other.

13. A twin moves only half the number of squares thrown by the dice: e.g. a throw of 4, 1, 4, 2 = 11, and would only allow a twin to move five squares, one half of ten squares. The player could of course move the twin four squares representing eight of the throw and then move some single piece three squares, utilizing the whole of the other three points scored.

14. If a twin is hit by a twin and sent off the board there are two alternative methods of play and it should be decided at the start of the game which is to be used.

(*a*) On being hit and sent off the board the twin becomes two single pieces again and they are entered singly on throws of 1, in the ordinary way.

(*b*) When a twin is sent off the board it can only be reintroduced as a twin, and only on throwing two 1's in a single throw, e.g. 4, 1, 4, 1, 8, 2. The first 4 could be used to move a piece on the board, then the two 1's could reintroduce the twin to the palace, the 8 and 2 could be used to move the twin on five squares or some other piece on ten squares and the 4 between the 1's could move some other piece four squares.

15. When a twin reaches the central keep it becomes two single pieces, and a double throw of 1 is not required in the final escape from the board.

I am indebted to Dr. M. Thillai-nayagam for the account of this game. He also mentioned a more elaborate form known as 'The King's Thayyam'. The boards are double the size and eight tamarind seeds are used instead of four. The game is played in Tamil schools but he was unable to give any details.

4. PEG SCORING BOARDS

THE PALM TREE GAME

In his five years excavating at Thebes Lord Carnarvon found a gaming board in a tomb of the Late Middle Kingdom, which is usually regarded as embracing the Twelfth Dynasty (2000 to 1788 B.C.) and is generally known as The Feudal Age.

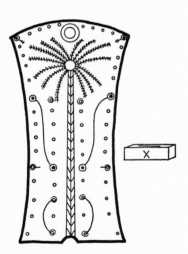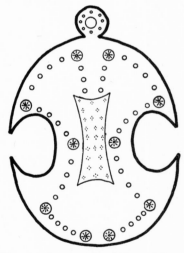

FIG. 13. Board found at Thebes; c. 2000 B.C. (redrawn from Lord Carnarvon and H. Carter's *Five Years' Excavations at Thebes*)

FIG. 14. Ivory and gold board from Megiddo in Palestine, c. 1300 B.C. (drawn from a photograph of a fragment in *Illustrated London News*, 23 October 1937, p. 709)

The board (fig. 13) is six inches long and three inches wide with an ivory top, and dog- and jackal-headed pieces which were contained in a drawer secured by copper staples and an ivory bolt.

Suggested Rules for the Palm Tree Game

1. The right side of the board belongs to Black, and the left to White. The pieces travel from the gold point beside the trunk of the palm nearest its fronds down the tree, round the perimeter of the board, and back up the other side of the tree; the five pieces taking up the upper five positions along the tree trunk on the opponent's side of the board. Exact throws are needed to enable them to take up these positions.

2. The two players throw the four-sided die alternately and only on the throw of four (X) can a piece be introduced on to the board at the gold point near the top of the tree. In virtue of Rule 3 the player then throws again and he may use this extra turn to move any of his pieces in play the indicated amount.

3. A piece landing on a gold point earns the player an extra turn.

4. If a piece lands on a point connected with a gold line it moves to the other end. This may be a promotion or a demotion, the line acting as both a snake or a ladder.

5. If a piece lands on a gold point marked with a short horizontal line the player loses a turn.

6. A player cannot move a piece on to a point already occupied.

7. A player must move if he can; if he is unable to use a score his opponent may do so in addition to his own turn which follows.

8. If the pieces become blocked and neither player can pass those of the opponent, the game is drawn.

9. The first player to marshal his five pieces on the upper five points of his opponent's side of the tree wins the game.

Archaeologists know the Palm Tree Game as the game of Dogs and Jackals as the pieces are often in the likeness of these animals. It appears to have originated in Egypt and the board from Thebes is one of the oldest known.

The board shown in fig. 14 was made in the thirteenth century B.C. of ivory and gold and was found at Megiddo in Palestine.

The board in fig. 15 was found at Ur by Sir Leonard Woolley in 1932. It is 13 cms. long and has the broken ends of gaming pieces protruding from the short side of the board. It was probably made during the Assyrian occupation of Ur, about 700 B.C. Similar boards have been found in Assyria itself and one has an inscription on its reverse which reads:

'Palace of Esarhaddon, the great king, the mighty king, king of all, king of Assyria, governor of Babylon, king of Sumer and Akkad, son of Sennacherib, the mighty king, king of all, king of Assyria, son of Sargon, the mighty king, etc. . . .'

Esarhaddon conquered Egypt *c.* 675 B.C.

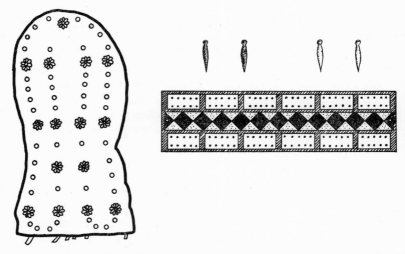

FIG. 15. Board of baked clay found at Ur by Sir L. Woolley; *c.* 700 B.C. (redrawn from Murray's *History of Board Games other than Chess*)

FIG. 16. Cribbage board of inlaid woods (author's collection)

An eighteenth- or early nineteenth-century cribbage board in the author's collection is shown in fig. 16. The resemblance to the earlier boards is striking. Cribbage was invented by Sir John Suckling (1609–1642) and was an improvement on an older card game, Noddy. There seems little doubt that an existing form of score board was utilized for the new games, and the humble cribbage board obtainable in any games shop may have a lineage reaching back to the board from Thebes.

5. THE BACKGAMMON GROUP

GAMING BOARDS FROM THE ROYAL
TOMBS AT UR

Sir Leonard Woolley found five gaming boards in the royal tombs
at Ur in Mesopotamia which were of the same type, though each
had individual variations in the decoration of the squares. The
boards date from about 3000 B.C. and are the earliest in existence.
Sir Leonard's book *The First Phases* contains a plate showing two
of these boards. One is very simple and consists of little discs of
shell with red or blue centres set in bitumen which covered the
wood and formed a background. The more elaborate board is completely covered with an incrustation of shell plaques inlaid with lapis

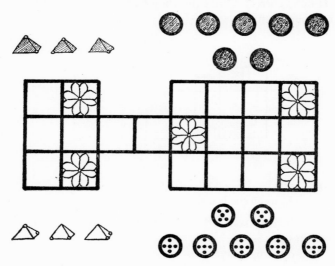

FIG. 17. Gaming board from the Royal Tombs of Ur, *c.* 3000 B.C. (drawn
from photographic plate in Sir L. Woolley's *The Royal Cemetery*)

lazuli and red limestone and divided by lapis lazuli strips; in other
examples the majority of the plaques and also the white 'pieces' are
engraved with animals (see frontispiece); but all agree in having the
coloured rosette in the middle row of the larger section next to the
'bridge'. The boards were hollow and inside were found seven
black and seven white counters and six curious dice, pyramidal in

shape with two of the four points dotted with inlay. Three white and three lapis lazuli dice made a set; perhaps three for each player. No account of how to play the game has survived but one may guess that there were lucky and unlucky squares. The two sides of the elaborate board are identical, suggesting that one side belonged to each player. The middle rank may have been neutral territory.

Suggested Rules for the Sumerian Game

1. Each player places an agreed sum into a pool which becomes the property of the winner at the end of the game. (In one of the finds there were twenty-one small white balls which may have been tallies.)

2. One player throws a single die, the other forecasting while it is in the air whether a tipped or an untipped corner will be uppermost. If he is correct he has the choice of colour, side of the board , and the opening move.

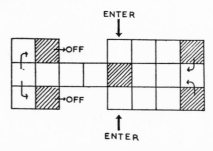

Fig. 18. Diagram to show the direction of movement of the pieces on the board

3. Both 'teams' start off the board. The direction of movement is shown in fig. 18.

4. The opening player throws his three dice and the possible scores are:

Three jewelled corners up	..	5 and another throw
Three plain corners up	..	4 and another throw
Two plain corners up	..	0 and the turn finishes
One plain corner up	..	1 and another throw

5. A piece can only be entered on the board on the throw of five and then it moves forward by the indicated numbers on the additional throws.

6. If a piece moves on to a marked square the opponent pays a fine into the pool.

7. When a piece moves on to the central file it is at war with the enemy pieces and if it lands on a square occupied by an enemy piece the latter is sent off the board and must start again with a throw of 5. There are eight 'fighting' squares and six 'safe' squares on the board for each player.

8. An exact throw is needed to bear a piece off the board.

9. A player may have any number of pieces on the board at once but only one piece is allowed on one square at a time.

10. The first player to bear all his pieces off the board wins the pool.

Fifteen hundred years later the Egyptians used boards which appear to have been derived from those of Ur, and several have been found in tombs of the 'Empire' age, about 1580 B.C. A board found at Enkomi in Cyprus which was within the Egyptian Empire is shown in fig. 19. See also fig. 153 on Plate XVII.

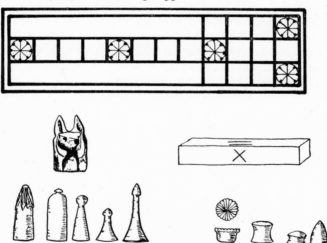

FIG. 19. Board for the Egyptian game of Senat found in Enkomi in Cyprus; *c.* 1580 B.C. (redrawn from *Journal of Hellenic Studies*, 1896, p.288). A long die and types of pieces used at that time are included

The group of squares at the smaller end of the Sumerian board have been unfolded into a straight tail but the rosettes have been retained and the game may have been played in a similar way. The Egyptian boards were usually made in a box form containing a drawer to hold the pieces and dice. The game was called Senat by the Egyptians. The under-surface of the box often had a second game of 3 × 10 or 3 × 12 squares.

THE GAME OF THIRTY SQUARES

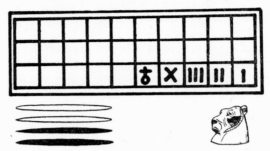

FIG. 20. Egyptian board now in the British Museum marked with the cartouche of Queen Hatshepsut, *c.* 1500 B.C., with one of twenty lion-headed pieces found with it. The gambling-sticks were found elsewhere

Fig. 20 shows an example now in the British Museum and marked with the cartouche of Queen Hatshepsut. The fifth square from the lower right-hand corner is marked with the hieroglyph which means a door or an exit. The fourth square is marked with an X (4) the third III (3), the second II (2), and the first I (1).

Many of these Egyptian boards contained two sets of men, one side being pawn shaped and the other like cotton reels (figs. 19 and 153 on Plate XVII).

The drawer of the board which is now in the British Museum contained twenty lion-headed pieces (fig. 20), ten of a light coloured wood, nine of a dark coloured wood, and one of ivory which may have been a replacement for a lost piece of the set. In addition to pieces there were four staves. A board from Tutankhamen's tomb contained two knuckle bones, and in the board from Ak-hor (fig. 21) was a long die. Four elaborate gaming pieces are also shown in fig. 21.

There is a picture in the Fifth Dynasty tomb of Rashepses at Sakkarah, *c.* 2500–2400 B.C., of two men squatting on the ground playing a game.

The pieces are placed alternately along the board, although the Egyptian artistic convention of only drawing in profile makes this observation of limited value. A similar painted relief from the Eleventh Dynasty tomb of Baqt at Benihasan, *c.* 2000–1780 B.C., shows two boards and four men. Over one board is written in hieroglyphs 'To play with five'. Over the other board is 'Consumed', possibly meaning that the game was finished. These two pictures are close together and may show two stages of the same game (fig. 22).

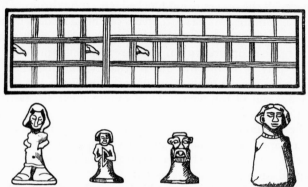

FIG. 21. Board from Ak-hor now in the Cairo Museum. The four elaborate gaming-pieces were found elsewhere

Several papyri exist containing similar drawings but the texts give no clue whatever to the method of play. It appears to have been a race game of the backgammon type and may have been an early forerunner of Nard, later so popular among the Arab peoples.

FIG. 22. Wall drawing from a tomb at Benihassan, *c.* 2000 B.C. (redrawn from Falkener's *Games Ancient and Oriental*)

Suggested Rules for the Game of Thirty Squares

1. Each player has ten men. At the beginning of the game the men are placed alternately on the top and second row (fig. 158 on Plate XXI).

2. The players throw the long die and the higher throw gives the advantage of first move, though this player's pieces occupy the second positions.

3. The opening player throws the die again and moves a piece the indicated number of squares, landing on an empty square, or one containing an enemy piece which is captured and removed. A piece may not move on to a square occupied by one of its own team.

4. If an opening player's first throw is a 2, he can only move his front piece, all the others being blocked, and if he throws a four (X) then only one of his two forward pieces can be moved. With a throw of 1, he can move any piece and make a capture, and with a throw of 3, he can make a capture with any piece except his front one.

5. The players throw the die alternately, making their moves before passing the die to their opponent. The pieces can only move towards the end of the board, They cannot move backwards.

6. A piece reaching one of the marked squares—X, III, II, I— cannot be captured but rests on it until an exact throw allows the piece to escape from the board and wins the player a point. A piece reaching the square marked ð is safe from attack, but must move on to a marked square as soon as possible.

7. A piece must vacate a marked square at the first possible throw.

8. The player guiding most pieces safely off the board wins the game.

In 1929 the Egyptian Government decided to raise the level of the Aswan Dam which involved the flooding of the southern area of Lower Nubia and the destruction of archaeological sites from Wadi es Sebua to Adindan on the Sudan frontier. An expedition under Walter B. Emery was sent to explore the area and to rescue as much material as possible before it was covered with water. In the six winter-months of 1931 they explored the tombs at Ballana and Qustul. Those at Qustul were constructed about the fourth century A.D. and belonged to the kings and nobility of a race known to archaeologists as the X-group people. They were probably the Blemyes, a powerful nation who lived south of the First Cataract. Between A.D. 250 and their final defeat in the middle of the sixth century, they were often at war with Roman forces in Egypt. About A.D. 550 Silko, the king of the Notabae who were allies of Rome, attacked and utterly routed the Blemyes and drove them out into the desert where they lingered for a few years and finally disappeared from history, and with them the last traditions of Pharaonic Egypt.

The Qustul tombs were buried beneath tumuli and in the base of tomb 3 near the surface the expedition found an elaborate gaming board lying face downwards, and beneath it a leather bag containing fifteen ivory and fifteen ebony gaming pieces; a dice box and five ivory dice. The board was 32 in. long and 15 in. wide and was made of a single piece of wood with a framed border, strengthened at the corners with silver brackets attached with small silver nails. There was a loop handle also of silver which was fastened to the frame with gudgeon pins. The playing surface of the board contained thirty-six squares marked by a delicate fretwork of ivory in conventional floral design. The squares were arranged in three rows of twelve, and each row was divided by centre markings, also of ivory fretwork. The outer rows were bisected by half circles, and the middle row by a full circle (fig. 23).

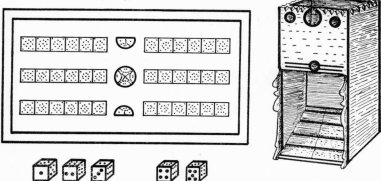

FIG. 23. Gaming-board from Qus-   FIG. 24. Copy of a fritillus or dice-
    tul, *c*. A.D. 350 (drawn from   box based on plate XXXII in
    plate XXXII in Emery's   Emery's *Nubian Treasure*
    Nubian Treasure)

The five dice were cube-shaped and of ivory. They were marked from one to six with tubular drill holes which were filled with red paint. The dice box (fig. 24) was made of wood and was $6\frac{1}{2} \times 3 \times 3$ in. The fittings were of silver. The dice were dropped through the open top and fell on to an inclined grooved board which turned them over before they rolled out through the opening at the bottom between two carved dolphins. Similar dice boxes were used by gamesters throughout the Greco-Roman world as late as the end of the fifth century. They prevented cheating by sleight of hand.

The Qustul board, pieces, dice, and box were used for a game probably similar to those played by their ancestors, the Ancient Egyptians.

LUDUS DUODECIM SCRIPTORUM

There are frequent references in Roman literature to a popular game called 'Ludus Duodecim Scriptorum'—the game of the twelve lines. On the back of a silver mirror which was made in the second or third century B.C. and found in Palestrina is an engraving of a youth and a maiden both partially undressed sitting in front of a gaming table (fig. 25).

FIG. 25. Back of a silver mirror, *c*. 200 B.C. (redrawn from D. Comparetti, Rendiconti della reale accademia dei Lincei, 17 Feb. 1887)

The youth has his hand half closed and looks as if he is about to throw a die. There are no pieces shown on the table; possibly the game has only just begun and the pieces were entered on the board according to the throws of the dice. The word OFEINOD is archaic and unknown. DEVINCAMTED may be translated 'I believe I have beaten you'. Comparetti who examined the mirror when it was in a private collection believed the work was Roman even though it was in the style of Greek art, and he suggested that the game may be the original form of Ludus Duodecim Scriptorum. Apparently this indigenous game was later replaced by the more elaborate thirty-six space game, coming either directly from Egypt or via Greece. The newcomer soon supplanted the native Roman game and also took its name in the same way that 'Sphairistike' invented by Major Wingfield in England about 1874 became known as 'Lawn Tennis', and within fifty years as 'Tennis'. Real tennis is an entirely

different game played in a penthouse and there are barely a score of
courts left in the whole of Europe.

A crude board made of buff ware but closely resembling the
Qustul board was found at Holt in Denbighshire and is now in the
National Museum of Wales. It apparently belonged to a soldier of
the Twentieth Legion stationed on the Marches of Wales in the first
half of the second century A.D. A raised moulded border surrounds
the playing area which consists of two outer rows of twelve roughly
inscribed ivy leaves, separated into groups of six by a central geo-
metrical pattern. The middle row consists of twelve pairs of scrolls
bisected by a compass-drawn pattern of a circle with a six-armed
rosette inside it (fig. 26).

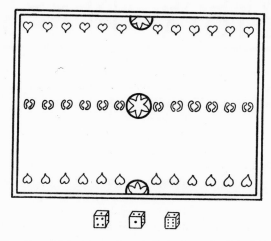

Fig. 26. Ludus Duodecim Scriptorum board from Holt in Denbighshire,
   c. A.D. 125; now in the National Museum of Wales (redrawn from
   Austin's *Roman Board Games*)

More than a hundred boards for this game were found in the city
of Rome alone during the lifetime of Rodolfo Lanciani, professor of
Archaeology in the University, clear evidence of its one-time
popularity. The commonest form consisted of three horizontal lines,
each line being split up into twelve spaces. These spaces varied in
almost every board; there were circles, squares, vertical bars, leaves,
letters, monograms, crosses, crescents, and even erotic symbols.
Sixty-five of the boards contained six words of six letters. See fig. 27.

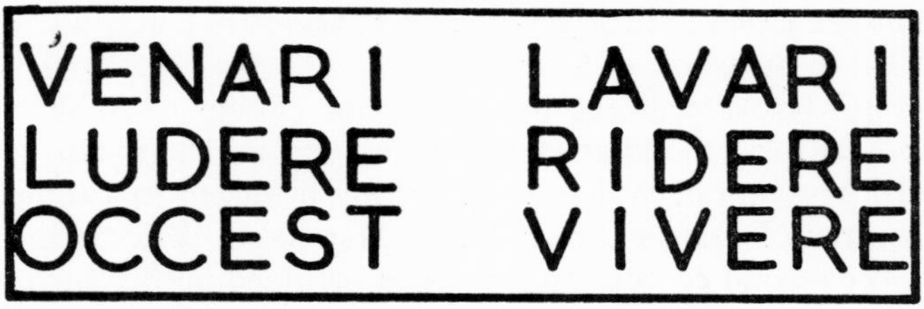

```
VENARI    LAVARI
LUDERE    RIDERE
OCCEST    VIVERE
```

A

```
LEVATE    DALOCV
LVDERE    NESCIS
IDIOTA    RECEDE
```

B

FIG. 27. Ludus Duodecim Scriptorum boards found at Timgad (A) and Rome (B) (redrawn from Austin's *Roman Board Games*)

(A) was found at Timgad; a rough translation is:

To hunt—to bathe
To play—to laugh
This is—to live.

(B) was found in Rome.

Jump up—push off
You can—not win
Get out—Baboon.

The players used three dice marked from 1 to 6, and the highest throw was three sixes, called by Cicero 'Venereus' (*de Divin.* 1. 13). The lowest throw was three aces known as 'Canis'. Cheating was prevented by throwing the dice into a Fritillus or Pyrgus, a wooden tower about a foot high which had a spiral staircase inside.

In the later days of Rome gambling became a mania. Nero played for huge stakes, up to 400,000 sesterces a point (about £6,000), while Lampridius tells us that Commodus turned the Imperial Palace into a casino replete with every form of shameless dissipation. Once, when he was pressed for money, he pretended that he was about to visit the African Provinces of the Empire, but when the Treasury made him a grant for the purpose, his enthusiasm evaporated rapidly and he spent it all in gambling and in immoral excesses.

In 1876 two paintings were found in a tavern in Pompeii, a Roman city partially buried with lava in A.D. 63, and finally overwhelmed by Vesuvius in A.D. 79. In one painting two players are seated opposite each other on stools, holding a gaming-table on their knees, and on it arranged in various lines are several LATRUNCULI of yellow, black, and white. The player on the left is shaking a yellow dice box and shouts 'Exsi!' (I am out!) The other points to the dice and answers 'Non tria, dvas est!' (Not three points, but two!) See fig. 28.

FIG. 28. Tavern wall-painting in Pompeii, *c.* A.D. 70 (redrawn from Gusman's *Pompeii, the City, its Life and Art*)

FIG. 29. Tavern wall-painting from Pompeii, *c.* A.D. 70 (redrawn from Gusman's *Pompeii, the City, its Life and Art*)

In the next picture the same players have sprung to their feet to fight, and the innkeeper, acting as his own chucker-out, is pushing them into the street, shouting 'Itis foras rixsatis!' (Get out if you want to fight!).

The game is mentioned by Ovid (*A.A.* iii. 363 f., *Trist.* ii. 475) and other writers but unfortunately no description of the rules has survived.

During the first century A.D. Ludus Duodecim Scriptorum became obsolete in fashionable circles and was replaced by Tabula, a variant with only two rows of points. Emperor Claudius (A.D. 41–54) was very fond of the game and Suetonius states that he wrote a book on the subject and had a board fixed to his chariot so that he could play while travelling.

Four centuries later Emperor Zeno (A.D. 475–81) suffered so remarkable a misfortune in a game that the position was described in an

D

epigram half a century later by Agathias, a scholastic of Myrine in Asia (A.D. 527–67). The position has been recovered by M. Becq de Fourquière and this sixth-century record enables us to recon-struct the game of Tabula with a fair degree of certainty.

TABULA

Fig. 30 shows the board and the position of the pieces. The Emperor was playing White and the throw of his three dice was 2, 5, 6. As he was unable to move the men on (6) which were blocked by the black men on (8), (11), (12): or the singleton on (9),

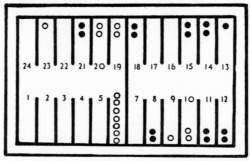

FIG. 30. Diagram of Zeno's disastrous throw at Tabula, *c.* A.D. 480 (redrawn from Austin's *Zeno's Game of Table*)

which was blocked by the black pieces on (11), (14), (15): he was forced to break up his three pairs, a piece from (20) going to (22), one from (19) going to (24), and one from (10) going to (16). No other moves were possible and he was left with eight singletons and a ruined position.

Rules for Tabula

1. The game was played on a board of twenty-four points by two players, each having fifteen pieces of a distinguishing colour.

2. The moves of the pieces were controlled by the alternate throws of three six-sided dice. If, for example, the numbers 1, 3, 5, were thrown:

(*a*) Three pieces could be moved, one 1 point, one 3 points, and one 5 points, as long as each resting point was not blocked by enemy pieces; or (*b*) two pieces could move, e.g. one piece by 1 point, and the other piece by 3 plus 5, or 5 plus 3, or any other combination desired; or

(*c*) one piece could move 9 points if each resting place were free, i.e. 1 plus 3 plus 5, or any reorientation of these numbers, e.g. 5 plus 1 plus 3.

3. The pieces were entered on the board in the first quarter and travelled anti-clockwise round the track. Apparently both colours travelled in the same direction, and it improves the game if no piece is allowed to enter the second half of the board until all the player's pieces are entered into the first half.

4. If a player had two or more men on a point, this point became closed to the enemy and the pieces on it could not be captured. They were called PILED MEN or ORDINARII.

5. If a player moved a piece on to a point occupied by an enemy singleton, the latter was sent off the board and had to re-enter the game at the next possible throw. Probably no other piece could be moved until it was re-entered. Singletons were known as VAGI.

6. Pieces unable to move because they were blocked by enemy ordinarii were known as INCITI. A player was forced to use the whole of his throw if this was possible even if, as happened to the unfortunate Emperor Zeno, it was to the player's disadvantage: any part of a throw, however, which was unplayable was lost and the turn passed to his opponent.

7. An additional rule not mentioned by classical writers which improves the game is that no piece may be borne off the board until all the player's pieces have entered the last quarter. If a player starts bearing off and a vagus is hit, no further pieces can be borne off until it has re-entered the final quarter again.

All gambling games were forbidden by law except during the festive licence of the Saturnalia at least as early as the time of Cicero (106–43 B.C.) but the laws were never rigidly enforced, and under many emperors were entirely disregarded.

Towards the end of the sixth century the name Tabula became replaced by Alea. Isidore of Seville who was born in the sixth century and died in the seventh, wrote in his *Origines*, 'Alea, id est ludus tabulae. . . .' (Alea, that is the game of tabula. . . .)

The Codex Exoniensis, a collection of Anglo-Saxon verse given to Exeter Cathedral by Leofric, the city's first bishop, about A.D. 1025, contains the first English references to Tables. Two lines run:

> 'Hy twegen sceolon
> Taefle ymsittan.'

meaning in modern English:

> 'These two shall sit at Tables.'

A superb manuscript was compiled between A.D. 1251 and 1282 at the command of Alfonso X, King of Leon and Castile. It is now in the library of the monastery of St. Lorenzo del Escorial, a few miles from Madrid. It contains ninety-eight pages, 16·5 in. high and 11·7 in. wide, bound in sheepskin. The manuscript is written in two columns to the page in a beautiful hand with many illuminated initials, both small and large. It is also illustrated with 150 richly coloured drawings, ten being full plates. The book is divided into four sections. Part one deals only with chess; part two with games played with three dice; part three with some fifteen varieties of Tables; and part four contains a miscellaneous collection of games starting with an enlarged chess, the Grande Acedrez, then a game consisting of a combination of chess and tables, Tablas de Alcedrez, and it ends with the game of Alquerque.

Some of the medieval boards used for Tables were magnificent works of art. One of them on view at the Munich Art Exposition of 1876 had been found in 1852 in the *mensa* of the altar of the diocesan church of St. Valentine in Aschaffenburg and had served as a reliquary. The plain points were pieces of red-veined oriental jasper, which were polished only on their upper surfaces, the sides being inlaid; and the adorned points were overlaid with thick pieces of split rock-crystal, themselves inlaid, and beneath were small terra-cotta figures, variously painted with green, red, yellow, blue, and white tints lying on a gold ground. They represented partly twin-tailed sirens, partly dragon-like monsters, centaurs, and battles between beasts and men. The spaces between the points as well as the borders and edges of the sides were covered with very thin silver leaf laid on hard cement, in which foliage and other orna-mental designs were impressed by means of metal stamps, which appeared as if they were in high relief when seen from the front. The flowers and leaves on the two sides were enamelled in red, green, and blue. At each end of the board were small drawers for holding the men which were missing. The covers of these containers were of rock crystal adorned with silver.

Backgammon boards were favourite objects for the expression of a craftsman's skill and it is not surprising that this superb board became a treasured piece of church furniture in spite of its secular origin.

In isolated parts of Iceland, Table boards are still used whose points are made of wooden strips tacked to an underlying plank similar to the Tabula boards of the late Roman period. One of the rustic games, AD ELTA STELPUR, or CHASING THE GIRLS, may date back to this period. Fig. 31 shows the opening positions of the two players' pieces.

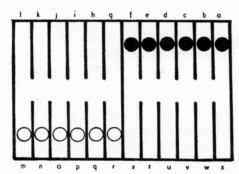

FIG. 31. Opening position in Chasing the Girls

CHASING THE GIRLS

Rules

1. The players throw a single die and the lower score gives the advantage of first move.

2. Two cubic dice are thrown but only throws of 6, 1, and any doublet are used. On throwing a doublet the player has another turn.

3. A throw of 6, 6, counts as a double double and the player may move four of his pieces six places each.

4. A throw of any other doublet allows two pieces to move the indicated number and the player has another turn.

5. A throw of 6, or of 1, allows one piece to move this number of points.

6. No other throw scores.

7. All the pieces move in an anti-clockwise direction and continue to circulate round the board until one player has lost all his men.

8. If a piece lands on a point occupied by an opponent's piece the latter is removed from the board and is out of the game.

9. Doubling up on a point is not allowed and if a throw brings a piece to a point on which the player already has a piece the former is placed on the first vacant point beyond.

10. When a player has only one man left, called a HORNASKELLA or CORNER-RATTLER, the method of play changes:

(*a*) The corner-rattler can only land on the corner points of the four quarters of the board, e.g. on a, f, g, l, m, r, s, and x.

(*b*) A throw of 1 moves it on to the next corner point.

(*c*) A throw of 6 moves it on two corner points.

(*d*) Throws of 1, 1, and 6, 6, count double a single throw of these numbers, but no other double enables the corner-rattler to move. The player, however, wins another throw: e.g. if a piece became a corner-rattler on p and the player threw 6, 1, then it would move to point r in virtue of the 1, and then to point x in virtue of the throw of 6. If he then threw 2, 2, he would have another throw. If this were 5, 1, he would move to a, etc.

11. The corner-rattler can only capture pieces standing on corner points and can itself only be attacked on these points. It is also safe from capture if it stands between enemy pieces; e.g. if Black has men on q, r, s, and White has a corner-rattler on m, and White throws 3, 1, the corner-rattler moves to r and captures the Black man on the point. If Black then throws 1, 2, the black piece on q cannot move to r and capture the corner-rattler because it is between two hostile pieces. Thus Black can only move his piece on s to t or his piece on q to t, the next vacant point.

If Black threw 1, 6, however, the black piece on s could move to a, using the 6, and then the black piece on q could move to r and capture White's corner-rattler and win the game. Both players may be reduced to corner-rattlers, when the game may develop into a long chase before one of them is beaten.

TOURNE-CASE

This simple game from France is played with a Tabula or Backgammon board and two cubic dice.

Rules

1. Each player has three pieces which are entered on the player's side of the board and travel along it to the twelfth or HOME point.

2. A player's pieces remain in their order of entry. No piece can pass over one in front of it, nor can two pieces rest on the same point except on the home point.

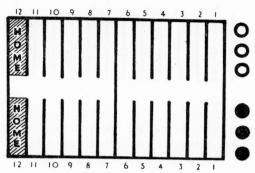

FIG. 32. Opening position in Tourne-case

3. If a player plays a piece on to a point, other than the home point, and an enemy piece is on the point immediately opposite, the latter is sent off the board and has to re-enter at the next throw.

4. Doublets count only as a single throw: e.g. a throw of 4, 4, allows the player to move only one piece four places.

5. The first player with three pieces home wins the game. If he does so before his opponent has any pieces home he gains a double win.

SIXE-ACE

The Alfonsine codex mentions this game as 'sies dos e as' and it is therefore at least seven hundred years old. Twelve pieces of the same colour are taken and each player arranges six on his side of the board (fig. 33).

Two dice are used and the score of a die is reckoned as:

1: A piece is handed over to the opponent and added to his pieces.

6: A piece is borne off the table and is laid aside.

5: A piece is put in the central pool between the tables.

2: A piece is taken from the pool and added to the player's pieces.

3 and 4: These throws are disregarded.

Each die's score must be taken separately and uncombined. On a throw of 3, 2, the 3 is disregarded and a piece is taken from the pool (if there is one in it) and is added to the player's pieces. The throw cannot be counted as 5.

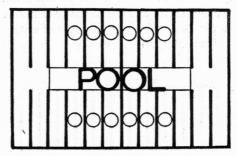

Fɪɢ. 33. Opening position in Six-Ace for two players

If doublets are thrown each die counts separately and the player has another throw, unless he casts 2, 2, when he has to pick up two pieces from the pool (if it contains so many) and he does not get another turn. Alternatively, it was sometimes played that on a throw of 2, 2, the player had to add all the pieces in the pool to his own, but he had another turn as well. When a player has cleared his side of the board he must throw a 6 to win.

In the *Compleat Gamester* by Charles Cotton (1674) there is a drinking variant of this game, which paraphrased might read:

'Up to five may play at Six-Ace, each having six pieces. [There are thirty pieces in a backgammon set.] On the throw of a 1, a player passes a piece to his neighbour; on the throw of 6, he bears a piece off; and a player throwing a 2, must drink and throw again. The last two players on the board, or sometimes the last one, pay for the drinks.'

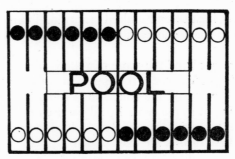

Fɪɢ. 34. Opening position in Six-Ace for four players

Fig. 34 shows the opening position in a four-handed game. The turn moves anti-clockwise round the table and on the throw of an Ace a piece is passed to the player on the right.

FAYLES

Fayles is also mentioned in the Alfonso manuscript under the name of Fallas and was still played in the time of Ben Jonson (1572–1637). See figs. 35 and 141 on Plate XI.

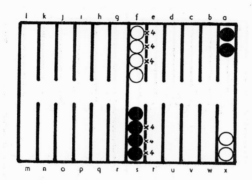

FIG. 35. Opening position in Fayles

Rules

1. Black started with 13 of his men on s and 2 on a and moved his pieces in the direction a to x. White had 13 men on f and 2 on x and moved in the direction x to a.

2. Three dice were used or, if only two, then at each throw the smaller score of the pair was counted twice, e.g. 6, 4, was scored as 6, 4, 4.

3. A piece was moved for the throw of each die or the same piece could be moved again if desired, and if a piece landed on a BLOT or singleton the latter was sent back to its starting point.

4. A piece could not move on to a point held by two or more enemy pieces.

5. If a player at any stage of the game threw a number which could not be played he FAILED and immediately lost; otherwise the player first bearing all his men off the board was the winner.

BACKGAMMON

Nard was a favourite game of the Arab world and was apparently invented before A.D. 800 in south-west Asia or, according to one tradition, in Persia. A Babylonian Talmud, the Gemara, compiled between A.D. 300 and 500, contains the word Nerdshir, and several early European Hebrew philologers, including Nathan ben Jechiel (Rome, 1103), suggested that it represented a game similar to or identical with Nard.

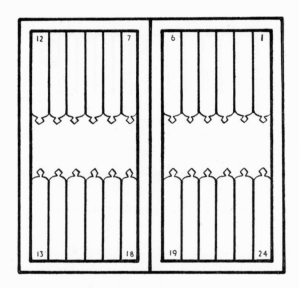

FIG. 36. Tables in an English thirteenth-century manuscript (redrawn from Fiske's *Chess in Iceland*)

Nard and its variants are found throughout Asia. Himly collected the Chinese references and the Hun Tsun Sii which was written during the Sung period (A.D. 960–1279) states that t'shu-p'u, its Chinese name, was invented in western India, spread to China in the time of the Wei Dynasty (A.D. 220–265) and became popular in China between A.D. 479–1000. Each player had sixteen pieces in the Chinese game. An antique ivory specimen forms the tailpiece of this chapter (p. 46). In Japan the game was called Sunoroko and it was declared illegal by the Empress Jito who reigned from A.D. 690–697.

Nard appears to have been introduced into Europe by the Arabs either into Spain or into Italy during the Arabic occupation of Sicily. Thirty pieces were used on a board of twenty-four points and the movements were controlled by the casts of two dice. King Alfonso's manuscript (A.D. 1251–1282) refers to 'Todas tablas' which was almost certainly the Tables of the Middle Ages. Fig. 36 shows an illustration of a board from an English thirteenth-century manuscript.

By 1475 chess had become the popular game and by the end of the sixteenth century the word Tables was used as a generic term for any game played on a flat surface or table, and was no longer applied to a specific game. Early in the seventeenth century a new variant appeared and, coupled with improvements in the boards, finer dice boxes and other attractive changes, the old game enjoyed a tremendous revival and swept through Europe, being played in England as backgammon, in Scotland as gammon, in France as tric-trac, in Germany as puff, in Spain as tablas reales, in Italy as tavole reale.

Just before the 1939–45 war there was a craze for backgammon among the intellectuals, especially the London literary set, but now in the middle of the twentieth century the game is once more suffering an eclipse. Pamphlets of rules can be bought in the better games shops in England, but few sell boards or pieces; occasionally they can be found in antique shops. The seller may be unaware of their purpose!

In America there are a few clubs of enthusiasts in the larger cities and two or three books have been published in the last twenty years, but the game only enjoys anything approaching its former popularity in the Middle East. Tric-trac is still commonplace in the Lebanon and surrounding countries.

Unfortunately, backgammon has inherited a number of technical terms and these may be partially responsible for its disfavour. They are reduced to a minimum in the following account.

POINTS. Each player's side of the board contains two sets of six elongated triangles known as points, separated from each other by the BAR.

INNER TABLE. This consists of the player's first six points.

OUTER TABLE. This consists of the points from seven to twelve.

THE BAR. This separates the inner from the outer table.

Fig. 37 shows the initial positions of the pieces. By a convention the inner tables are always those nearer the source of light. The object of the game is to bring all one's pieces home to one's inner table and when they are all assembled there they are BORNE OFF the board. The first player to remove all his pieces wins the game.

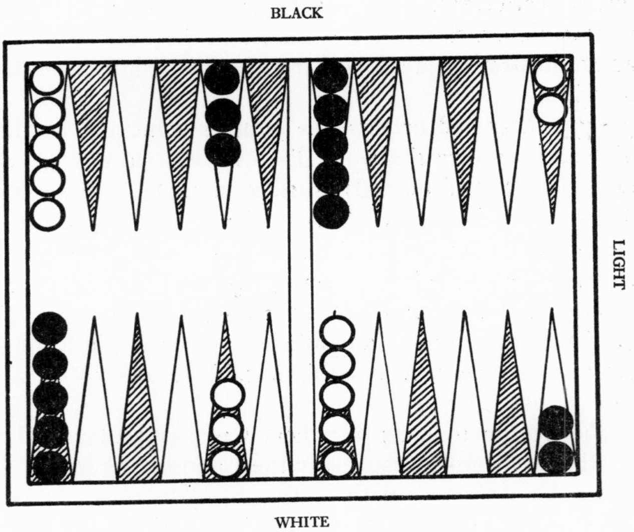

BLACK

LIGHT

WHITE

FIG. 37. Opening position of pieces in Backgammon

Rules

1. At the beginning of the game each player throws a single die and the player with the higher score has a choice of the sides of the board and the colour of his men. He then makes the first move using the numbers of both the dice to move his pieces. His opponent then throws both dice and moves his pieces accordingly and throughout the rest of the game the players throw both dice alternately. The players retain the same sides and pieces in succeeding games.

2. The pieces move in a direction from the opponent's inner table to the opponent's outer table and then from the home outer table to the home inner table and when all the pieces are congregated in the inner table the player begins to bear them off the board.

3. The opposing pieces travel in opposite directions.

4. The two units of a throw may be used separately to move two pieces the indicated amounts, or they may be combined to move one piece the sum of the units as long as it is possible to move the piece first by the throw of one die and then the other. Either number

may be played first; if only one number can be played and there is a choice, the higher must be played.

5. When a pair is thrown this throw is known as a DOUBLET and the player plays double the score, i.e. if 2, 2, is thrown the player counts it as a throw of 2, 2, 2, 2, and can move four men two points, or one man eight points or any other possible combination.

6. When a player has two or more men on the same point his opponent is barred from moving on to the point. This is called MAKING A POINT. A player may not have more than five men on any point.

7. A player must play the whole of a throw if he can, and any part of a throw which cannot be played is lost.

8. If a single man rests on a point this is known as a BLOT, and if the opponent plays a piece on to that point the blot is hit and is removed from the table and placed on the bar where it remains until it can be played into the opponent's inner table.

9. If a player has a man on the bar he cannot move any other piece until it has been re-entered into the game and this is only possible if the pips of one of the dice thrown corresponds to a point on the opponent's inner table which is not held by him. If a player is unable to enter the man on the bar the throw is lost and the opponent follows with another throw. A player unable to enter a man may lose several throws in succession.

10. A player may hit two or more blots in the same throw and he also has the choice of hitting or not hitting a blot, unless no other move is possible.

11. When a player has moved all his men to his own inner table he begins to bear them off. The numbers on the dice may be used to move men forward or to bear them off, or both.

12. If a number higher than any point covered is thrown, a man from the highest point may be borne off.

13. If a number is thrown for an unoccupied point, no men below can be borne off if any man remains on a higher point.

14. A doublet may enable a player to bear off four men at the same time.

15. If a player has begun bearing his pieces off and has a blot hit, it must be placed on the bar and then re-entered into the opponent's inner table and must travel round the board to its own inner table again before any more of his men can be borne off.

16. The player first bearing all his men off the board is the winner

but there are degrees of victory. The simplest form of scoring is the points game.

A. THE POINTS GAME

The winner gets four points for each opposing piece in his inner table or on the bar; three points for each piece in his outer table; two points for each piece in the opponent's outer table, and one point for each piece in the opponent's inner table.

B. THE TRADITIONAL GAME

In the older method of scoring a player wins by:

A SINGLE GAME if his opponent has borne off one or more of his pieces;

A DOUBLE GAME (GAMMON) if no opposing piece has been borne off;

A TRIPLE GAME (BACKGAMMON) if no opposing piece has been borne off and there are one or more pieces on the bar or in the winner's inner table. The stakes for a single win are decided before the game and if a gammon or a backgammon is made the loser pays twice or three times the agreed stake.

DOUBLES. In the modern method of scoring if a doublet is thrown by the players on their initial throw of one die each to decide who moves first, the basic stake is automatically doubled and each tie of the opening throw may either double the previous basic stake or add one to the previous basic stake as decided upon by the players. This is known as AUTOMATIC DOUBLING.

At any time during the game either player may offer to double the stake. If the offer is refused his opponent loses the game and pays the stake in force at the time of the refusal. If the double is accepted, the game goes on with a doubled stake but an additional double can only be made by the player who accepted the previous double. This is known as VOLUNTARY DOUBLING. A voluntary double may only be offered by the player whose turn it is to play and before he has thrown the dice.

Antique Chinese Tableman in filigree ivory (author's collection)

CHAPTER TWO

War Games

1. THE ALQUERQUE GROUP

Seven different types of gaming boards were found cut into the great roofing slabs of the temple at Kurna in Egypt, which was built about 1400 B.C. One of these boards was unfinished, probably owing to a mistake in the cutting of a diagonal line (fig. 38).

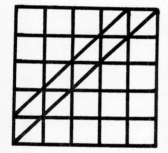

FIG. 38. Abandoned Alquerque board, Ancient Egypt, *c.* 1400 B.C. (from Parker's *Ancient Ceylon*)

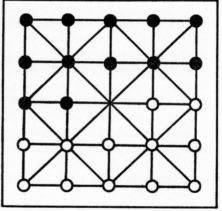

FIG. 39. Opening position of the pieces in Alquerque

Two thousand years later a game called Quirkat is mentioned in the Arabic work *Kitab-al Aghani*, whose author died in A.D. 976. When the Moors invaded Spain they took El-quirkat with them and it appears in the Alfonso X manuscript under its Spanish name of Alquerque (A.D. 1251–1282).

ALQUERQUE

Fig. 39 shows the Alquerque board with the pieces arranged ready for play. The pieces move from any point to any adjacent empty point along a marked line. If the adjacent point is occupied by an enemy piece and the next point beyond it on the line is empty, the player's piece can make a short jump over the hostile piece and remove it from the board. If another piece is then EN PRISE it is taken in the same move by a second short leap, a change of direction being allowed. Two or more pieces may be captured in one move. If a piece can make a capture it is forced to do so, otherwise it is HUFFED and is removed from the board. These rules from the Alfonso manuscript are not sufficient to play a game.

Suggested Additional Rules

1. No piece can move backwards; only forwards, diagonally forwards, or sideways.
2. No piece may return to a point that it has been on before.
3. A piece reaching the opponent's back line is unable to move except by making a capture by a short leap over an enemy piece.
4. The game is over when:
   (*a*) *One player has lost all his pieces*. He then pays two points for losing the game and two points for each of the victor's pieces left on the board.
   (*b*) *A player cannot move any of his pieces*. He then pays two points for losing the game and a single point for each enemy piece on the board in excess of his own. Should the loser have more pieces on the board than his opponent he pays two points for defeat, minus one point for each piece he has in excess of the winner.

When the Spaniards settled in New Mexico they introduced a quadruple alquerque which the Zuni Indians modified into a new game.

THE GAME OF THE STONE WARRIORS

The boards were often cut into one of the stone slabs used in the flat roofs of the native houses. There were 168 squares (fig. 40) and at the beginning of a game between two players each had six warriors in the six nearest squares on his side of the board. The warriors were discs of pottery about 1 in. in diameter, plain for one side and and with a hole drilled through the centre for the other. The object of the game was to cross over and take the opponent's place, capturing as many men as possible on the way. The pieces moved diagonally one intersection at a time.

A capture was made by a player blocking an enemy piece diagonally between two of his own, when it was removed from the board (custodian capture). The first piece a player lost was replaced by a special piece called the PRIEST OF THE BOW which could move diagonally or orthogonally. No piece could move backwards.

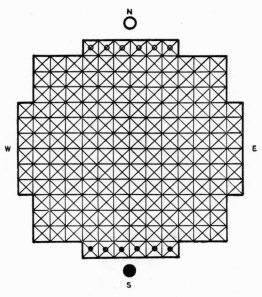

FIG. 40. Game of the Stone Warriors (after Culin, *Games of the North American Indians*)

When the game was played by four, North and West played against South and East. Each player had six pieces making a total of twelve perforated and twelve plain, and each side had one Priest of the Bow, a larger piece, which was exchanged for the first piece captured by the enemy.

The Zuni Indians played another game on the roof-tops called Kolowis Awithlaknannai. (Kolowis is a mythical serpent and Awithlaknannai means 'stones kill'.)

E

FIGHTING SERPENTS

The length of the board and the number of pieces was not constant. Fig. 41 shows a common size. Small black and white stones

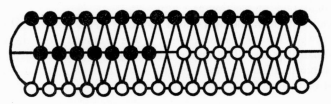

FIG. 41. Board for Fighting Serpents (after Culin, *Games of the North American Indians*)

were used for markers. All the intersections were covered with pieces except for the central one and the two at the extreme ends of the board. The opening player moved a piece on to an empty point. This piece was captured by a short leap at the opponent's next move and was taken off the board, taking being compulsory. The players moved alternately and the pieces could move one intersection in any direction along the lines. Capture was by the short leap and more than one piece could be lifted in one turn of play. The game ended when one player had lost all his pieces. See fig. 137 on Plate IX.

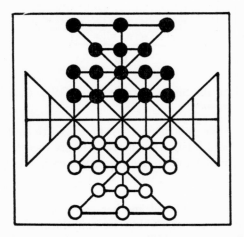

FIG. 42. Board for The Sixteen Soldiers (author's collection)

THE SIXTEEN SOLDIERS

This game is played in Ceylon and parts of India. The initial position is shown in fig. 42. The players move alternately and all pieces can move in any direction along the lines of the board, orthogonally or diagonally, to the next point of intersection.

A capture is made by jumping over an enemy piece on to a vacant point beyond and any number of pieces may be captured in one move by a series of jumps similar to the move of a king in English draughts. The player capturing all the opposing soldiers wins.

As a variant each player may have seven more men placed on the points of the triangle on his left. Three empty points remain along the central transverse line. The same board is used for the game of COWS AND LEOPARDS described on p. 81.

2. THE CHESS GROUP

SHATURANGA

In Ancient India a race-game called Ashtapada was played on a board of sixty-four squares (fig. 43). It was probably similar to Thayaam (p. 17). See also Plate IIa facing p. 15.

About the fifth century A.D. the Ashtapada board was used for a new game, Shaturanga, which was a miniature battle between four armies each under the control of a Rajah and each containing four corps: Infantry, Cavalry, Elephants, and Boatmen.

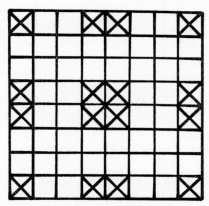

FIG. 43. An Ashtapada board (from Hyde, *De Ludis Orientalibus*)

One of the early Sanskrit writings, the Bhavishya Purana, contains the tale of a prince who lost all his possessions including his wife, playing at dice. He went to an old friend to learn the mysteries of Shaturanga hoping to win his fortune back. His instruction is contained in a poem and the following account is based on the translation by Professor Duncan Forbes, Department of Oriental Languages, at King's College, London (1860).

The pawns in Shaturanga represent the infantry, a ship the boatmen, a horse the cavalry, an elephant the elephants, and a human figure the rajah. Each piece had a different type of move.

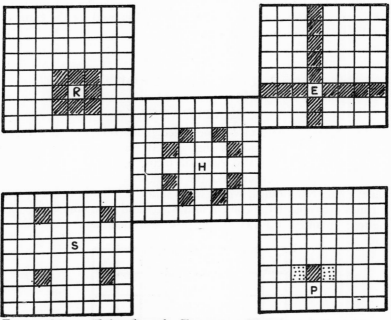

FIG. 44. Moves of the pieces in Shaturanga. The pieces indicated by a letter can move to any shaded square at the next move
R=rajah, E=elephant, H=horse, S=ship, P=pawn

Power of Movement

The RAJAH moved orthogonally or diagonally one square in any direction (fig. 44).

The ELEPHANT moved orthogonally forwards, sideways, or backwards any number of unoccupied squares. The elephant could not jump over a piece (fig. 44).

The HORSE moved one square orthogonally and one square diagonally (the knight's move in modern chess). The horse could jump over any intervening piece (fig. 44).

The SHIP moved two squares diagonally and could jump over any intervening piece (fig. 44).

The PAWNS moved one square orthogonally forwards, unless they were making a capture when they moved one square diagonally forwards (fig. 44).

Ships and pawns were minor pieces and could capture each other but were not allowed to capture the major pieces. The moves of the pieces were controlled by a long die marked 2, 3, 4, 5. On a throw of:

> 2: The ship moved
> 3: The horse moved
> 4: The elephant moved
> 5: The rajah or a pawn moved.

If a piece moved on to a square occupied by an enemy piece, the latter was removed from the board.

Fig. 45 shows the arrangement of the board with the Black Army

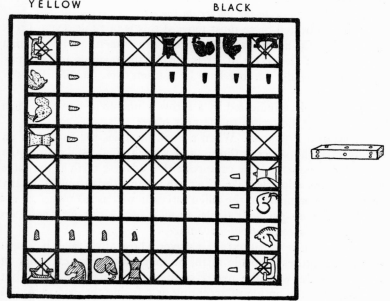

FIG. 45. Shaturanga pieces arranged for a game on an ashtapada board.

at the north, the Red at the south, the Green at the east and the Yellow at the west. Each army is drawn up in the same formation with a boat on the marked corner square, next is a horse, then an elephant, and the king stands on a marked central square known as the THRONE. The pawns stand in front of these pieces and move orthogonally forwards towards their ally's side of the board. This opening position of the pieces is taken from al-Beruni's work *India*. Al-Beruni was a Persian born in Khiva in Khwarizm in A.D. 973 and he lived in Hyrcania on the southern shores of the Caspian. He travelled to India and wrote extensively about the people of the Punjab. He died at Ghazna in A.D. 1048.

Rules

(Additions in italics fill obvious deficiencies in the ancient account.)

    1. *At the beginning of the game each player puts an agreed stake into a pool. This is shared by the victorious allies at the end of the game.*

    2. *Each player throws a die in turn and the player with the highest number throws again and makes his opening move in accordance with this throw, unless it is a 4: when the elephant is unable to move and the turn passes clockwise to the player on the left.*

    3. An indicated piece must move if this is possible, even if it is to the player's disadvantage. A throw can sometimes be satisfied by a choice of pieces, e.g. if a 5 is thrown the rajah or a pawn may move, or if the ally's troops have been taken over, one of his pawns or rajah.

    4. If the piece indicated by a throw is unable to move the turn is lost and the die passes to the next player.

    5. SEIZING A THRONE. When a rajah occupies the throne of an enemy rajah he seizes a throne and wins a single stake from the despoiled opponent. If he captures either adverse rajah at the same move he wins a double stake. If a rajah mounts the throne of his ally he assumes command of the allied forces as well as his own . . . *and at his own or his partner's throws he may move either his own or his ally's pieces: a considerable advantage.*

    6. REGAINING A THRONE. If a player whose ally's rajah has been captured captures a hostile rajah, he may propose an exchange of prisoner rajahs with the player owning the remaining rajah, but the latter has the option of accepting or refusing the exchange. . . . *Rescued rajahs re-enter the board on their own throne squares, or, if these are occupied, on the nearest vacant square.*

7. If a player whose own rajah is still on the board but whose ally's rajah is a prisoner captures both enemy rajahs he may claim the restoration of his ally's rajah without exchange or ransom. . . . *This would, however, also restore to his ally the control of his pieces.*

8. BUILDING AN EMPIRE. A player who succeeds in seizing his ally's throne and in capturing both enemy rajahs builds an empire.

(*a*) If the player's rajah made the capture on the hostile rajah's throne square he wins a quadruple stake . . . *from both opponents.*

(*b*) If the player's rajah made the capture on some other square he wins a double stake . . . *from both opponents.*

(*c*) If the capture of the second hostile rajah was made by any other piece the player wins a single stake . . . *from both opponents.*

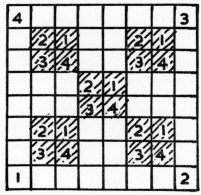

FIG. 46. The original positions of the ships are marked 1, 2, 3, 4. The five possible Concourses of shipping are shaded

9. CONCOURSE OF SHIPPING. Each ship sails on a different course and controls different squares and they can never attack each other directly, but if three ships are on adjacent squares and the fourth moves into position to occupy the fourth square this player completes a concourse of shipping and he captures the two enemy vessels and takes control of the moves of his ally's ship . . . *and when he throws a 2, he may move his own or his ally's ship on to a square favourable to himself even if it is not in his ally's interests!* There are only five positions on the board where a concourse of shipping can occur (fig. 46).

10. PROMOTION OF PAWNS. If a pawn reaches an unmarked square on the opposite side of the board it is promoted to the piece of that square, either a horse or an elephant. Promotion only occurs,

however, if the player has already lost one or more pawns. He is not allowed to have a promoted piece and three pawns on the board, and promotion is delayed until a pawn has been lost. . . . *A pawn reaching a marked square is not promoted and can take no further part in the game except to be captured by an enemy piece unless he should become a* PRIVILEGED PAWN.

11. PRIVILEGED PAWN. If a player has only a ship and a pawn left, this pawn becomes privileged and on reaching any square on the opposite side of the board can be promoted to any piece at the choice of his owner. This appears to be a chivalrous courtesy towards a weak adversary.

12. DRAWN GAME. If a player loses all his pieces except his rajah he is considered to have fought to an honourable peace and the game is drawn. . . . *His ally may still be in a position to fight on alone.*

13. *When a player has lost all his pieces he is out of the game. His turn does not pass to his partner who is forced to fight on with only one turn to his opponent's two.*

14. *Each player pays any special debts acquired in the course of the game to the player winning them; e.g. a stake to the first enemy player seizing his throne; a double stake if his rajah is captured in the same move; and a quadruple stake if one of his opponents builds an empire. The allies do not win from each other.*

Gambling became forbidden at an early date in Hindu culture and in the ninth book of the Laws of Manu is written:

'Let the king punish corporally, at discretion, both the gamester and the keeper of the gambling house, whether they play with inanimate objects such as dice, or shaturanga, or with living creatures as in the blood sports of cock and ram fighting.'

Shaturanga players evaded the gambling laws by discarding the die and removing the element of luck. Other changes followed. One of the first appears to have been the amalgamation of the allied forces into a single army and the game for four players became one for two. This explains the duplication of the pieces in modern chess. The allied kings were reduced in rank to prime ministers and their power of movement was halved, making them weak pieces.

About the same time the moves of the ship and the elephant were transposed, the elephant moving diagonally two squares, while the ship, called in Sanskrit *roka*, assumed the powerful orthogonal moves of the ancient elephant. With these changes the game ceased to be Shaturanga; it had developed into the early medieval variety of chess, Shatranj.

SHATRANJ

There is a tradition which places the introduction of Shatranj from India into Persia during the reign of Naushirawan (A.D. 531–79). He is better known in the west as Chosroes I. The earliest reference to Shatranj occurs in a Persian work called the *Karnamak-i-Artakh shatr-i-Papakan* which was written about A.D. 600. The poet Firdausi writing four centuries after Chosroes' death composed a great epic poem of a hundred and twenty thousand lines called the *Shahnama*, based on earlier historical works which have been lost. In the poem he relates a traditional story of how chess came to Persia. Forbes made a collation of six manuscripts in the British Museum and the following account is taken from his work.

'One day an ambassador from the king of Hind arrived at the Persian court of Chosroes, and after an oriental exchange of courtesies, the ambassador produced rich presents from his sovereign and amongst them was an elaborate board with curiously carved pieces of ebony and ivory. He then issued a challenge.

'"Oh great king, fetch your wise men and let them solve the mysteries of this game. If they succeed my master the king of Hind will pay you tribute as an overlord, but if they fail it will be proof that the Persians are of lower intellect and we shall demand tribute from Iran."

'The courtiers were shown the board, and after a day and a night in deep thought one of them, Buzurjmihr, solved the mystery and was richly rewarded by his delighted sovereign.'

(Perhaps the twenty-four hours were spent in bribing the Indian ambassador rather than in heavy thinking.)

In the following fifty years Shatranj became known to the Arabs and also to the Byzantine Court through the marriage of Khusru Parviz, the grandson of Chosroes I, to the daughter of the Byzantine emperor Maurice. In A.D. 591 Khusru became king of Persia and after the assassination of his father-in-law, the Emperor Maurice, he declared war on the Roman Empire. At first he was successful and conquered Asia Minor, Syria, Egypt, and North Africa, but after a crushing defeat by the Emperor Heraclius he lost them all again.

The Greeks probably knew the game soon after A.D. 600 and about the same time it reached the cities of Mecca and Medina. Shatranj was in high favour at the court of the Caliphs of Damascus

from A.D. 661 to 774. The first Arabian writer on chess of whom we
have any record was as-Sarakhsi, a physician of Bagdad who died
in A.D. 899. As-Suli, the greatest of the Arab chess players, died in
the city of Basra about A.D. 946 and several of his games have been
preserved.

FIG. 47. Chess set based on early eleventh-century fragments found at
Bambra-ka-Thul

The oldest-known Muslim chessmen (fig. 47) were found in
1855 in India by Mr. A. F. Bellasis while excavating the ruined
Muslim city of Mansura at Bambra-ka-thul, 47 miles north-east of
Haidarabad. The city was destroyed by an earthquake a little before
the time of al-Beruni (A.D. 1030). They are now in the British
Museum. A long die (2, 5; 1, 6;), a cubic die (1, 6; 2, 5; 3, 4;), and
fragments of a small box were found with them.

When and where Shatranj entered Europe is uncertain but claims
have been made for at least three routes. In the seventh century A.D.
the Saracens captured North Africa, and they crossed the Straits
of Gibraltar and settled in Andalus early in the eighth. They probably
took chess with them and the game may have spread from Spain
to the court of Charlemagne in France about A.D. 760.

The game may also have reached France from the Byzantine
Court. There is a story that at one time a marriage was contemplated
between Charlemagne and the Empress Irene. The two monarchs
exchanged courtesies and presents and among those from the aged
Empress was a chess set in which the two prime ministers were
replaced by two queens whose power had been increased beyond
that of any piece on the board. Charlemagne sensed future diffi-
culties and the marriage did not materialize!

The most frequently suggested avenue of entry was the Crusades.
In 1171 Saladin founded the Ayubite dynasty in Egypt and Syria,
and Shatranj was held in considerable respect at his court. We
know that the Christians learnt medical secrets from the Arab

physicians and Shatranj also may have appealed to the knights of the Cross. On their return home the game would have reached every castle in Christendom.

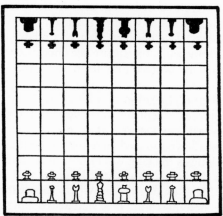

FIG. 48. Arrangement of pieces in Shatranj (using thirteenth-century symbols from Alfonso X and Cotton manuscripts)

A Shatranj board is shown in fig. 48 and the symbols used for the pieces are taken from the thirteenth-century Alfonso and Cotton manuscripts. There are no chequered squares and the advantage of the first move was decided with a die. See also fig. 154 on Plate XVIII.

Moves of the Pieces

The KING (Shah) moved one square orthogonally or diagonally in any direction.

The PRIME MINISTER (Firz) moved one square diagonally forwards or backwards. The two prime ministers could not attack each other.

The ELEPHANT (Fil) moved diagonally two squares. He could jump over a piece on the intervening square but could not attack it. The four elephants were unable to attack each other as each had a different circuit.

The WAR HORSE (Faras) moved one square orthogonally and one square diagonally. He was allowed to jump over intervening pieces.

The RUHK moved orthogonally any number of vacant squares in any direction. He could not jump over a piece.

The PAWNS (Baidaq) moved one square orthogonally forwards, but captured by moving one square diagonally forwards. When a pawn reached the far side of the board he was promoted to the rank of a prime minister and he could then move diagonally one square at a time backwards or forwards. There could be any number of promoted pawns on the board at the same time.

There were three ways of winning:

1. By CHECKMATE. If a checked king was unable to move out of check, or it was impossible to capture the checking man, or to interpose another man to protect him from the check, the game was lost.

2. By A BARE KING (Isolation of a king). If a player captured all the opponent's pieces except his king, he won the game.

3. By STRANGLED STALEMATE. If a player was stalemated in Shatranj, he was allowed to exchange his king with any other piece on the board as long as the king was not in check in the new position. This counted as the king's move, and the game then continued. The exchanged piece was known as the VICTIM because it was usually captured in the new position. If a stalemated king was unable to exchange position with any of his remaining forces the game was lost.

DRAWN GAME. Because of the peculiar powers and limited range of some of the pieces a powerful force was sometimes unable to defeat a much weaker one stationed on favourable squares, and in spite of there being three ways of winning, drawn games were frequent.

PERPETUAL CHECK was considered a drawn game.

The opening moves of Shatranj were rather tedious as several of the pieces were more restricted than their modern counterparts, and so the players often agreed to allow the opening player to make ten moves at once to arrange his forces; no piece, however, was allowed to cross the middle of the board. The second player then made his first ten moves in reply and from this opening position, called the Ta'biyat, or battle array, the play proceeded by alternate moves. Sometimes twelve moves constituted the Ta'biyat instead of ten.

During the next four centuries there was little change in the game and the European form of medieval chess described in Caxton's *The Game and Playe of the Chesse* printed in Bruges in 1474 was little different from the Persian Shatranj of the Crusades. Caxton's work was a translation of a translation of the famous chess morality of Jacobus de Cessolis, a native of Lombard who was a friar belonging to the order of the Friars Preachers, now known as Dominicans. The monk's work was in four books, written in Latin and called *Liber de Moribus Hominum et Officiis Nobilium*. It was written between A.D. 1275 and 1300, and was immensely popular. Several manuscripts have survived.

Caxton's *The Game and Playe of the Chesse* was reprinted in London in 1480 with the addition of twenty-four woodcuts. Several reprints were made during the nineteenth century, the last being in 1883 by W. E. A. Axon, London. At an auction of Lord Cunliffe's library a copy of the 1474 edition sold for £1,900. The book had been bought for £54. 12s. 0d. in 1813.

During the long evolution of chess many exotic forms were invented, enjoyed an ephemeral popularity, and then passed away. One such was Tamberlane's or the Great Chess which was the form played by the Mogul conqueror. After it had been forgotten for several hundred years it was recovered from a Persian manuscript in the possession of the Royal Asiatic Society and it is fully described in Forbes's *History of Chess*. There were twenty-eight pieces on each side and the game was played on a large board of 112 squares. Another medieval form which may be of more interest to the modern player was the Circular, or Byzantine Chess.

FIG. 49. Byzantine chess (after Strutt, *Sports and Pastimes of the People of England*). Bland (*Persian Chess*) gives an alternative arrangement with the King and Queen at the periphery, then the Bishops, then Knights and the Rooks placed centrally

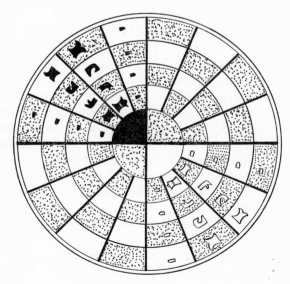

CIRCULAR CHESS

The circular board contained sixty-four spaces and four citadels. Ordinary chessmen were used. The board and opening position of the pieces is shown in fig. 49. The pieces had the same moves and powers as in Shatranj with one exception. There was no pawn promotion, and if two of a player's pawns were played around the board and met face to face blocking each other, the opponent removed them both and then made his own move.

If a player's king was hard pressed and he managed to enter his opponent's citadel he was considered to have reached a sanctuary and the game was drawn.

 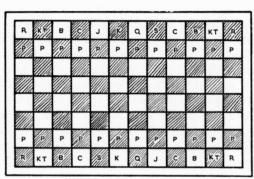

FIG. 50. Courier chessmen
from Van Leyden's *Chess
Players*; c. A.D. 1520

FIG. 51. Opening positions
in Courier chess
(after Murray's *History of Chess*)

THE COURIER GAME

Early in the thirteenth century this enlarged form of chess appeared in Germany and was played for several centuries. The village of Ströbeck near Halberstadt, in the Hartz mountains, still possesses a board which was presented to the village in 1651 by the Elector-Prince Frederick William of Brandenburg. The original silver pieces were lent in the eighteenth century and were never returned; but there is a complete set of wooden men for the game. A set based on Van Leyden's 'Chess Players' is shown in fig. 50. See also Plate III facing p. 64.

Fig. 51 shows the arrangement of the pieces.

Moves

The KING moved one square in any direction. He had no power of leaping and could not castle.

The QUEEN moved one square diagonally forwards or backwards but in the opening move she jumped to the third square.

The BISHOP moved two squares diagonally and had the power of jumping over a piece on the intervening square.

The KNIGHT moved one square orthogonally and one square diagonally or vice-versa. It had the power of leaping over an intervening piece.

The ROOK moved any number of vacant squares orthogonally.

The COURIER moved any number of empty squares diagonally. This is the move of the modern bishop.

The JESTER moved to an adjacent square horizontally or vertically.

The SAGE moved to any adjacent square, and unlike the king was not limited by being in check.

The PAWNS could only move a single square forwards with the exception of the Queen's and Rooks' pawns which could make a double step forwards on their first move.

Rules

1. The board was placed with a white corner square at the player's right hand.

2. To develop the game more quickly the opening player moved his two rooks' pawns and his queen's pawn to the fourth square, and the queen made a JOY-LEAP to her third square. His opponent replied with the same four moves and then the game continued one move alternately as in other forms of chess.

3. Nothing is known about the pawn promotion of Courier chess but it may have been the same as in another variety of chess played in Ströbeck. In this a pawn reaching the eighth row had to make three joy-leaps to the sixth, fourth, and second rows on the same file before it was promoted. It then became a queen only. It could not leap over, or take a piece during the joy-leaps. It was immune from capture when on the eighth row, but not in its leaps backwards to its original square. These leaps did not have to be in consecutive moves.

The game is mentioned in the *Wigalois* of Wirnt v. Gravenberg (A.D. 1202) and therefore it was played at least as early as this date. Gustavus Selenus in *Das Schach-oder König-Spiel* (Leipzig, 1616) gives woodcuts of the pieces. The courier was a man galloping on horseback with a horn to his lips; the sage had a long beard; and the jester, cap and bells. Plate III (opposite), a painting of 'The Chess Players', *c*. A.D. 1520, shows a Courier game in progress. It is attributed to Van Leyden, and before the Second World War formed part of the famous collection of the Kaiser Friedrich Museum in Berlin. In September 1939 these works of art were removed to the vaulted stone cellars, but in 1943, when the air-raids increased and the building was severely damaged, the collection was placed in an air-raid shelter in Dönhoffstrasse, and a little later in a huge concrete anti-aircraft flak tower near the Alexanderplatz.

Early in 1945 the air-raids became excessive and the art experts urged the military authorities to transfer the treasures to a safer home. All requests were refused until a direct order was received in March from Hitler himself for the immediate evacuation of the most valuable items. By this time only two small open trucks could be spared but the removal began on 12 March 1945. The two drivers left the city a little before 8 p.m. when the raids usually began. As they could not drive by night for fear of accidents in the blackout, they stopped and slept in the woods a few miles from Berlin. There was no covering of any sort for the priceless cargo but fortunately it did not rain. When they arrived at Merker's salt mine which is south-west of Erfurt the treasures were placed 2,000 ft. below ground. The two trucks made several journeys until conditions became impossible.

On 7 April 1945 General Patton's Third Army entered the area and two elderly French women who were in a German slave-gang stopped Lt.-Col. Russell of the American 90th Infantry Division and indicated with gesticulations and a torrent of French that he should follow them into the mine. There he found a fantastic reincarnation of Aladdin's cave. There were millions of pounds' worth of gold coins, bullion, jewels, art treasures, and crate after crate of great paintings, Van Leyden's being among them.

Nazi loot was returned to its rightful owners while the Kaiser Friedrich collection was taken to Wiesbaden. In November 1945 instructions arrived for their transfer to the U.S.A. The roads were appalling; ice and snow added to the dangers from bomb craters and weakened bridges, and it was decided to send them by rail. The only rolling stock left in the shattered railway yard were two German hospital cars complete with huge red crosses. The masterpieces were placed inside, and the journey to Le Havre began.

A game of Courier chess, *c.* A.D. 1520. Reproduced from Van Leyden's oil-painting
'The Chess Players'

IV

FIG. 52. Blind player's chess set, twentieth century. The white pieces have pointed tops and the black smooth. The black squares are raised above the general level of the board. The pieces have pegs to prevent accidental displacement

In America the pictures were stored in the National Gallery of Art in Washington until a home was ready for them in Germany. Early in 1948 they returned to the Fatherland, to a modern exhibition hall in Munich, the Haus der Kunst.

MODERN INTERNATIONAL CHESS

Information is so readily available that it will not be described here. Fig. 52 (opposite) shows a twentieth-century chess set for blind players.

THE MAHARAJAH AND THE SEPOYS

A chess board and set is used. One player arranges his pieces in the normal way; the other has a single piece, the Maharajah, which can move as a Queen or a Knight and is placed on any free square on the board (fig. 53).

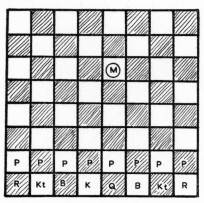

Fɪɢ. 53. Opening position in The Maharajah and the Sepoys

The game provides interesting problems, though a careful player who never leaves a piece unsupported will finally hem the Maharajah in. If he makes a mistake, however, the Maharajah's great mobility may allow him to win quickly by trapping the King behind his own men; or later when the board is clear, he may drive the King into a corner which is followed by an inevitable checkmate.

ORIENTAL CHESS

When Shatranj spread westwards into Europe it also re-entered Northern India and travelled eastwards into Burma, China, and

F

Japan. Each of these countries developed its own form. Only the Chinese will be described.

CHINESE CHESS (SIANG K'I)

The original Shatranj was considerably modified and elephants, horsemen, infantry, cannon, and war-chariots fight for the capture of the enemy general. Each army has a fortress within which the general and his mandarins direct operations; the enemy fortress must be taken by storm to win the game. Between the two armies is a river which the heavily-laden elephants are unable to cross. The other field pieces pass over it at will.

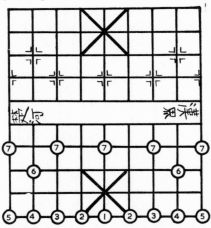

FIG. 54. Chinese chess board with one player's pieces arranged in opening positions

The Chinese chess board consists of two halves of 8×4 squares which are separated by a space one square wide known as the RIVER. Each half of the board contains four squares marked with diagonals. The resulting square of nine points is known as the FORTRESS. The pieces are placed on the intersections of the lines instead of on the spaces, and the board becomes one of 9×10 points (figs. 54 and 150 on Plate XV).

The chessmen are circular discs of wood, ivory, or other material, all alike in size and shape. The ranks are written on the upper face, one side in red and the other in green. Some of the green characters differ from those of the red on pieces of the same power, as if one side were given English titles and the other German. This increases

the atmosphere of rival armies but it makes recognition more difficult for players who do not read Chinese. The author has found it
helpful to add small triangular marks to the pieces confined to the
fortress, and small circular marks to the field pieces outside, the
soldiers being left unmarked (fig. 55).

FIG. 55. Chinese chess pieces. The characters for the Horse, Chariot and
Cannon are the same for both colours (from pieces in author's
collection)

Moves of the Pieces

The GENERAL moves one point vertically or horizontally, but he
is confined to the nine points of the fortress.

The MANDARINS move one point diagonally, but they are confined to the nine points of the fortress.

The ELEPHANTS move diagonally to the next point but one, the
intervening point must be unoccupied and they are unable to
cross the river into enemy territory.

The other pieces are free to move over the whole board.

The HORSEMEN move one point vertically or horizontally followed
by a point diagonally; the intervening point must be unoccupied.

The CHARIOTS move any distance vertically or horizontally, if
the intervening points are unoccupied.

The CANNONS move any distance vertically or horizontally, but they can only capture if they have jumped over some piece on the way to the point which they are attacking. The intervening piece, known as the SCREEN, may be of any power and of either side. The cannons cannot, however, jump over more than one piece in a single move.

The SOLDIERS move one point vertically forwards on their own side of the board. In enemy territory they can move one point forwards or sideways, but on reaching the opponent's back line they can only move sideways. There is no promotion.

The object of the game is to checkmate or stalemate the opposing General. A player cannot give perpetual check, he must vary the move. A General is in check:

1. When he is under attack by any piece, and could have been taken on the following move, if nothing were done to thwart the attack.

2. When the Generals face one another upon the same file with no intervening piece.

When a check is given there are three possible replies:

1. The attacking piece may be taken and removed from the board.

2. The General may move out of check.

3. The check may be covered. If a horseman is the attacking piece, a man placed on the ANGLE of its move blocks its attack.

If a cannon is attacking, either the screen may be removed, as a cannon can only attack over an intervening piece, or a second piece may be interposed which protects the General as a cannon can only jump over one piece at a time. If the check cannot be relieved the General is defeated and the game is lost.

Chess is the game of the middle and lower classes and they usually play for small stakes; the aristocracy and the intelligentsia prefer Wei-ch'i. The earliest reference to Siang k'i is in the *Book of Marvels* (Hüan Kwai Lu) attributed to Nui Seng-ju who died in A.D. 847.

THE JUNGLE GAME

No information is yet available about the history of this curious game. It may be a development of Chinese chess comparable to Draughts in Europe.

The board is shown in fig. 56. The pieces of one side are blue, and the other red. Each player has eight animals. In the list below the numbers represent their respective strengths.

Piece	*Power*
Elephant	8
Lion	7
Tiger	6
Panther	5
Dog	4
Wolf	3
Cat	2
Rat	1
Trapped	0

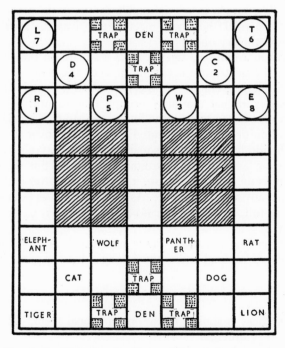

FIG. 56. Board for The Jungle Game. The shaded squares represent water. One player's pieces are arranged in the opening positions (author's collection)

At the beginning of the game the pieces are placed on the appropriately marked squares. Blue moves first.

Rules

1. Each turn consists of moving one piece one square orthogonally in any direction.

2. An animal may eat any animal smaller than itself by moving on to its square. (The method of capture in chess.) The only exception to this rule is that the rat can kill the elephant since it can run into the elephant's ears and so gnaw into its brain. If similar animals meet, the animal moving on to a square eats the animal already there.

3. Three pieces have special powers.

(*a*) When the rat reaches the river it can enter it and move on the water squares as if it were on dry land. If it is in the river no other animal can attack it since they cannot move on to a water square. The rat, however, is unable to attack the elephant from a water square. If both rats meet in the river the moving piece eats the stationary one.

(*b*) When a lion or a tiger reaches a square on the edge of the river, at the next move it can jump over the water in any orthogonal direction, landing on the nearest land square. It destroys any smaller animal that may occupy that square: if, however, there is a rat in the river in the line of the jump, it blocks the way and the lion or tiger is prevented from leaping over the water.

4. Each side has three trap-squares and the player's own pieces may move on and off them without restriction, but if an enemy animal moves on to a trap-square, it loses all its power and becomes weaker than any defending piece. As soon as it moves out of the trap it regains its full strength. Animals of either side may enter and leave traps at will.

5. A player may not move any of his animals on to his own den.

6. When any animal enters the enemy's den the game is won.

TIBETAN CHESS

Tibetan chess is similar to the international form, although the pieces are very different.

A set in the author's collection is shown in fig. 156 (on Plate XIX). The King also forms the tailpiece to this chapter, p. 90. The pieces of this particular set are made of human bone.

3. DRAUGHTS

About A.D. 1100 someone unknown, probably living in the south of France, invented a new game using tablemen on a chequered chess board with the moves of Alquerque. Each player had twelve pieces called FERSES, the name of the queens in medieval chess, and the ferses in the new game moved in the same way as in the old, one square diagonally in any direction. A piece in FIERGES, however, made a capture by jumping diagonally over the enemy piece to land on an empty square immediately beyond.

In the *Chronique* of Philip Mouskat (A.D. 1243), lines 23617–20, is a reference to a KING of Fierges, indicating that a fers could be promoted to a king at this early period. When the name of the fers in chess was changed to dame, the same change occurred in the new game, a piece being known as a DAME, and the game as DAMES. In Dames there was no compulsion to take an enemy piece, a survival of chess practice. When a compulsion rule was introduced in France about 1535 the old non-huffing game became known as LE JEU PLAISANT DE DAMES or simply as PLAISANT in contrast to the huffing game called JEU FORCÉ. Modern English draughts is the jeu forcé of the sixteenth century.

ENGLISH DRAUGHTS

The board is shown in fig. 57. The pieces move only on the black squares and Black begins. The players change colours at the end of each game. The double-black corner must be on the player's right. The draughtsmen move diagonally forwards one square at a time. They cannot move backwards.

The object of the game is to capture or immobilize the twelve opposing pieces. A capture is made by a piece jumping over an enemy piece and landing on a vacant square immediately beyond. If the capturing piece can continue to leap over other enemy pieces they are also captured and removed from the board. When a piece finally comes to rest the move is finished.

If a draughtsman reaches the opponent's back line it becomes a king (fig. 58). Crowning ends a move. After crowning a king can move diagonally backwards or forwards one square at a time, and captures by a SHORT JUMP over an enemy piece. There may be several kings on the board at the same time.

If a player has a choice of captures he may take a smaller rather than a larger number if he wishes, but if he chooses the larger then he must capture all the pieces possible. If he does not make a complete capture he becomes liable to one of the three penalties below, which are also levied against a piece failing to make a single capture when this is possible.

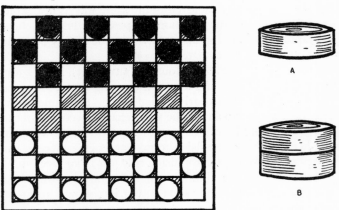

FIG. 57. English draughts board   FIG. 58. A, a draughtsman; B, a king

Penalties for failing to take an Enemy Piece

1. The opponent may insist that the piece which was moved is returned to its position, and the proper capturing move made.

2. The opponent may accept the move which was made and let it stand. If this is done the piece able to make the capture must do so at the player's next move or the penalties may be inflicted a second time.

3. The opponent may remove the piece which should have made the capture, and then continue with his own move. This is called HUFFING and does not constitute a move in itself.

The early settlers took the English game to North America where it is known as CHECKERS. There are two variants of the English draughts which make a pleasant change from the orthodox game.

THE LOSING GAME

Each player has twelve men arranged in the conventional manner and the moves and methods of capture are as in the English game except that only Rule 1 under penalties applies. Each player tries to force his opponent to capture his pieces, and the first player to lose them all wins the game.

DIAGONAL DRAUGHTS

The rules are the same as in the English game except that the pieces are arranged as in fig. 59.

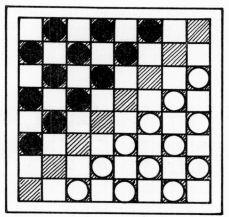

FIG. 59. Opening position in Diagonal draughts

ITALIAN DRAUGHTS

This game was played in Italy at the end of the sixteenth century. The two differences from English draughts were:

1. A man could not take a king.
2. A player had to take when possible or lose the game, and if he had a choice of capture he was forced to take the greater number; and if the number were equal, then the more valuable pieces: e.g. he was compelled to take a king in preference to a man. This rule was known in Italy as 'il più col più' ('the greater to the greater').

TURKISH DRAUGHTS

An uncheckered board is used but the familiar one is satisfactory. Each player has sixteen men and the opening arrangement is shown in fig. 60.

Rules

1. A man moves one square forwards or sideways but not diagonally, and on reaching the eighth row becomes a king.

2. A man captures by the short jump forwards or sideways and may take more than one piece in a turn of play.

3. Captured pieces are removed as taken and a turn continues until the piece can make no more captures.

4. A king can move forwards, sideways, or backwards any number of vacant squares, and the king can place himself on any vacant square beyond the captured piece to make further captures.

5. The first player to capture or immobilize all his opponent's pieces, or reduce the enemy to a single man against a king, wins the game.

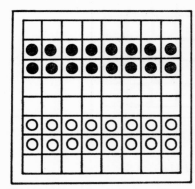

FIG. 60. Opening position in Turkish draughts

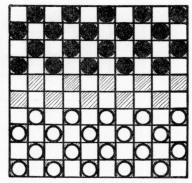

FIG. 61. Opening position in Polish
draughts

REVERSI

Reversi was invented between 1880 and 1890 and is played on a draughts-board. There are sixty-four pieces which are black on one side and white on the other.

Black begins by placing a piece black side up on one of the four central squares on the empty board. White replies by placing his first piece white side up on another of these squares. The central four squares must be filled first and then the players play alternately, each piece being placed on a square adjacent to one occupied by an enemy piece. Any enemy pieces directly intervening between this piece and another of the player's own colour, orthogonally or diagonally, are captured and turned over to show the player's colour uppermost. A piece may change owners several times in a game. When all the squares of the board are covered with pieces, the player with most of his colour showing wins the game.

CONTINENTAL OR POLISH DRAUGHTS

The jeu forcé (English draughts) only lasted a few years in France and was replaced about 1650 by a variety known as 'Le Grand Forçat'. This also became obsolete within fifty years and was replaced by the game now known as Polish or Continental draughts, first played in the cafés of Paris in 1727. Modifications in the rules have been made and as now played, Polish draughts must rank as one of the great board games of the world. See fig. 142 on Plate XI.

Rules

1. The opening position of the pieces is shown in fig. 61.
2. A man moves one square diagonally forwards.
3. A man captures by the short jump both diagonally forwards or backwards.
4. A king can move diagonally any number of unoccupied squares.
5. A king may land any number of vacant squares beyond a captured piece.
6. If a player has a choice of captures he must choose the one in which the greatest number of captures are made, or if equal numbers are at risk, then the more powerful pieces must be taken.
7. Captured pieces are only lifted at the end of the move and a dead piece forms an impassable barrier.
8. A man is only promoted to a king when he remains on the opponent's back line; if on reaching the crownhead more captures are possible, they must be made and the move completed, the man remaining unpromoted until he again reaches the crownhead and remains there at the end of the move.

4. THE TAFL GROUP

These games originated in northern Europe and are miniature battles fought between unequal forces. The smaller force has a piece, or pieces, with special powers and the larger force tries to hem them in; while the smaller force tries to break out, or destroy the larger.

FOX AND GEESE

Thirteen geese are arranged on the board as in fig. 62 and the fox is placed on any vacant point. The fox and the geese can move in any direction along a line to the next contiguous point. If the fox jumps over a goose and lands on an empty point beyond, the goose is killed and removed from the board. Two or more geese can be killed in one move by a series of short jumps by the fox. The geese cannot jump over the fox, but they try to crowd him into a corner

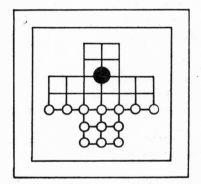   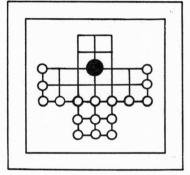

FIG. 62. An early form of Fox and   FIG. 63. Fox and Geese. A later
        Geese   form with seventeen geese

and make it impossible for him to move. If the fox is immobilized he loses the game, but if he can deplete the gaggle of geese until they are unable to trap him he wins.

If the geese are correctly played the fox must lose. In later forms of the game the geese were increased to seventeen, but were deprived of the power of moving backwards (fig. 63).

Hala-tafl, the Fox Game, is mentioned in the Icelandic 'Grettis saga'. Dr. Finnur Jonsson, the literary historian, believed that this saga was written after A.D. 1300 by an anonymous priest who lived in the northern part of the island.

During the reign of Edward IV of England (1461–83) an entry was made in the accounts of the Royal Household for the purchase of two foxes and twenty-six hounds of silver over-gilt for two sets of Marelles.

Fiske suggested that Fox and Geese may be the same game as Freystafl which is mentioned in the late sagas. Tafl itself, frequently appearing in the early literature of northern Europe, was later replaced by Hnefatafl. No record of either game has survived.

FIG. 64. Embroidered Tablut board (redrawn from Linnaeus's *Lachesis Lapponica*)

In 1732 Linnaeus, the Swedish botanist, visited Lapland when he was a young student and his diary contains the description of a game played there by the Alpine Lapps called Tablut which appears to be closely related to Hnefatafl. The following account is taken from the entry in his diary for 20 July.

TABLUT

The Tablut board (fig. 64) is marked out with 9 × 9 squares, the central one being distinctive and known as the Konakis or throne. Only the Swedish king can occupy this square. One player has eight blonde Swedes (fig. 65A) and their monarch (fig. 65B); the other has sixteen dark Muscovites (fig. 65C). The king is larger than the other pieces. The Muscovites are placed on the embroidered squares. (This remark suggests that the board was made of reindeer skin ornamented with needlework as the Lapps had no cloth.)

Rules

1. All the pieces move orthogonally any number of vacant squares (the move of the rook in chess).

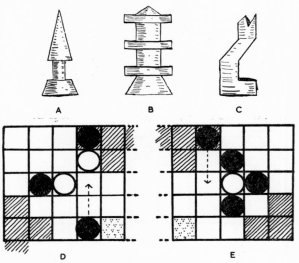

Fig. 65. Tablut pieces and method of capture
 A, a Swede; B, the Swedish king; C, a Muscovite; D, two pieces captured in one move; E, capture of the Swedish king.

2. A piece is captured and removed from the board when the opponent occupies both adjacent squares in row or column (fig. 65D). This is the CUSTODIAN method of capture. A piece may move safely on to an empty square between two enemy pieces.

3. The king is captured if all four squares around him are occupied by enemy pieces (fig. 65E); or if he is surrounded on three sides by enemy pieces and on the fourth by the Konakis. When the king is captured the game is over and the Muscovites are victorious.

4. The Swedes win if the king reaches any square at the periphery of the board. When there is a clear route for the king to a perimeter square the player must warn his opponent by saying 'Raichi!' When there are two clear routes he must say 'Tuichi!' This is the equivalent of 'Checkmate' since it is impossible to block two directions in the same move.

Linnaeus's journey through Lapland was an incredible feat. He travelled 3,798 miles on foot and by small boat in 153 days, an average of 24 miles a day, in spite of most of the route being over trackless wastes. He depended for food upon the hospitality of the peasant people. His diary, written in a mixture of Swedish and Latin, is crammed with observations and drawings: pages of records of flowers and plants, descriptions of animals, fish, insects, parasites, and geology; details of diseases and their treatment; folk-lore; cooking recipes, marriage ceremonies, scythes, skis, cross-bows, making garments, building houses. . . .

Before he died this traveller occupied a professorial chair and became a preceptor of the learned world, invented a system of plant classification still in use today, and was honoured throughout Europe.

SAXON HNEFATAFL

A fragment of a gaming board (fig. 66) was found at Wimose in Fyn, the second largest of the Danish islands, in a Roman Iron-Age grave. This period ended about A.D. 400.

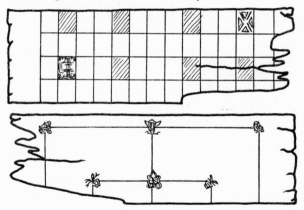

FIG. 66. Fragment of a board found at Wimose, Denmark, *c.* A.D. 400 (from Du Chaillu's *The Viking Age*, Vol. II). The patterns in the shaded squares are similar to those shown. On the reverse was a Nine Men's Morris board.

Eighteen squares are visible along one side and if the board was symmetrical it contained at least 18 × 18 squares, and each square was about 1 in. × 1 in. in area. The Scandinavians took tafl with them to Iceland and Britain. The later sagas mention the development of tafl into hnefatafl and an English manuscript written during the reign of King Athelstan (A.D. 925–40) contains a diagram of the Saxon form of hnefatafl which corresponds with the Wimose fragment. See Plate V, opposite.

The Latin text describes the game as a religious allegory, but it is valuable in preserving the form of hnefatafl played in England in the tenth century.

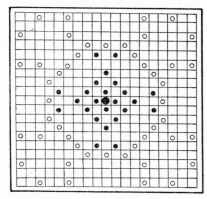

FIG. 67. Saxon Hnefatafl pieces. A, a hnefi; B, a hunns found at Woodperry (after Murray's *A History of Board Games other than Chess*)

FIG. 68. Saxon Hnefatafl board and opening position of the pieces (reconstruction)

A bone piece found at Woodperry in Oxfordshire gives the shape of the hunns or ordinary pieces (fig. 67B). The king or hnefi was larger and more ornate (fig. 67A). (This is a reconstruction.)

The following reconstruction of the game is based on the translation of the Athelstan manuscript in Robinson J. Armitage's *Time of St. Dunstan* (Oxford, 1923). The board (fig. 68) has been modified to allow the pieces to move on the squares instead of on the points. See also fig. 155 on Plate XVIII.

Reconstructed Board and Suggested Rules

1. The two forces begin in the positions shown in fig. 68. The king is on the central square.

2. The king's force has the first move and then the players move alternately.

V

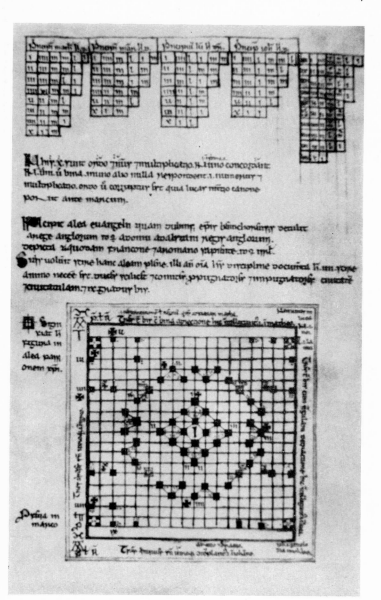

Photograph of a page from a tenth-century manuscript with a
diagram of a Hnefatafl board

DE SHAHILUDIO

cè vocant *Shatrangi: non enim dicitur Fortuna aut Infortunium* (i. e. bona fortuna aut mala fortuna,) *in Bello Shatrangico, quemadmodum dicitur de duobus Regibus contra se invicem belligerantibus. Causa enim Belli Shatrangici comperte sunt, ut sc. sapiens prudenti ductu suo semper vincat, & non metuat causam naturalem.*

Impressa exemplaria pro *Cubia,* melius legunt אשקוקין *Escaques.* At in illis pessima interpolatione interseritur אשפשיר *Asfasfir,* ut legatur אשפשיר ובמלחמת השחוק aut *infortunium in Asfasfir & in Bello Scachorum.* Pessima inquam est hæc interpolatio: cum enim Author Philosophicè differendo, introduxisset exemplum Ludi *Shatrangi* seu *Scachorum* tanquam rei quæ fortunæ & casui non esset subjecta; Interpolator injicit mentionem τȣ *Asfasfir* seu *Tesserarum Ludi,* qui fortunæ & casui omnino obnoxius est; quod itaque Authoris scopo non quadrat, sed potius totius Argumenti vim enervat, & loci sensum plané pervertit.

In dicta pericope etiam innuitur hunc Ludum esse repræsentationem Belli. Ideòque *Abmetres* in *Oneirocriticis* observat, quòd ὁ Βασιλεὺς, ἡ Μέγιςος, ἡ Ἄρχων παλίμιος, ἐὰν ἴδῃ ὅτι τὸ Ζατρίκιν αὐτȣ ἀπώλετο, ἡ ἐκλάδη, ἡ ἐκλάδη, ἀπολέσει τὸν ςρατὸν αὐτȣ. Et *Ahmed Bashá* Epigrammatista idem innuit, in suâ Epigrammatum Turcicorum collectione adducens نظر شطرنج de *Shatrangi* ænigma elegans, MS Seld. superius, p. 236, اول

PROLEGOMENA CURIOSA.

اول دھ طرقھ دلھ دررز تدبیر لتنگ
دور زنگ
دور زنگ اسر الزر وزر ازاریر صلر ویجانک خزان
جاسر الزر وزر ازاریر صلر ویجانک خزان
صاح السر اول قلجی دجمی دیسی درنک

Illud quâ plagâ fiat Castello, ubi duorum colorum Examines viri sunt qui faciunt pacem & Bellam? Pax facit illud Castellum momento desolatum: Bellum verò illud statim habitatum reddit?

Nempe Scaccarium affimilatur Castello, quia armatis viris defenditur; quod in pace (quando nempe non luditur,) incolis vacuum & quasi desolatum est, quòd non adsint Scachi seu Milites. In bello autem, (viz. quando luditur,) tum incolis frequens est, & Scachis seu Militibus refertum. Adeò ut Bellum quod omnia vastare solet, heic è contra istud Castellum non desolatum, sed habitatum, reddat.

Hieronymus Vida etiam suum Librum cui Tit. *Scachias,* sic inchoat,

Ludimus effigiem belli simulataque veris
Prælia, buxo acies fictas, & ludicra regna:
Ut gemini inter se Reges albúsque nigerque
Pro laude oppositi certent bicoloribus armis.

Et *Sokeikr Damascenus* in Libello Arabico quidem folio
(a 2)

Reproduction of two consecutive pages from Hyde's *De Ludis Orientalibus.*

3. Any piece can move orthogonally any number of vacant squares (the rook's move in chess).

4. A capture is made by trapping an enemy piece between two of the player's pieces on rank or file but not diagonally.

5. A piece may move between two enemy pieces without being captured.

6. The king can only be captured by being surrounded on all four sides by enemy pieces.

7. White wins if the king reaches any square on the periphery of the board and loses if the monarch is captured.

COWS AND LEOPARDS

This game is not one of the Tafl group, but the sides are unequal and the objectives of the two players are different. It is the best of a

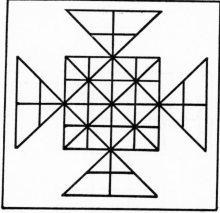

FIG. 69. Board for Cows and Leopards (after Parker's *Ancient Ceylon*)

group of related games which are widely played throughout southern Asia and appear to be quite independent of Scandinavia. One player has two leopards, and the other has twenty-four cows which try to imprison the leopards. The leopards can KILL a cow by jumping over her on to a vacant point beyond. Cows and leopards move from one point to the next orthogonally or diagonally.

The leopard player begins the game by placing a leopard on any point, usually the centre one. A cow is next put down, and then the second leopard on any other chosen point. Another cow follows, and then a cow is added to the board after each move of a leopard,

G

until they are all in play. Only then can the cows on the board be moved. While the cows are being introduced some will be KILLED and if the leopards can kill eight cows they should win, but with careful play the cows always succeed in trapping the leopards. See fig. 145 on Plate XIII.

5. THE LATRUNCULORUM GROUP

War games with the custodian method of capture are played in north-east Africa, but the two sides are equal and the games have two phases: the first when the pieces are introduced on to the board, and the second when they fight for supremacy.

SEEGA

In *The Modern Egyptians* Lane described the game of Seega which was popular with the fellaheen in the early nineteenth century. Marin, a hundred years later, found the same game played by the Somali.

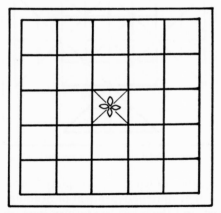

FIG. 70. Board for Seega (after Lane's *Modern Egyptians*)

A board of 5×5 squares is marked out on the ground (fig. 70). The two players each use a set of twelve coloured stones.

First Phase

1. The players place two stones at a time on any vacant squares except the centre square which is left uncovered in the first phase.

2. When the twenty-four stones have been placed, the player placing the last couple in position begins the second phase.

Second Phase

3. A stone can move orthogonally to any adjacent vacant square, including the central one.

4. If a player can trap an enemy stone between two of his own (the custodian capture), he removes it from the board and continues to move the same stone as long as he makes captures with it.

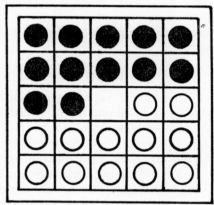

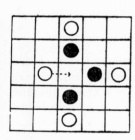

FIG. 71. Multiple custodian capture

FIG. 72. Opening positions in High Jump

5. A stone may make more than one capture in a single move. In fig. 71 the white stone captures three black ones by moving on to the centre square.

6. A player can move a stone between two enemy stones without harm.

7. A stone on the centre square cannot be captured even though it is trapped between two enemy pieces.

8. When a player cannot move, his opponent must make an opening for him by taking an extra turn.

9. The boards may be increased to 7×7 or 9×9 squares, each player then having 24 or 40 pieces.

A weak feature of the game is the frequency of a draw.

Each player may make a barrier behind which there are only his own pieces and he can move these without any chance of attack. The placing of the stones in the first phase is an important factor in planning such barriers. If a player captures all the enemy stones he has a clear win; if a barrier position arises the player with most pieces has a points win; if each player has the same number of pieces in a barrier position the game is drawn.

HIGH JUMP

The Somalis play another game called High Jump on the same board. The initial positions of the stones are shown in fig. 72. The stones move as in Seega but they capture an opponent's piece by jumping over it orthogonally, and several pieces can be taken in succession in one turn of play. It is not compulsory to make a capture.

LUDUS LATRUNCULORUM

In the museum at Chesters, Northumberland, is a stone board which was found on Hadrian's Wall (fig. 73). Several small pieces of tile were lying near and are now in the Black Gate Museum, Newcastle-upon-Tyne. Some are plain and others have a hole drilled through the centre. They appear to have served as pieces for the game.

In a Richborough find there was a board of 8×8 squares with eighteen flat discs; eleven were marked with concentric circles and seven were plain. Many other boards have been found in Roman sites in Britain. They are usually marked with 7×8, 8×8, or 9×10 squares. Their frequency suggests a popular game which may have been Ludus Latrunculorum. The first reference to this game was made by Varro (116–27 B.C.) but it was probably much older. He implies that it was played on a board marked with lines and spaces.

Ovid tells us that the pieces were of different-coloured glass or even precious stones. He also states that a piece was taken by being surrounded by two enemy pieces in rank or file and that backward moves were allowed. Our chief source of information about the game comes from an obscure account in a poem known as *Laus Pisonis* which was written by Saleius Bassus during the middle of the first century A.D. The following translation is taken from Professor Austin's article, 'Roman Board Games'.

'Cunningly the pieces are disposed on the open board, and battles are fought with soldiery of glass, so that now White blocks Black, now Black blocks White. But every foe yields to thee, Piso; marshalled by thee, what piece ever gave way? What piece on the brink of death dealt not death to his enemy? Thousand-fold are thy battle tactics: one man in fleeing from an attack himself overpowers him, another, who has been standing on the look-out, comes up from a distant coign; another stoutly rushes into the mêlée, and cheats his foe now creeping on his prey; another courts blockade on either flank, and under feint of being blocked, himself blocks two men; another's objective is more ambitious, that he may quickly break through the massed phalanx, swoop into the lines, and razing the enemy's rampart do havoc in the walled stronghold. Meantime, although the fight rages fiercely the hostile ranks are split, yet thou thyself are victorious with serried lines unbroken, or despoiled may be of one or two men, and both thy hands rattle with the prisoned throng.'

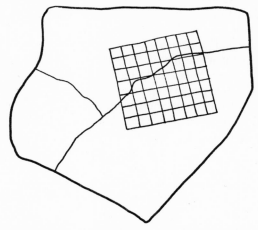

FIG. 73. Stone board for Ludus Latrunculorum found at Chesters, Northumberland; c. A.D. 150–400

Allowing for the demands of the metre and rhetoric this is a fair description of the game of Seega; the cunning disposition of the pieces on the open board refers to the first phase of the game when the pieces are placed in position. The attack by trapping an enemy piece between two of one's own is described, while a piece may be supported by moving another alongside; impregnable lines of pieces may be created, and the captured pieces are removed from the board and held in the hands. The game was won by the player who succeeded in making most captures.

Becq de Fouquière and others have suggested that some of the pieces may have had increased power: perhaps there was a leader who could move more than one square at a time by jumping over an enemy piece and trapping another of the player's pieces. This would allow a player to break up an otherwise impregnable position and thus prevent a game finishing with many pieces still on the board. There is nothing in the literature to support these suggestions, nor is there anything to contradict them. One of the Pompeii wall-paintings shows a board with yellow, black, and white pieces on it, while in 1924 twenty-one white, five black, and two blue counters were found in a room of one of the barrack buildings in a late first-century deposit at Chester. No trace was found of a board or dice. The game may have been played on the ground marked out into squares. The two blue counters may have been leaders.

Egypt was within the frontiers of the Roman Empire in the days of Trajan, and Somaliland was just outside. Ludus Latrunculorum may well have survived among the unsophisticated fellaheen and Somali tribesmen while it was forgotten elsewhere after the fall of the Roman Empire. Seega and High Jump may be survivals of the Roman game, each preserving one of its forms of movement. The last reference to Latrunculorum being played in the interior of the Empire was about A.D. 400 when Macrobius rebuked those who played at Tabula and Latrunculi. See fig. 140 on Plate X.

Suggested Rules for Ludus Latrunculorum

1. Using an 8 × 7 board each player has 16 pieces. They are placed two at a time by alternate turns of play anywhere on the board. During this first phase no captures are made.

2. When the thirty-two pieces are in position each player adds a blue piece to the board. This is the DUX. The second phase then begins. The pieces can move one square orthogonally in any direction.

3. A capture is made by trapping an enemy piece between two of one's own pieces on rank or file.

4. When a piece makes a capture it has another turn, and from this it follows that an isolated piece may endanger itself and several of its fellows by starting a sequence of captures.

5. The dux may move in the ordinary way, or it may make a short orthogonal jump over an enemy piece, landing on an empty square beyond. It does not capture by this manœuvre, unless it traps another enemy piece between itself and one of its own men. The power of jumping enables it to penetrate a defensive position which may start a whole series of captures from within a walled stronghold. It is captured in the same way as any other piece.

6. A piece may move between two enemy pieces without being captured.

7. The game continues until one player has lost all his pieces, or a blockade has developed which neither player can break. The player with most pieces left on the board then wins.

8. If no captures have been made in thirty moves a blockade has been established and the game is over.

6. RUNNING-FIGHT GAMES

Lane's *Modern Egyptians* contains the description of a game TAB which is played on a board of 9×4 squares. The board is very similar to the 10×3 board of Ancient Egypt and it may be another example of a race board being adapted for a war game. TABLAN is simpler than TAB although it belongs to the same group.

TABLAN

This traditional game is still played in some of the villages in Mysore in south-west India. See fig. 143 on Plate XII.

Rules

1. The board (fig. 74A) consists of four rows of twelve squares and each player has twelve pieces of his own colour. At the beginning of the game one piece stands on each square of the player's back row.

2. The four dicing sticks are painted on one side and plain on the other. They are thrown from the hand into the air, caught and thrown up again two or three times before they are allowed to fall to the ground.

Scores

1 plain surface up	..	2 and throw again
4 plain surfaces up	..	8 and throw again
4 painted surfaces up	..	12 and throw again

No other throw scores and the sticks are passed to the opponent.

3. The first move of a piece can only be made on a throw of 2, though this throw can be split into two 1's if required, and two pieces can be moved one square, instead of one piece two squares.

4. Throws of 8 and 12 can similarly be split in half into two 4's or two 6's.

5. The pieces move in the directions shown in the diagram (fig. 74B). White's pieces move A to L, L to X, X to m, m to x and then into Black's back row. Black's pieces move in the opposite direction and finish in White's back row.

6. The pieces can only capture enemy pieces when they are on the two central rows, or when displacing them on the opponent's back row. Captured pieces are removed from the board.

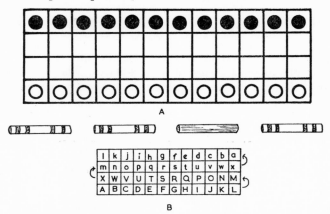

FIG. 74. Tablan board with the pieces in the opening position. Below are four dicing-sticks. (The diagram shows the direction of movement.) (author's collection)

7. Once a piece lands on a square on the opponent's back row it is immobilized and does not move again during the game. It cannot be captured.

8. The enemy home row is captured, square by square, starting from a to l.

9. More than one piece can be moved in any turn of play and more than one capture can be made; but the pieces must move in the directions shown, and when they reach their last square on the middle rows they must turn off into the enemy home row and become immobilized. If they displace a home piece in doing so it is captured.

10. There is no DOUBLING UP of pieces.

11. At any stage of the game a player has to use a throw, convenient or not, unless he has only one piece left near the end of the middle row next to the enemy camp and the throw does not allow him to occupy a square in the enemy camp. These squares must be occupied one after another in the order of a to l (Rule 8).

12. The player occupying most enemy home squares wins the game.

PULUC

This is another running-fight game played by the Kekchi Indians of Central America who are descended from the Mayas. This description is taken from the German text of von Karl Sapper in the Boas Anniversary volume, article 190, p. 283. I am indebted to Miss Agnes Kramer, F.R.C.S. Ed., for her translation.

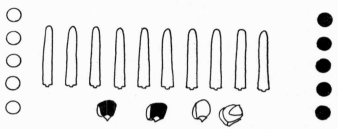

FIG. 75. Maize Highway and pieces for Puluc. The maize-ear dice are drawn to a larger scale

Ten corn cobs are laid on the ground like the rungs of a ladder. The players sit at either end of the MAIZE HIGHWAY and each has five counters of his own colour, made of little pieces of stick. Four flat maize ears are used as dice with one surface blackened and the other left natural (fig. 75).

Scores

2 yellow surfaces up	.. 2
3 yellow surfaces up	.. 3
4 yellow surfaces up	.. 5
4 black surfaces up	.. 4

Rules

1. At the beginning of the game each player throws the dice, and the higher scorer throws again to begin the game; the players then throw alternately.

2. At the player's first throw he enters one of his team on to the highway. At his next throw he may enter another piece or move his first piece on the indicated number of spaces. Any number of his team may be on the highway at the same time. He must not move a piece on to a space which is already occupied by one of his own pieces; there is no doubling up.

3. A player may move a piece forwards on to a space occupied by an enemy piece; the latter is taken prisoner by being placed beneath the winning piece and is moved backwards along the highway by its conqueror in his journey towards the far end of the board.

4. If the victor and the vanquished reach the end of the board (an exact throw is not required), the victor returns to his team ready to be re-entered on the highway for another journey along it, while the poor prisoner is SLAIN and is out of the game.

5. If a player moves a piece on to a space occupied by an enemy piece in charge of a prisoner, the player's piece is placed on the top of the stack, and the whole stack reverses its direction towards the goal of the new victor. Possession of the stack may change sides several times before it eventually arrives at the end of the highway when the top piece and all the others of the same colour are returned to their team ready for new journeys, while the prisoners are out of the game.

6. If a piece journeys along the highway to the far end without incident, it returns to its team to begin the journey again.

7. A stack may capture a single piece or another stack.

8. When a player has no pieces left he has lost the game.

Green king of a Tibetan chess set (author's collection)

CHAPTER THREE

Games of Position

1. MORRIS GAMES

NOUGHTS AND CROSSES

This simple game is played on a diagram drawn on a slate or piece of paper (fig. 76).

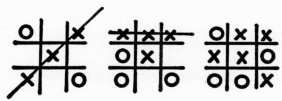

FIG. 76. Noughts and Crosses

The opening player places an X in any position on the board. His opponent then adds an O and the players make their marks alternately until one of them has three of his symbols in a straight line. This wins the game. If neither player can make a line the game is drawn. The players alternate in having first move in successive games.

A. S. White pointed out that the opening player has only three possible moves: centre, middle of side, and corner of side. There are only twelve positions after the second player has moved and in six of these the first player should win, and in six draw. The second player can never win unless his opponent makes a mistake.

THREE MEN'S MORRIS

The board contains nine points and each player has four counters of his own colour. The players place one counter alternately on a point, and if one player can place three in a straight line he wins the game (fig. 77).

A more complicated board was cut into the roofing slabs of the temple at Kurna in Egypt, *c.* 1400–1333 B.C. (fig. 78).

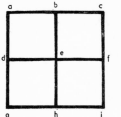

FIG. 77. Three Men's Morris (from Fiske's *Chess* ←   *in Iceland*)

FIG. 78. A second form of Three Men's Morris (from Fiske's *Chess in Iceland*) →

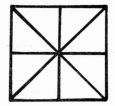

Each player had three men of his own colour and entered them in turn on any vacant point on the board, and then the game continued with alternate moves until one player succeeded in placing his three men in a straight line. As the first player could always force a win by correct play, dice may have been used to decide the advantage of first entry.

More than a thousand years later Ovid mentions the game in his *Ars Amatoria*. The Roman boards were usually of wood or stone, though exotic materials were sometimes used to satisfy the eccentricities of the rich. Trimalchio had one of turpentine-tree, and Martial speaks of an ivory board.

The game was widely played in England in A.D. 1300 and visitors to the cathedrals of Norwich, Canterbury, Gloucester, Salisbury, and Westminster Abbey can see boards cut into the cloister seats by monks who found their long devotions tedious.

Hyde tells us that on the other side of the world the Chinese were playing the same game, Luk tsut K'i, in the time of Confucius, *c.* 500 B.C.

SIX MEN'S MORRIS

Six Men's Morris was popular in Italy, France, and England during the Middle Ages but was obsolete by 1600. Each player had six pieces and they were entered alternately, one at a time; each player trying to form a row along one of the sides of either square. If a player succeeded in this he removed any one of his opponent's pieces. When all the pieces had been entered the game continued by alternate moves of a piece along a line to an adjacent empty point. When a player was reduced to two men the game was over (fig. 79).

NINE MEN'S MORRIS

Two players have nine men each and enter them alternately one at a time, on any vacant point. Each time a player forms a row or MILL of three pieces along a line he removes one of his opponent's pieces from the board, but not one which is in a mill. When all the men have been entered the turns continue by moving a piece to an adjacent vacant point along a line, with the object of making a mill and capturing an enemy piece. A player blocking all his opponent's men so that they cannot move, or reducing him to two pieces, wins the game. See fig. 147 on Plate XIV.

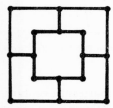

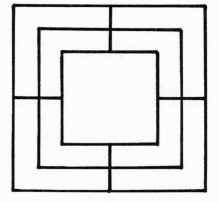

FIG. 79 (*above*). Six Men's Morris (from Fiske's *Chess in Iceland*)

FIG. 80 (*right*). Nine Men's Morris (from Fiske's *Chess in Iceland*)

Cut into the roofing slabs at Kurna is a design $15\frac{1}{2}$ in. square for this game, *c.* 1400 B.C. Two similar diagrams are cut into the great flight of steps which ascend the lower part of the hill at Mihintale in Ceylon. They were carved by the masons who laid the thirty-foot-wide stairway during the reign of Mahadathika Maha-Naga, A.D. 9–21. The design has been used in Ceylon as a charm against evil influences. In Europe it has been found on articles from Lake Dwellings, the first city of Troy, and a burial site of the Bronze Age at Cr Bri Chualann, Co. Wicklow, Ireland.

In 1880 a large grave-mound was opened on the Gokstad farms near Sandefjord in Norway. Inside was a Viking ship and on the deck was the burial chamber of a king. Many of his possessions were with him, including a portion of a gaming board, cut on one side for Nine Men's Morris (fig. 81) and on the other for a game which may have been Hnefatafl.

The Alfonso X manuscript of the thirteenth century A.D. describes a variant using three cubic dice. During the entry phase throws of 6, 5, 4, or 6, 3, 3, or 5, 2, 2, or 4, 1, 1, gave the caster the right to break into an enemy mill and capture a piece, in addition to introducing one of his own pieces on to the board, and if a mill was formed with this piece he removed two of the opponent's men. With any other throw only a single piece was entered. At the end of the first phase the dice were discarded and the game continued in the usual way.

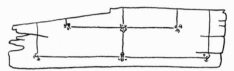

FIG. 81. Fragment of a Nine Men's Morris board from the Gokstad ship, *c.* A.D. 900 (after Du Chaillu)

Nine Men's Morris reached its zenith in the fourteenth century. Superb illustrations of the game are contained in the codices of the North Italian Academies; manuscripts designed for the use of the court. There is an illustrated account of the game in one of the redactions of the *Civis Bononiae*, a remarkable volume in the Victor Emmanuel library at Rome. The perimeters of the boards are drawn with double lines in two colours while the pieces are dissimilar and each player controls the movements of MOONS, STARS, SHIELDS, CROSSES, SQUARES, and ROUNDS. The Moon is shown as a crescent orb, the Star has long shimmering rays, the Shield is triangular, the Cross is in the Greek form, and the Squares and Rounds are in solid colour.

These codices contain collections of Morris positions, with the sides differentiated in red or gold, contrasting with the black and white of chess diagrams. Unfortunately, the manuscripts contain very little information on how to play the games. Only six names are given for the pieces and in some of the diagrams more than one Square or Round is shown. All the pieces seem to have had the same value and movement and von der Lasa has suggested that the names and shapes may merely represent a method of recording the order of play.

Triple-purpose boards built in the form of a shallow box with a hinged lid were popular in Europe from the fourteenth century onwards. When closed, one surface was used for chess, and the other for Nine Men's Morris; when open, the interior displayed a backgammon table. Some were most elaborately worked in mother-of-pearl, ivory, and metals.

2. THREE-IN-A-ROW GAMES

DARA

Several games of this group are played in North Africa, one of the best being Dara of the Dakarkari people, Nigeria. The board consists of thirty small depressions made in the ground in five rows of six each.

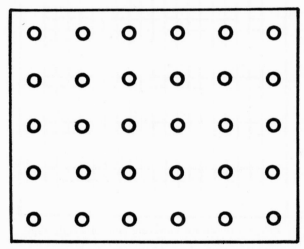

FIG. 82. Arrangement of holes in Dara (after Fitzgerald)

First phase. Each player has twelve distinctive stones or pieces of pottery. They are placed one at a time in the holes in alternate turns of play. When all the pieces have been positioned the second phase begins.

Second phase. Alternately, one piece is moved orthogonally to the next hole, the object being to form a line of three pieces in consecutive holes orthogonally, but not diagonally. When a THREE is formed the player removes one of his opponent's pieces from the board.

The game ends when one player is unable to make further lines of three pieces. Lines of four pieces do not count. Skilful placing of the pieces in the first phase of the game may be decisive in the second.

3. FIVE-IN-A-ROW GAMES

GO-BANG

This Japanese game is played chiefly by children, women and Occidental visitors. It is a poor relation of the intellectual I-go, described on pp. 99ff. under its Chinese name of Wei-ch'i.

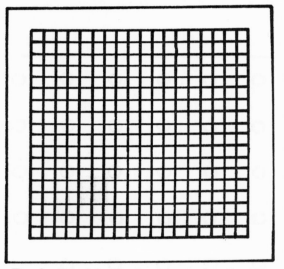

FIG. 83. Board for Go-Bang (author's collection)

Go-bang is played on the I-go board of 18 × 18 squares and each player has 100 counters of his own colour. They are placed one at a time in alternate turns of play on the squares of the board. The object of the game is to form a contiguous line of five pieces on a row, column, or diagonally; this formation winning the game. If all the counters are used up before a FIVE is formed the game may be drawn, or the players may move one piece one square alternately in orthogonal directions until a FIVE is formed.

Go-bang was introduced into Europe about 1885 and is known in England as Spoil Five.

HASAMI SHOGI (1)

This game, also from Japan, is played on a quarter of the I-go board (9 × 9 squares). Each player has 18 pieces of his own colour and they are placed on the two back rows. The object is to form five men in a row excluding the two home rows. No diagonal moves are allowed.

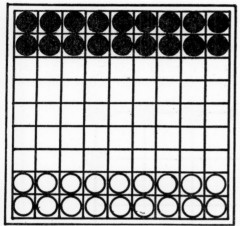

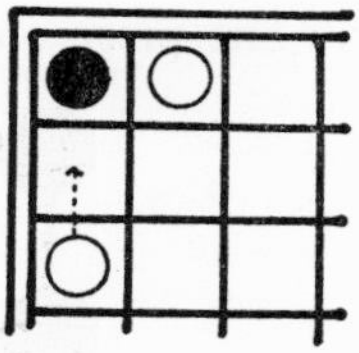

FIG. 85. Custodian capture in a corner in Hasami Shogi

FIG. 84. A quarter of a Wei-ch'i board arranged for playing Hasami Shogi

Method of Play

1. A piece cannot land on a square occupied by another piece.

2. A piece can jump over an adjacent piece to land on a vacant square beyond; but it cannot jump over a vacant square and an occupied square in the same move.

3. When a player traps an opposing piece between two of his own on a rank or file (custodian capture), it is removed from the board.

4. A piece may move between two enemy pieces safely.

5. A player wins the game when he has five pieces in a row on a file, rank, or diagonally.

HASAMI SHOGI (2)

The first variety of Hasami Shogi belongs to the games of position but the second is a war game.

H

1. Each player has one row of men on his back row.

2. The moves and the method of capture are as in the first form.

3. The object of the game is to capture all an opponent's pieces and remove them from the board. A man on a corner square may be captured by blocking his movement with pieces on the two adjacent orthogonal squares (fig. 85).

4. REPLACEMENT GAMES

FIVE FIELD KONO

The board and opening position are shown in fig. 86. The players move one piece one point at a time diagonally across the squares,

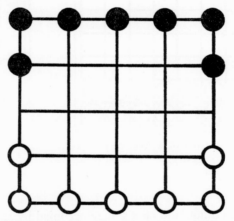

FIG. 86. Opening position in Five Field Kono (after Culin's *Korean Games*)

either backwards or forwards. The object of the game is to move the pieces across to the other side of the board to occupy the places vacated by the opponent, and the first player to do so wins the game.

HALMA

This game was invented about 1880 and in the two-handed form each player has nineteen men arranged in his own CAMP, the walls of which are marked by a thicker or double line. Only one man may be moved in any turn of play: either as a single step in any direction

on to an empty adjacent square, or by leaping over a man in any
direction on to an empty square immediately beyond. A number
of leaps may be made over his own or hostile pieces, and each player
tries to make ladders to enable his pieces to move several squares in

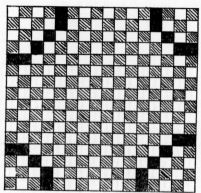

FIG. 87. Halma. Two corners are marked for 19 pieces (two-handed
game). If four play each player has 13 pieces

a single turn of play. Each also tries to use an opponent's ladder, or
alternatively tries to block it to prevent its use by his adversary. The
first player to move all his pieces into the enemy camp wins the game.
In a four-handed game each player has thirteen men arranged in his
own corner.

Cheap boards are made of cardboard and the pieces are wooden or
plastic; expensive boards are of veneered wood with light and dark
squares and in the centre of each is a drill hole to receive the pegs
of the halma men which are made of bone or ivory.

5. TERRITORIAL POSSESSION

WEI CH'I

This Chinese game, pronounced Way Key, is one of the great
intellectual games of the world. Chinese boards are often made of
paper and are thrown away at the end of the game, but in Japan more
serviceable wooden boards about twenty inches square are used.
They are marked with eighteen squares each way, and the pieces
are played on the 361 points, not on the squares. The four intersections four points along the principal diagonals are strategically

30102

important and are specially marked. These points are covered first (fig. 88).

The pieces, known as TZE, are discoid and about the size of a shilling. The author's are made of black and white china. Each player has some two hundred kept in a wooden bowl (see tailpiece, p. 110).

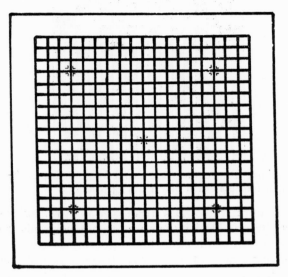

FIG. 88. Wei-ch'i board (author's collection)

The Chinese notation is extremely confusing and a simpler method suggested by Murray, based on the Japanese form, is shown in fig. 89.

Players are graded according to their skill, and the weaker player takes Black and has first move except when White gives odds. If the players are ill-matched White may concede a considerable handicap (see below).

The object of the game is to control as many of the 361 points as possible. Black begins by placing a tze on a marked point. White replies by placing one of his on another. Thereafter the players move alternately entering one tze at a time on any empty point except when a PERPETUAL ATTACK would result, as explained later. After entry, no tze may move.

Wei ch'i is difficult to describe, but an anachronism may be helpful. Let us assume that each tze represents a paratroop unit. If it is surrounded orthogonally on all sides or is pinned against the edge of the board by enemy pieces it is overwhelmed and is removed (fig. 90).

More than one unit may be surrounded at a time and captured (fig. 91).

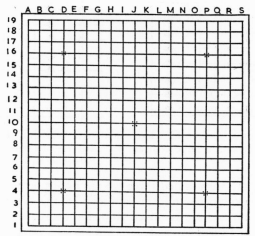

FIG. 89. Notation for Wei-ch'i (after Murray's *History of Board Games other than Chess*)

If the paratroopers are in contact with an empty point they may hold out indefinitely: they have an airfield on which supplies can be landed. The players, therefore, try to form rings of troops surrounding an empty central space in any portion of the board (fig. 92).

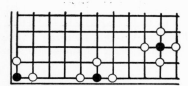

FIG. 90. Wei-ch'i. Three positions of capture

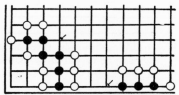

FIG. 91. Wei-ch'i. Multiple captures by placing a white tze on either arrowed point

The paratroopers are in contact with each other if there is continuity between the tze in orthogonal directions, but not diagonally.

In fig. 93 the white pieces are all in orthogonal contact with an empty space and are safe.

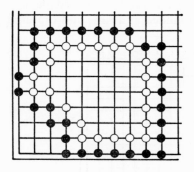

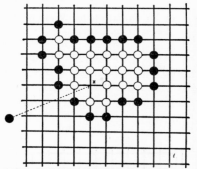

FIG. 92. Wei-ch'i. A safe white formation with a large central airfield

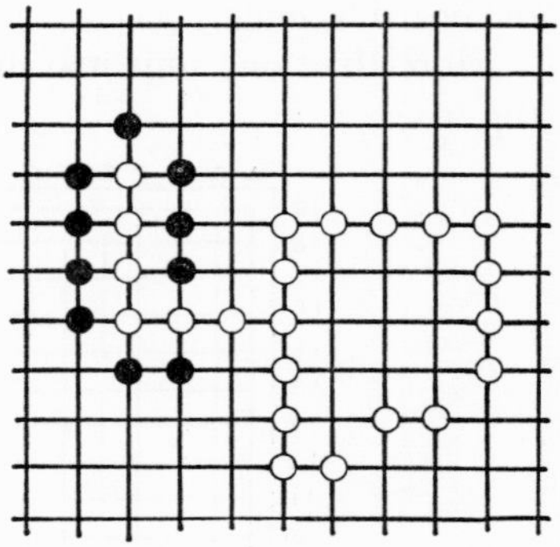

FIG. 93. Wei-ch'i. The white tze are in orthogonal continuity with the airfield and are safe

In fig. 94 the surrounded three tze are not in orthogonal contact with the empty space and are captured by the black pieces surrounding them and are removed from the board.

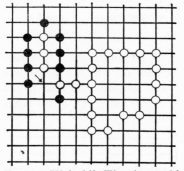

FIG. 94. Wei-ch'i. The three white tze can be captured by placing a black tze on the marked point

FIG. 95. Wei-ch'i. By placing a tze on x Black captures eighteen white tze

If a force is surrounded by enemy pieces and has only a single empty point and the enemy lands a unit on it, the air supplies are cut off and the whole force is captured. See fig. 95 where Black captures and removes the eighteen white tze by placing a black tze on the vacant point.

In fig. 96 the white force is quite safe from attack for it has two small airfields. If a black tze is placed on either field it is immediately captured, since it is surrounded on all sides by white tze while the white force can still be supported by supplies landing on the other field. Thus a tze cannot land on a single-point field without being captured, unless the moment it lands it cuts off the enemy's sole supply line, and then instead of being destroyed it captures the enemy. To be safe a force must have either a double airfield, or a very large airfield that can be divided into two under attack.

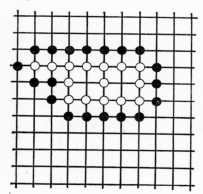
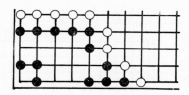

FIG. 96. Wei-ch'i. The white form- FIG. 97. Black's formation is safe
ation is safe with two single
airfields

No tze can commit suicide. If a player places a piece in a position of capture, the move is illegal and must be altered without penalty. Thus a player cannot decide the moment when an indefensible formation of his pieces is captured—once it is doomed, however, it is known as a DEAD MASS.

In fig. 97 Black has two airfields, one of one point, and the other of nine. If White were to fill in this larger space he would capture the ten outer black tze, but of course Black would prevent this. He would wait until White had filled in eight of the points, and then Black would place a unit on the ninth point and capture the surrounded white pieces. The larger airfield would then consist of only eight points. If White repeated this attack seven more times there would be only one vacant point remaining of the larger field, but Black would have two one-point airfields and if an enemy unit landed on one of them it would be immediately captured and removed because the other was still open. Such a formation is quite safe from attack and both players would leave it and pass on to other parts of the board. Unlike chess, where the squares containing the kings are of supreme importance, in Wei-ch'i a reverse in one area can be offset by a victory in another.

A group of pieces which are not enclosed, but which are certain to become so are regarded as DEAD and to save moves both players abandon the position and turn to the capture of territory elsewhere (fig. 95).

An IMPASSE is also left alone. This arises when a vacant space is surrounded partly by white pieces and partly by black in such a way that if either player enters a man his opponent could capture the whole group (fig. 98).

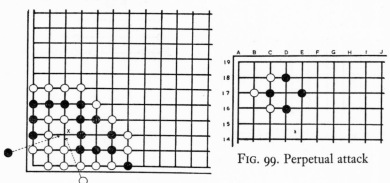

FIG. 99. Perpetual attack

FIG. 98. An impasse. Neither player can harm the other

If White entered a piece at x, Black would fill the point at the corner of the board and White's inner pieces would be captured. If Black entered a piece at x, White would fill the other single point airfield and all Black's pieces would be captured.

PERPETUAL ATTACK is the one position which limits a player's free choice of placing his pieces. In the position in fig. 99 it is White's turn to play and he enters a tze on D 17. This captures the black tze on C 17 which is removed. Black is then not allowed to reply by placing a tze on C 17, taking the white tze on D 17 which would lead to a perpetual repetition of move; but he must play elsewhere and can only play on to C 17 after White has moved again.

The game ends when the two territories are in absolute contact, or when both players agree that no more territory can be won.

There are several ways of scoring, the simplest being the modern Japanese method. All captured tze are placed on vacant points held by the opponent. Then each player counts the number of vacant points under his control and this is his score. Vacant points between the formations are neutral and do not count to either player. The degree of the victory is the difference between the two player's scores.

Tactics

Oriental scholars have devoted years to the study of this game and it is quite impossible to describe finer points of play in a few pages. Only an outline of the basic principles will be attempted.

(*a*) Do not make purposeless moves: they lose valuable time and space.

(*b*) A game on a full board generally lasts about an hour, but may take three. Beginners are advised to use only a quarter of the board in the early games until they have grasped the principles of play.

(*c*) When no handicap is given, each player occupies two of the four marked squares on the third line. This line is very strong and it can be used as a base for attack or defence.

(*d*) As the object of the game is to enclose territory quickly, the fences should be as light as possible consistent with strength to resist assault and capture. The size of the enclosure must be balanced against the number of men required to defend it. The wider the space, the further the fence is from support and the stronger it must be. Fig. 100 shows examples of fence formations.

    1. Very strong but slow.
    2. Faster and still very strong.
    3. Strong.
    4. Nearly as strong as 3 and faster.
    5. Strong and fast for penetrating new territory.
    6. A variant of 5.
    7.
    8. } Rather flimsy but useful in some situations.
    9. Weak, but fast and can be converted quickly into 5 or 6.

(*e*) A fence built at about half strength is secure, i.e. piece and space alternately: the opponent usually cannot play between without loss. But if the pieces are further apart a struggle for the intervals may develop, the success of the attack depending upon the positions of other groups.

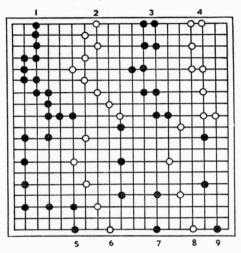

FIG. 100. Diagram of fence formations (after Cheshire's *Goh or Wei Chi*)

(*f*) If a lightly constructed fortification is attacked it is often better to extend it and to counter-attack enemy positions rather than to spend time and pieces in strengthening its walls. In this way other airfields may be gained, flimsy at first but capable of being strengthened later. Solid walls round small plots lead to inevitable defeat.

(*g*) A player should make every effort to prevent his opponent from linking dead formations with live ones.

(*h*) When men are surrounded without an airfield they are removed at once from the board.

(*i*) When a player makes a move which forces his opponent to defend, he has THE FIRST HAND. This is valuable and it is sometimes worth losing a few pieces to retain the initiative.

(*j*) Three vacant points cannot be defended against the move, but they can with it, by making two one-point airfields.

(*k*) Four vacant points in a straight line can be defended with or without the move, but if they are in a square they are indefensible even with the move. Four empty points like a stunted T can be defended with the move, but not against it.

(*l*) A fortification with more than seven empty points is safe and it is a waste of time to strengthen it unless attacked.

(*m*) The reduction of enemy-held spaces by neutralization is always profitable. If White holds six vacant points it will cost $5+4+3+2+1=15$ pieces to neutralize it, before the formation is captured. But there must be at least six men in the wall of the fortification, and five more will have been played into it$=11$. Therefore, White loses eleven pieces taken prisoner and Black gains eleven empty points. White has also lost six points and, therefore, Black has improved his position by $6+11+11=28$ at a cost of fifteen.

(*n*) When trying to hinder the development of an enemy piece in a clear field it is generally unwise to play on an adjacent point: this invites an attack that may be disastrous. It is better to leave a vacant point between the pieces and then any attack will develop too slowly to be successful.

(*o*) Towards the end of a game considerable time may be saved by abandoning men that cannot be defended, and who are then taken prisoner; any doubtful position, however, should be fought out.

Novices will have more pieces on the board at the end of a game than experts, who may only half cover it when the game is finished,

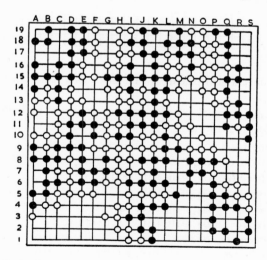

FIG. 101. End of a game (from Falkener's *Games, Ancient and Oriental*)

each recognizing positions which are beyond defence; and neutral points which cannot be incorporated in fortifications (fig. 101).

Three PERPETUAL POSITIONS on the board results in a draw.

Etiquette

1. When a player places a tze on the board no previous move can be revoked.

2. When a player wins three consecutive games he usually gives his opponent a handicap of one piece, and if he continues to win the handicap is gradually increased.

3. A player receiving a handicap plays Black and plays second.

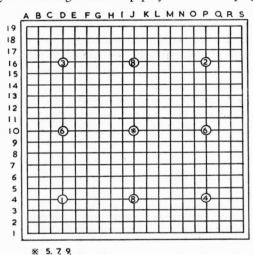

FIG. 102. Conventional placings of tze given as a handicap to a weaker player

4. The conventional positionings of tze given as handicaps are shown in fig. 102 and are:

One tze	D4
Two tze	D4, P16
Three tze	D4, P16, D16, or J10
Four tze	D4, P16, D16, P4
Five tze	D4, P16, D16, P4, J10
Six tze	D4, P16, D16, P4, D10, P10
Seven tze	D4, P16, D16, P4, D10, P10, J10
Eight tze	D4, P16, D16, P4, D10, P10, J16, J4
Nine tze	D4, P16, D16, P4, D10, P10, J16, J4, J10

When an opposing piece is within one move of being captured it is usual to tap the board with a tze. This courtesy is optional.

Wei-ch'i is first mentioned in Chinese writings from Honan about 625 B.C. Confucius advised the idle rich to play Wei-ch'i rather than allow their minds to stagnate. According to tradition the game was taken to Japan in A.D. 735 by the Lord Kibi.

Skill at Wei-ch'i was a strong recommendation to promotion in Cathay and Japan before the twentieth century. It corresponded as an index of mental ability to a university degree in a standard sub-ject in the West. In Japan tuition classes were held and diplomas of proficiency awarded, players being divided into nine grades.

6. PATIENCE GAMES

SOLITAIRE

In the eighteenth century a new game reached England from the Continent called Solitaire. It was a form of patience for one player using a traditional Fox and Geese board and said to have been invented by a French count when in prison.

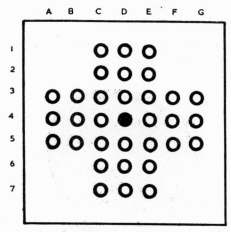

FIG. 103. Fox and Geese board used for Solitaire

Fig. 103 shows a Fox and Geese board with a notation to record solutions of solitaire problems. The basic problem is to remove the marble in D4, and then at each turn of play one marble must jump orthogonally over an adjacent marble into a vacant hole beyond. The marble passed over is removed. The object of the game is to remove all the marbles from the board except one, and this should be left in the central hole.

Method

1.	D2 into D4 remove D3		17.	C2	C4	C3
2.	F3	D3	E3	18.	A3	C3	B3
3.	E1	E3	E2	19.	D3	B3	C3
4.	E4	E2	E3	20.	A5	A3	A4
5.	C1	E1	D1	21.	A3	C3	B3
6.	E1	E3	E2	22.	D5	D3	D4
7.	E6	E4	E5	23.	D3	B3	C3
8.	G5	E5	F5	24.	B3	B5	B4
9.	D5	F5	E5	25.	B5	D5	C5
10.	G3	G5	G4	26.	D5	F5	E5
11.	G5	E5	F5	27.	F4	D4	E4
12.	B5	D5	C5	28.	C4	E4	D4
13.	C7	C5	C6	29.	E3	E5	E4
14.	C4	C6	C5	30.	F5	D5	E5
15.	E7	C7	D7	31.	D6	D4	D5
16.	C7	C5	C6				

This sequence of moves leaves the last marble in the centre, D4. Other problems can be set and solved.

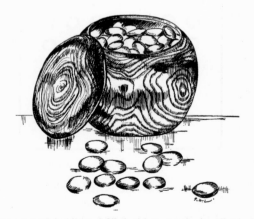

Wooden Wei-ch'i bowl filled with tze (author's collection)

CHAPTER FOUR

Mancala Games

1. TWO-RANK MANCALA

MANKALA'H

In Lane's *Modern Egyptians*, written when he was living in Egypt in the 1830's, is a description of MANKALA'H, a popular game in the coffee shops. The loser paid for the coffee! The board (fig. 104) consisted of two rows of six small pits.

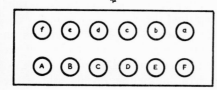

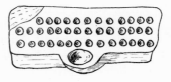

FIG. 104. Board for Mankala'h (after Lane's *Modern Egyptians*)

FIG. 105. Limestone mancala board from Ancient Egypt (from Petrie's *Objects of Daily Use*)

Those marked A, B, C, D, E, F, belonged to P, and a, b, c, d, e, f, to p. Each began the game with thirty-six pebbles. One player took all the pebbles and without counting, distributed them in one or more pits on each side; usually choosing the central pits and leaving the end pits empty. Another common arrangement was to place about half into pit A and the remainder in pit a. If the other player did not like his opponent's arrangement he could turn the board round but he then surrendered his right to first move.

The player opening the game started from any one of his pits by lifting all the pebbles out of it and sowing one in each pit in an anti-clockwise direction. When he reached the end of his row he passed over into the opponent's row, sowing a pebble into each pit in turn. At the end of the opponent's row, if he still had pebbles left in his hand, he returned to the beginning of his own row and continued sowing until he had used them up. If the last pebble was sown into an empty pit his turn ceased and his opponent began to play.

If the last pebble was sown into a pit containing one or three pebbles, making two or four, the player took these pebbles together with those of the pit opposite and put them into his store as captured pieces. If one or more of the preceding pits also contained either two or four pebbles, with no pit with any other amount intervening, he also took the contents of these preceding pits together with the contents of those opposite.

If the last pebble fell into a pit containing two, four, or some other even number, thus making an odd number after the sowing, he lifted all the pebbles out and sowed them in the same way as before: e.g. if the last pebble was placed in pit D, he lifted out all the pebbles in it and sowed one into E, another into F, and a third into a, etc. and he continued in this way until either his last pebble fell into an empty pit or into a pit with one or three pebbles, thus making two or four, when he captured them.

After the first win of a lap, the player could play from any pit on his side of the board. After any other win in a lap he had to lift the pebbles in the next loaded pit on his side of the board.

When one player had more than one pebble on his side of the board, and his opponent had none, he was obliged to put one of his pebbles into his opponent's first hole. When only two pebbles remained on the board they became the property of the player first having them both on his side of the board. When the board was empty each player counted his pebbles, and the winner scored the difference for that round. A new round then began, and the score of each round was added to the last until one player reached sixty.

Professor Flinders Petrie found a rough block of limestone at Memphis containing three rows of fourteen pits which appears to be an early form of Mankala'h (fig. 105). The store suggests that pieces were captured and the pits are so small that the pieces were probably beans or seeds.

There are several sets of deeply cut holes in the roofing slabs of the Kurna temple at Thebes, c. 1400 B.C. Other sets of boards are cut into the summit of the damaged portion of the great pylon built in Ptolemaic times at the entrance of the temple of Karnak, and also at the Luxor temple. The boards consist of two rows of six, seven, and eight saucer-shaped holes, the largest being $3\frac{1}{2}$ in. wide and 1 in. deep.

Boards have been found in Arabia dating from before the time of Muhammad, and the followers of the prophet carried variations of the game to the countries influenced by their culture. MANCALA is used as a generic noun for all the games of the Mankala'h type.

PALLANGULI

Pallanguli is played by the Tamil women of southern India and Ceylon, though it is sometimes used as a gambling game by men. Antique boards were made of wood or ivory and were usually plain, though they might be beautifully carved and ornamented. The modern board in fig. 152 on Plate XVII came from Ernakulam in Travancore-Cochin and is made of a white metal chromium-plated. The little wheels are an unexpected embellishment!

The players start with seven holes and place six seeds in each. The opening player then lifts the seeds from any hole on his side of the board, leaving it empty, and moving anti-clockwise sows one seed into each pit. If he reaches the end of his side of the board he continues sowing in his opponent's holes, still in an anti-clockwise direction. When the last seed of a lift falls into a hole, either on his own side of the board or his opponent's, he picks up all the pieces in the next hole and continues sowing as before in the same direction. If the last seed of a lift falls into a hole with an empty hole beyond, any seeds in the hole immediately beyond the empty hole are captured and put into the player's store hole; he then continues play from the next loaded hole beyond; but if the last seed of a lift falls into a hole with two empty holes beyond he wins nothing and his turn ceases.

His opponent then plays by lifting the seeds or seed from any hole on his side of the board and sowing in an anti-clockwise direction. His turn also ceases when he sows the last seed of a lift into a hole next to two empty ones. The game continues by alternate moves.

Four seeds in a hole is called a COW and, irrespective of the sower, becomes the property of the owner of the hole and is lifted at once and put in his store while play continues.

At the end of the first round each player lifts the seeds from his

I

store hole and puts six into as many of the holes on his side of the board as he can, any remainder being returned to his store. The loser of the first round will be unable to fill all his holes and these are marked with a little stick and are known as RUBBISH HOLES. The winner of a round fills all his seven holes and the surplus remains in his store.

The player having the first move in the first round, has second move in the second round, and first move in the third round, etc., each round being played in the same way as the first except that the rubbish holes are not used. The game ends when one player is reduced to less than six seeds and is unable to fill even one hole at the beginning of a round.

During any round the losing player may win enough seeds to re-open one or more rubbish holes, and eventually he may turn the tables and finally defeat his opponent. A game between well-balanced players can last a very long time. A player is not allowed to count his pieces before making a move, but a good player can tell at a glance the best moves on the board. An antique Pallanguli board is shown as the tailpiece on p. 122.

WARI

The beautiful board carved from one piece of Osese wood in fig. 138 (Plate IX, facing p. 176) came from Ghana. The stem is hollow and contains the seeds when they are not in use. The design is traditional.

Each player begins with four seeds in each hole on his side of the board (fig. 106).

Rules

1. The opening player lifts all the seeds out of one of the holes on his side of the board and sows one into each of the holes in an anti-clockwise direction, cup F being followed by cup a and cup f by cup A.

Example. If the opening player P emptied cup C at the beginning of the game the position would become $\frac{444445}{440555}$.

The second player, p, then lifts the seeds from any hole on his side of the board. If he chose cup e he would sow one seed in cups f, A, B, C, and the position would be $\frac{504445}{551555}$.

2. If the last seed of a lift drops into an enemy hole to make a

final score of 2 or 3, these seeds are captured and are placed in the player's store. The seeds of any unbroken sequence of 2's and 3's on the opponent's side of the board contiguous with and behind the plundered hole are also lifted. A player is not, however, allowed to capture all the pieces on the opponent's side of the board as this would leave him nothing to lift at the next turn of play.

Example. If the position were $\frac{121122}{442710}$ and it was P's turn to play, and he emptied D, he would capture 3 from e, 2 from d, 2 from c, 3 from b, and 3 from a, leaving 1 in f for p to lift at the next turn.

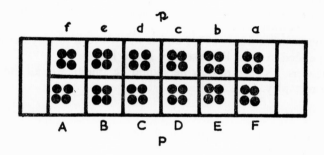

FIG. 106. Wari board at the beginning of a game (redrawn from Rattray's *Religion and Art in Ashanti*)

If the position were $\frac{121710}{111106}$ and P emptied cup F, he would capture 2 from f, 3 from e, and 2 from d. The new position would become $\frac{000821}{111100}$.

3. A heavily loaded cup may contain more than 12 seeds and the sowing from such a cup will be more than one complete cycle of the board. The emptied cup is omitted from the sowing on the second or subsequent cycles and remains empty.

Example. If the position were $\frac{361100}{42800}{}_{15}$ and P lifted the fifteen seeds in cup F, he would drop the last seed in cup d making 3 in that cup and would capture 3, 3, 2, 2, from cups d, c, b, a.

4. When an opponent's cups are empty a player must, if possible, feed seeds into them. If he cannot do so the game is over and all the seeds left on the board become the player's.

Example. If the position were $\frac{000000}{103216}$ and it was P's turn to play he would be obliged to empty cup F. No other cup would feed seeds into p's side of the board.

If the position were $\frac{000000}{103210}$ P could not pass seeds over into p's cups by any lift and therefore the game would be finished, and all the seeds on the board would belong to P.

An extreme example occurs when it is P's turn to play and the position is $\frac{000000}{543210}$. The game is finished and the fifteen seeds left on the board all belong to P.

5. If all a player's cups are empty and it is his turn to play, the game is over.

6. When only a few seeds remain in play they may circulate with no captures possible for either player. Each then takes the seeds on his own side of the board.

Example. If the position were $\frac{100000}{000001}$ each player would take the seed on his own side.

If the position were $\frac{100000}{000011}$ and it was p's turn to play, he would take the seed in f and P the seed in E and F.

If it were P's turn to play he should be able to win all the seeds by correct play.

Tactics of Wari

A threat occurs to a cup containing one or two seeds when any enemy cup contains a number of seeds equal to the number of cups intervening between them.

Example. If cup B contains 1 or 2 seeds, it is threatened by 2 in f, 3 in e, 4 in d, 5 in c, 6 in b, or 7 in a. In looking for a threat it is quicker to count backwards from the threatened cup, noting when the number of intervening cups agrees with the number of seeds in the cup reached. If a cup contains more than eleven seeds the same rule applies after the subtraction of eleven.

A player's position is strongest when his cups are bearing on several different enemy cups. It is usually a weakness to have several cups all bearing on one opposing cup.

Example. If p has 3 in e, 4 in d, and 6 in b, they all threaten cup B.

If a single seed is threatened it may be defended by:

1. Moving it on to the next cup.

2. Adding a seed to the threatening hole and then the sowing will overshoot the singleton.

3. The player may leave the threat undefended and prepare an immediate reprisal which equals or exceeds it.

Two seeds in a cup may be defended in the same ways and in addition they may be converted into a three by playing a seed into it.

A cup loaded with more than eleven seeds may threaten an

empty cup, or one containing one seed. An empty cup is difficult to defend. Only overloading the threatening cup, or preparing reprisals are possible. A singleton may be defended by increasing it to two, which would make four seeds in the cup after the opponent's sowing. If the singleton were moved on, an empty cup is left which would entail the loss of two seeds when the opponent has finished his sowing.

Example. If the position were $\frac{^{14}0\,0\,0\,0\,0}{1\,1\,1\,0\,0\,0}$ and it was P's turn to play, his only move to save immediate loss of seeds is to lift the seed in B, making 2 in cup C which is then safe from the threat of the 14 seeds in f.

If the position were $\frac{^{14}0\,0\,0\,0\,0}{1\,1\,0\,0\,0\,1}$, loss is inevitable, but if P played from cup A, only two would be lost while if he played from B or F he would lose eight.

The position after p's move in the first alternative would be $\frac{0\,1\,1\,1\,1\,1}{2\,\underset{\times}{4}\,2\,1\,1\,2}$.

The position after p's move in the second alternative would be $\underset{\times\times\times}{\frac{0\,1\,1\,1\,1\,1}{3\,2\,3\,1\,1\,2}}$; and if the seeds in F were moved it would be $\underset{\times\times}{\frac{0\,1\,1\,1\,1\,2}{3\,3\,2\,1\,1\,1}}$.

In the position $\frac{5\,4\,0\,5\,0\,0}{2\,0\,2\,0\,0\,5}$ with P to play he is presented with a difficult problem. He is threatened with losing 3 at C if p at his next move plays e. He may:

1. Empty the threatened cup C, then p can play f and win four, 2 from D and 2 from E.

2. Overload e by playing F, but p can win 3 at C by playing c.

3. If P plays A, converting C into a safe 3, p can win 2 at B by playing c. This move gives the smallest loss and appears to be the most attractive, but it should be noted that the move giving the smallest *immediate* loss is not always the best in the end.

The End Game

Each player tries to retain as many seeds in his own cups and as few in his opponent's as possible. By keeping the seeds spread in many cups instead of a few, and by playing from lightly loaded cups in preference to the heavier, a player can slow the progress of seeds on his side of the board, and may manage to make the outflow smaller than the inflow.

> Lifting one seed from a cup advances 1 unit.
> Lifting two seeds from a cup advances 3 units.
> Lifting three seeds from a cup advances 6 units.
> Lifting four seeds from a cup advances 10 units.

Example. The effect of slow-motion play is seen in the position $\frac{000000}{300001}$. If it is P's turn to play he can win all four seeds. The play is FaAbDcCdBeCf. Any other play will not win all four pieces. This introduces the problem of recording Wari games.

Notation

As player P must always start from a cup on his side of the board (A, B, C, D, E, F) and p must start from one on his side (a, b, c, d, e, f), it is possible to record a game by noting the letters representing the holes, and then the game may be replayed later and the positions recovered. If the opening four moves of a game were CeFd the resulting position would be $\frac{620556}{662550}$. The reader is advised to check

this for himself to make sure he understands this method of notation. Player p would win 2 from cup C.

Group Movement

When the board is nearly empty, a diminishing sequence of seeds in consecutive cups with empty cups ahead may be advanced unaltered. If P has 432100 in his cups and he plays from A, the new position is 0432100. If p leaves this unaltered, on the next move P may play from B and the position becomes 004321. This process may continue round the corner Fa. An important application of this principle occurs when a player has two cups with a 1 in front of a 2 and empty cups ahead.

Example. Assume that P has advanced 2 seeds in one cup and 1 in the cup in front with empty holes ahead to the end of his row, 2 seeds being in E and 1 in F. On playing from E, he has two seeds in E and 1 in a. If b is empty p cannot play from cup a without allowing P to make a capture at b from F. This 2 and 1 method may be used repeatedly to capture seeds that must be passed to the other side of the board. Of the 3 passed, 2 are captured.

In the position $\frac{000000}{011121}$ with P to play, he may win 5 of the 6 seeds by playing EaFaDbCcBdCeDfEaF. The two seeds remaining in B and a would circle perpetually and are, therefore, shared by the players.

Heavily Loaded Cups

A heavily loaded cup may have a devastating effect on an opposing row of nearly empty cups, and this effect may sometimes be increased by delaying its use for a few moves.

Example. In the position $\frac{000001}{003211_2}$ with P to play, if he played F at once the position would become $\frac{111113}{114320}$ and he would win the three seeds in a.

If P played the moves EaDbEcCdEeDfF he would then gain 10 seeds at the last move.

If p had had 2 or 3 seeds in his cups he might have manœuvred so that the cup threatened by P always contained 2 seeds, or at least that a 2 occurred close behind the cup threatened and thus prevented a wholesale sweep by P from cup F.

Match Play

At the end of a game the players count their seeds, the one with most being the winner. If they are playing a match the winner of a game fills the holes on his side of the board and then begins to fill the holes on his opponent's side; and each hole filled with 4 seeds, or a hole with one or more of the leading player's seeds, becomes an extension of his side of the board for the next game. When a player has only two or three holes left he usually concedes the match to his opponent.

Early in the seventeenth century Richard Jobson saw Wari played in the Gambia territory and wrote:

'In the heat of the day, the men will come forth, and sit themselves in companies, under the shady trees, to receive the fresh aire, and there passe the time in communication, having only one kind of game to recreate themselves withall, and that is in a peece of wood, certaine great holes cut, which they set upon the ground betwixt two of them, and with a number of some thirty pibble stones, after a manner of counting, they take one from the other, until one is possessed of all, whereat some of them are wondrous nimble.'

AWARI

In the New World African slaves played their native games and taught them to their children. It is still possible to trace the ancestral origins of some West Indian negroes by their form of mancala. Four variants of Wari are found among the negroes of Guiana and the Caribbean which match with the games of Dahomey, Togoland, and Nigeria. The games have several names, one being Awari. As an intellectual exercise it is on a level with chess. The negroes play for amusement and the prestige accruing to a good player. They will not play for money.

Awari is a masculine pastime though women occasionally play. Herskovits saw an elder of the Saramacca people teaching a young girl, but if a woman became a strong player the men refused to play with her, for no man's reputation would bear the ridicule following defeat by a woman.

Awari also has a religious significance and is often played in a House of Mourning to amuse the spirit of the dead awaiting burial. It is only played during daylight; for when the shadows fall the Yorkas, or ghosts, would join the living players in their game and at the end carry off the spirits.

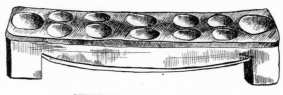

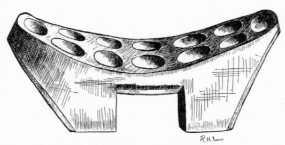

FIG. 107. Awari boards (redrawn from Herskovits' *Wari in the New World*)

Making Awari boards involves spiritual danger, and only old men who have lost a wife are allowed to make them. Although the Bush Negroes are fine carvers, their Awari boards are crude affairs roughly hacked out of a log; they feel that a board should not be brought to immediate perfection, but that the fingers of many players should caress the cups in many games to make them smooth.

The boards are made in two shapes, one with a straight top and the other curved. A village will have both types so that when a man dies who preferred to play on one shape, the villagers will use the other for a time to lessen the chance of his ghost joining in.

A negro on the island of St. Kitts explained that Awari was not played at night because of devils.

'But we're not as afraid of djombies as we used to be.'

'Why not?'

'There aren't so many now, sir. The motor cyars run 'em over, sir.'

2. FOUR-RANK MANCALA

Mancala games with four rows of holes are confined to eastern and southern Africa. The Swahili, Baganda, and a few other advanced tribes used beautifully made and finished boards, but most dig a series of holes in the ground.

CHISOLO

This is played by the Ba-ila speaking peoples of Northern Rhodesia. The board consists of four rows of seven holes scooped out of the earth. There is a larger store hole at one end. The counters are small stones and each player starts with thirty-three arranged as in fig. 108.

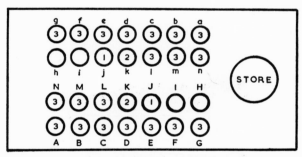

FIG. 108. The beginning of a game of Chisolo

Method of Play

1. The players move alternately and only along the two rows on their own side of the board.

2. On the first move each player must move clockwise; in the second move he may move either clockwise or anti-clockwise, but for the rest of the game he must move in the same direction as he did on his second move. The two players may, therefore, be moving in the same or different directions.

3. The player may begin his move from any hole on his side of the board. He lifts all the stones out of a hole and sows one into each

of the holes beyond. If the last stone of a lap falls into a loaded hole, he lifts all the stones in it and begins a second lap, sowing one stone into each hole beyond. A move may consist of several laps.

4. When the last stone of a lap falls into an empty hole the move is finished. If the empty hole was in the front row the player captures all the stones in the two holes on the same file on the opponent's side of the board; and when he makes a capture he also has the privilege of robbing all the stones out of one extra hole belonging to his opponent. If the two enemy holes on the same file are empty, and no capture is made, the player is also barred from robbing a third hole.

If the last stone of a lap falls into an empty hole in the back row the move finishes, but no captures are made.

5. When a player has no stones left on his side of the board the game is over and he has lost.

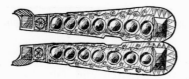

Antique Pallanguli board (redrawn from Durai)

CHAPTER FIVE

Dice Games

The history of lots is as old as the history of man. The pyramidal dice of Sumer have been described in the first chapter, also four-sided dice from Egyptian tombs. Etruscan dice found near Rome (fig. 109) and made about 900 B.C. are similar to the dice of today, with the opposite faces adding up to seven: 1:6, 2:5, 3:4. Similar dice have been found in Britain in the prehistoric earthworks of Maiden Castle.

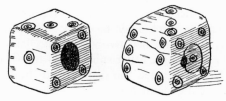

FIG. 109. Etruscan dice, *c.* 900 B.C. (after Culin's *Chinese Games with Dice and Dominoes*)

Gambling sticks have been found with Senat boards of the Empire Age of Egypt, *c.* 1500 B.C., and are still used today by the fellaheen for the game of Tab. The Arabs use them for Hyena, the Koreans for Nyout, and the Amerindians for many related games.

Gambling fever has not been confined to any nation or period in time. Tacitus wrote of the Germani in A.D. 99:

'They practise dice play, at which one will naturally wonder, soberly, and quite as if it were a serious business, with such hardihood in winning and losing, that, when they have nothing more left, they stake their freedom, and their person on the last cast of the die. The loser resigns himself voluntarily to servitude, and even if he is younger and stronger than his adversary, he allows himself to be bound and sold. Thus great is their staunchness in an affair so bad: they themselves call it "Keeping their word".'

During the twelfth and thirteenth centuries A.D. dicing spread throughout England. Hazard was the favourite game in low taverns, and although men could no longer stake their personal liberties on a throw, they played for everything else, even their clothing, on which the tavern-keeper, who acted as a pawnbroker, readily lent small sums of money. There are many accounts of travellers falling into the taverner's hands and playing and drinking themselves destitute; and in an early fourteenth-century manuscript there is an illumination depicting two such players; the older is stark naked, while the younger is reduced to his shirt!

Dice have even taken part in the destiny of nations. King Olaf of Norway, and his contemporary, King Olaf of Sweden, met at Konungahella in Norway in A.D. 1020 to decide the ownership of the isolated district of Hising. They agreed to throw two dice for its possession. The Swedish king threw two sixes, and smiled and said it was hardly worth the Norwegian's while to make a throw. King Olaf replied, while shaking the dice in his hands, 'Although these be two sixes on the dice, it would be easy, sire, for God to let them turn up again in my favour!' Then he threw and had sixes also. The Swede re-threw, and again had two sixes. On Olaf's second throw one die showed a six but the other split in two and there were seven pips showing. Norway gained the district and the kings parted at the end of the meeting staunch friends.

A   B

Fig. 110. (A) Roman die of silver. Some versions have the pips arranged with Rabelaisian humour. (B) Sixteenth-century German die of box-wood (redrawn from Wright's *History of Domestic Manners and Sentiments in England during the Middle Ages*, 1862)

Grotesque dice in human form have been made from time to time and the two shown in fig. 110 are separated by more than a thousand years. The first is Roman, and made of silver. Several Roman dice of the same type are known. The second is larger and is carved in

box-wood. In was apparently made in Germany at the beginning
of the sixteenth century. Both were in the collection of Lord
Londesborough.

1. GAMES WITH TWO-SIDED DICE

HEADS AND TAILS

Although this game is now only of interest to children or used
for gambling by the unintelligent, during the reign of Edward II
it even appeared at court. In one of his wardrobe rolls is the entry:
'Item, paid to Henry, the King's barber, for money which he lent
to the King to play at Cross and Pile [Heads and Tails]—Five
Shillings. Item, paid to Pires Barnard, usher of the King's Chamber,
money which he lent to the King, and which he lost at Cross and
Pile to Monsieur Robert Wattewille, Eight Pence.'

These sums were not trifles. A penny in those days had the pur-
chasing power of at least a modern pound; a whole sheep cost 3*d.*,
and a hind earned 6*d.* a week!

The Romans played the same game with a copper coin, the AS,
with the head of Janus on one side and the prow of a galley on the
other. They called the game CAPITA AUT NAVIM. Professor Lanciani
found a coin of Nero which had been sawn in two, and an iron weight
placed between the two halves to make one side come up more often.
Similar crooked coins are still used by a few pitmen today when
playing pitch and toss. Occasionally one may also find a coin which
has been split and joined to the halves of another so that one coin
has two 'heads' and the other two 'tails'.

Heads and tails is played by one player tossing a coin into the air
and the other calling when it is still in flight. If his guess is correct
he wins, if not he loses.

THE BOWL GAME

Long before Columbus discovered America the Amerindians
played bowl games. All-tes teg-enuk of the Passamaquoddy of
Maine is typical of the group. Three pieces of equipment are required.

  1. A bowl or shallow wooden dish about 12 in. across and 2 in.
deep (fig. 111).

  2. The dice are six thin bone discs about ¾ in. in diameter, plain
on one side and carved and coloured on the other (fig. 112).

3. Four dozen small sticks about 6 in. long, four larger ones, and a fifth stick which is notched (fig. 112; see also fig. 161 on Plate XXIII).

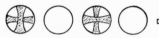

FIG. 111. Wooden bowl for All-tes teg-enuk. The dice are made of plum-stones (bone described in the text) (after Culin's *Chess and Playing Cards*)

FIG. 112. Equipment for All-tes teg-enuk: (A) Notched tally. (B) Four large tallies. (C) Forty-eight small tallies. (D) Six bone discs, plain on one surface and marked on the other

Method of Play

Two players sit facing each other with the bowl between them containing the dice which are arranged haphazardly. The sticks are heaped up in a store pile. One of the players takes the bowl and bangs it down on the ground, causing the dice to jump into the air. If a player scores he has another turn, otherwise the bowl passes to the opponent who also bangs it down and the turn of play passes alternately back and forth. If a die jumps out of the bowl the turn ceases. There are two phases in the game.

First Phase. If five of the discs are the same way up, either marked or plain, the player wins three small tallies from the store pile and places them in a cache.

If he succeeds twice in succession he wins nine small tallies from the pool.

If three times in succession he wins twelve small tallies or one big one; his turn then ceases.

If six discs are alike the player wins a big tally from the pile, or twelve small ones.

If this happens twice in succession the player wins three big tallies or thirty-six small ones.

If it happens three times in succession the player takes sixteen small tallies from the opponent's cache, or if this is impossible he turns a stick up on end; and then claims his win when it is possible and adds them, together with the marker stick, to his own cache.

If all the small tallies have been taken and only large ones are left in the pile, when a player throws five alike he places one of his sticks in front of his cache to show that he has a credit of three tallies. When a player has four sticks out, he takes a large tally from the pool and adds it together with the four marker sticks to his cache.

The notched tally is worth three small tallies and must be the last tally taken from the pile. When it has been won the second phase begins.

Second Phase. The values of the throws alter:
Five alike wins four small tallies from the opponent.
Five alike twice in succession wins twelve small tallies.
Five alike three times in succession wins a large tally or sixteen small tallies from the opponent's cache.
Six alike wins one large tally or sixteen small ones.
Six alike twice in succession wins three large tallies or forty-eight small ones.
When a player has no sticks left he has lost the game.

All-tes teg-enuk may become wearisome in a drawn-out second phase. A quicker ending is achieved by placing any tallies won from the opponent in the second phase back into the pool and out of play. The first player to lose all his tallies loses the game.

2. GAMES WITH SIX-SIDED DICE

GAMES USING ONE DIE

THIRTY-SIX

In this game for any number of players each puts a stake into a pool, and then throws the die to determine the order of play, the lowest cast opening and the highest having the advantage of playing last. Each player in turn throws the die, adding each number thrown to his previous score; the object being to reach thirty-six, or approach it as closely as possible without passing it. Players throwing more than thirty-six go OVER THE TOP and are out of the game. The player nearest to thirty-six wins, and if there is a tie the pool is divided between the winners.

PIG

Any number of players may play and each throws the die in turn. The player with the lowest throw begins the game and the one with the highest plays last. The opening player throws the die as many times as he wishes, each time adding the number on the upper face of the die to his score. If he throws an ace, however, he loses all the points for that turn, and has to pass the die on to the next player. He may stop throwing at any time and hand the die on, when he keeps the points scored in that turn and adds it to his total score. The first player to reach 100 points wins. In succeeding games the advantage of an early throw is decided afresh by each player casting the die, lowest starting and the highest being last.

GAMES USING TWO DICE

ACES IN THE POT

Any number can play and each player starts with two counters. The players make a single throw with two dice in rotation. On a throw of 1 one counter is placed in the pot; if two 1's are thrown both counters are put in. On a throw of 6 a counter and the dice are passed to the player on the left. On a throw of 6:6 the dice and both counters are passed to the left. The dice pass clockwise around the players until there is only one counter left outside the pot. A player without a counter cannot throw the dice but passes them on. The player with the last counter makes three consecutive throws and if he does not throw a 6 he wins the game; but if a 6 is thrown the counter and the dice pass to the player on the left who in turn throws three times. The first player to throw three times without a 6 wins the game.

BARBUDI

This popular Mexican gambling game is played by any number with two dice thrown from a cup.

Rules

1. Each player rolls one die and the highest scorer starts the game. He is known as the SHOOTER and the player on his right becomes the FADER who makes a bet on any amount up to an agreed

limit that the shooter will not win; and he places his bet in the centre of the table.

2. The Shooter may place an equal sum into the centre, or he may allow other players to make up part of, or even the whole of the second stake; or he may refuse the wager entirely and pass up the dice.

3. The Fader also has the right to refuse to fad, and if he does so the opportunity to fad is passed on to the next player on the right.

4. The other players make side bets on whether the Shooter, or the Fader, will make a winning, or losing, throw.

5. When the Fader makes his bet he calls for a ONE-SHOT or a TWO-SHOT decision (Rules 7 and 8).

6. When the Fader's bet has been covered the Shooter rolls the dice once. If the number thrown is not decisive the dice are passed to the Fader who rolls once. If this roll is also ineffectual the Shooter throws again, and they continue throwing alternately until a decisive throw is made.

7. In a One-shot decision the winning numbers are throws of 6:6, 5:5, 3:3, and 6:5, while the losing numbers are 4:4, 2:2, 1:1, and 1:2.

8. In the Two-shot decision if either the Shooter or the Fader throws a 6:5, he wins only half the bet, while a throw of 1:2 loses only half the bet. Either player can then call off the rest of the bet, or they may continue shooting for it.

When the Shooter loses with a throw of 1:2, or the Fader wins with a throw of 6:5, and the second half of the wager is refused by either player, the Shooter passes the dice to the Fader who becomes the new Shooter, and the player on his right the new Fader. If, however, they decide to shoot for the second half of the wager they change roles, the Fader of the first half of the bet becomes the Shooter, and the late Shooter becomes the new Fader. When a decisive throw is cast the dice are passed to the player on the new Shooter's right who becomes the next Shooter.

9. Except when the second half of a Two-shot decision has been contested, when a Shooter throws a losing number or the Fader throws a winning one, the dice pass to the Fader who becomes the new Shooter.

10. A Shooter retains the dice and continues to shoot as long as he continues to win.

K

HAZARD

In Flaundres whylom was a companye
Of yonge folk that haunteden folye
As ryot, *hazard*, stewes and tavernes.
    Chaucer. *Pardoner's Tale*, 1–3.

This game for any number of players became a mania among
gamblers in the seventeenth and eighteenth centuries, and it survives in a modified form in the modern American game of Craps,
so widely played by the United States and Canadian troops in the
Second World War. Two dice were thrown from a cup by one of
the players known as the CASTER.

Rules

1. The Caster threw the two dice to determine the MAIN point.
This had to be a 5, 6, 7, 8, or a 9; any other throw was disallowed
and he threw again until one of the valid points came up.
2. He then threw the two dice to determine the CHANCE point.
This had to be a 4, 5, 6, 7, 8, 9, or 10.
3. Then he continued to throw the two dice until either he
duplicated the CHANCE point when he won the stakes on the table,
or he threw the MAIN point when he lost them.
4. When the Caster was throwing to determine the CHANCE point
he lost the stakes outright if he threw an OUT.

A throw of 12 was OUT if the MAIN point was 9, 7, or 5.

A throw of 11 was OUT if the MAIN point was 9, 8, 6, or 5.

A throw of 2 or 3 known as CRABS was OUT regardless of the MAIN
point.

5. There were also advantageous throws for the Caster when he
was throwing for the CHANCE known as NICKS. If he duplicated the
MAIN point, i.e. if the MAIN was 5, and he threw a 5, he scored a
NICK and won the stakes.

He also won a NICK:

   On throwing a 12 when the MAIN point was a 6 or an 8.

   On throwing 11 when the MAIN point was a 7.

Methods of Betting

Any player wishing to lay money with the Caster placed it in a
marked circle in the centre of the table. The Caster had the option
of accepting or refusing the stake. A player betting with the Caster

could bar any throw if he did so before the throw was made, and with the agreement of the Caster. The players also wagered side bets among themselves and the table below taken from the 1786 edition of Hoyle give the odds accepted at that time against the Caster.

Table of Odds Against the Caster for Side Betting

Main	Chance	Odds
7	4	2 to 1
6	4	5 ,, 3
5	4	4 ,, 3
7	9	3 ,, 2
7	6	3 ,, 2
7	3:3	6 ,, 5
7	5	3 ,, 2
6	5	Evens
3:3	5	5 to 4
8	5	Evens
4:4	5	5 to 4
9	4	4 ,, 3
9	5	Evens

Great fortunes were won and lost at Hazard. William Crockford was born in 1775, the son of a fishmonger with a small business adjoining Temple Bar. After his father's death he sold fish for a time, but also made money at gambling and joined a gaming house in King Street, St. James's. He became a bookmaker at Tattersall's and later a race-horse owner. One of his horses, Sultan, won the Derby in 1836.

In 1821–22 luck went against Crockford's gaming establishment, and night after night his capital shrank. At last the evening came when there was only £5,000 left; and in the first hour's play £3,000 of it had been lost. Crockford left the room, meditating whether to hang or to drown himself, but scarcely was his back turned when the run of luck changed and within two hours the house had easily recouped their losses. By the end of the season he had won over £200,000. He opened a new club-house in 1827 and Captain Gronow has given us a contemporary description.

'In the reign of George IV a new star rose upon the horizon in the person of Mr. William Crockford; and the old-fashioned games of faro,

macao and lansquenet gave place to the all-devouring thirst for the game
of hazard. Crockey, when still a young man, had relinquished the peaceful
trade of a fishmonger for a share in a "hell" where, with his partner Gye,
he managed to win, after a sitting of twenty-four hours, the enormous
sum of one hundred thousand pounds from Lords Thanet and Granville,
Mr. Ball Hughes, and two other gentlemen whose names I do not now
remember. With this capital added to his former gains, he built the well-
known palace in St. James's Street, where a club was established, and
play organized on a scale of magnificence and liberality hitherto unknown
in Europe.

'No one can describe the splendour and excitement of the early days of
Crockey. A supper of the most exquisite kind, prepared by the famous
Ude, and accompanied by the best wines in the world, together with
every luxury of the season, was furnished gratis. The members of the
club included all the celebrities of England, from the Duke of Wellington, to the youngest ensign of the Guards; and, at the gay and festive
board, which was constantly replenished from midnight to early dawn,
the most brilliant sallies of wit, the most agreeable conversation, the most
interesting anecdotes, interspersed with grave political discussions and
acute logical reasoning on every conceivable subject, proceeded from the
soldiers, scholars, statesmen, poets and men of pleasure, who, when the
"House was up" and balls and parties at an end, delighted to finish their
evening with a little supper, and a good deal of hazard at old Crockey's.
The tone of the club was most excellent. A most gentleman-like feeling
prevailed, and none of the rudeness, familiarity and ill-breeding which
disgraced some of the minor clubs would have been tolerated for a
moment.

'The great foreign diplomatists, Prince Talleyrand, Count Pozzo di
Borgo, General Alava, the Duke of Palmella, Prince Esterhazy, the French,
Russian, Spanish, Portuguese, and Austrian ambassadors, and all persons
of distinction and eminence who arrived in England, belonged to Crockford's as a matter of course; but many rued the day when they became
members of that fascinating but dangerous coterie. The great Duke himself, always rather a friend of the dandies did not disdain to appear now
and then at this charming club; whilst the late Lord Raglan, Lord
Anglesey, Sir Hussey Vivian, and many more of our Peninsula and Water-
loo heroes, were constant visitors. . . .

'In the play-room might be heard the clear ringing voice of that agreeable reprobate, Tom Duncombe, as he cheerfully called "Seven" and
the powerful hand of the vigorous Sefton in throwing for a ten.

'Who that ever entered that dangerous little room can forget the large
green table, with the croupiers, Page, Darking and Bacon, with their
suave manners, sleek appearance, stiff white neck-cloths, and the almost

miraculous quickness and dexterity with which they swept away the money of the unfortunate punters when the fatal cry of "Deuce ace", "Aces", or "Sixes out" was heard in answer to the caster's bold cry of "Seven", or "Nine", or "Fives the main" . . . .

'A number of men who did not care to play at hazard used purposely to lose a hundred or two a year at the tables, to have the pleasure of dining and supping with their friends, who all flocked to the magnificent rooms. . . . '

Crockford won all the ready money of his generation. Twelve hundred thousand pounds were netted by the fortunate fishmonger, but when he died he was worth less than a sixth of this sum; unlucky speculations disposing of the rest.

Hazard was never very popular in America except among the negroes around New Orleans who began to play it about 1800. They soon simplified the intricate rules and betting odds and played a form known as THE NEGRO'S GAME, later developing into CRAPS. The sharper John Philip Quinn who reformed, and later when on an evangelical tour was imprisoned quite unjustly, wrote while in jail an exposition on gambling called 'Fools of Fortune'. He mentions travelling on the Mississippi steamboat *City of Chester* and hearing a negro calling, 'Come seven or eleven!' and 'Chill'en crying fo' bread!' Quinn tried his luck and lost fifteen dollars to the 'Crap Roller'.

While the new game of Craps was spreading up the Mississippi, its many variations settled into a standard form played by the workers on the steamboats, the wharves and docks, in the cotton fields and the saloons. About 1890 it began to appear in the clubs and gambling houses, competing with Faro as a banking game, and developing step by step into the Open Craps of the casino.

Private, or Military Craps, however, needs no layout, bank, or book: only two or more players with cash in their pockets, a pair of dice, and time on their hands. G.I. Joe has played Craps all over the world, for millions of pounds, but it is a dull game and its attraction depends entirely on money.

GAMES USING THREE DICE

BUCK DICE

Any number can play and each player throws the dice to determine the order, the highest leading and the lowest having his turn
last. The low man throws a single die to give the POINT NUMBER.

The opening player throws three dice and scores one point for
each point number thrown and he continues to throw as long as he
throws point numbers and they are added up as he goes along. When
he fails to throw a point number on any throw the dice are passed
to the next player. Each player drops out of the game as he reaches
exactly fifteen points. The last player left in the game is the loser.

If a player reaches a total above fifteen the whole throw does not
count and he passes the dice on. Any three of a kind except that of
the point number is a LITTLE BUCK and counts five points. When a
triple point number is thrown it is a BIG BUCK and the player is
immediately credited with fifteen, whatever his previous score may
have been. The player shooting first has a slight advantage.

MARTINETTI

Each player has a coloured counter and the board is marked from
1 to 12 (fig. 113). Each player throws the dice from a cup, the highest
scorer starting the game, while the lowest has his turn last. Ties
are thrown again.

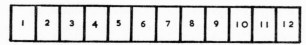

FIG. 113. Board for Martinetti (after Scarne's *Scarne on Dice*)

If the opening player throws an ace he places his marker on
space 1 on the board. If he throws a 1 and a 2 on the same throw, he
would put his marker on the second space, while a throw of 1:2:3
would advance it to the third compartment. Numbers may also be
added together to make required numbers. A throw of 1:4:6 could
be used to make 5 or 7 or 10 or 11. Each player's turn lasts as long
as he is using the numbers thrown. If he fails to score on any throw
the dice are passed to the player on his left.

If a player misses a number that he could have used any player
may make use of it by calling it out as soon as the player passes the

dice on and before they are rolled again. If two players call the number together the one who is nearest the player's left takes precedence.

The first player to travel from 1 to 12 and back to 1 again wins the game.

GAMES USING FIVE DICE

DROP DEAD

Any number can play and each player throws a single die to decide the order of play, low man going first and high last. Tying players throw again. Each player in turn throws the five dice, using a cup, and scores the sum of the numbers thrown, unless a 2 or a 5 appears, when he scores nothing on that roll and any die with 2 or 5 is put aside. The player puts the remaining dice back in the cup and rolls again and continues to score whenever 2 or 5 does not appear, eliminating any die that shows 2 or 5 until all the dice are dead. The next player then has his turn and the highest scorer wins.

INDIAN DICE

The players each throw a die to decide the order of play, high man playing first, the next highest second, etc. Sixes are high, deuces low, while aces are wild and can count as any number.

The opening player has a choice of making one, two, or three throws; the other players are only allowed the same number as he has chosen. After his first throw the opening player may put aside any of the five dice and place the others in the cup for a second throw, or he may re-throw all five. After his second throw, he may throw any or all of the five dice in a third throw, including any which were previously put aside.

Scoring Values

  Five of a kind (five 6's being above five 5's, etc.)
  Four of a kind
  Three of a kind and a pair (known as a FULL HOUSE)
  Three of a kind
  Two pairs
  One pair

A hand without a pair scores nothing and a sequence is useless. Whatever the dice show after the last throw is the final value of the hand.

Example. The first player throws 5:5:2:3:4. He may throw all five again hoping to get better than a pair; or he may put the 5:5 aside and throw the remaining three dice. If he throws 1:3:4 he would add the 1 to the 5:5 making three of a kind, as the ace is wild, and then he might stand or attempt a third roll, hoping to get another 5 or a pair which would give him a full house.

Each round is called a leg. If there are only two players the winner of two out of three legs wins the game. When there are more players they all enter in the first two legs, and the high man in the first leg plays a two-handed deciding game with the winner of the second leg. Alternately the two low men may play off and the loser pays a forfeit.

SHIP, CAPTAIN, MATE AND CREW

Each player throws a single die to decide on the order of play, the highest going first and the lowest last. Players tying throw again. Each player, in turn, is allowed three throws and first tries to get a 6:5 and 4 in that order, the 6 being the ship, the 5 the captain, and the 4 the mate. If 6 and 5 appear on the first throw they are put aside and the three remaining dice are rolled again trying for a 4. When a player has 6:5:4 in that order the points on the remaining two dice are his score, or the crew. If he has not used all his three throws he may, if he wishes, use any remaining throws of the two dice to try to make a higher total. If a 6 and a 4 appear on the first roll, only the 6 can be put aside, and the player then throws the remaining four dice trying for a 5 and then a 4.

The player with the highest score at the end of the round is the winner. If the two high players tie, the round is drawn for everyone and another round is thrown. The player on the left of the shooter in one round becomes the new shooter in the next.

GAMES USING SIX DICE

SEQUENCES

Any number can play and each throws the six dice once, and then passes them on clockwise around the table. A throw of 1:1:1 cancels a player's whole score and he has to start again. The first to reach a hundred wins.

Scoring

Throw	Points
1:2	5
1:2:3	10
1:2:3:4	15
1:2:3:4:5	20
1:2:3:4:5:6	25

1:1:1 cancels whole score. Start again.

GAMES USING TEN DICE

TWENTY-SIX

One of the players acts as banker and has a large pile of counters, the rest have smaller piles. A cup and ten dice are used. The player on the left of the banker chooses any number from one to six as his POINT, and puts a number of counters into the centre of the table and then throws the ten dice thirteen times, counting the number of times the point number appears. The banker pays:

4 to 1 if the player scores 26 or 27 point numbers
5 to 1 for 28 or 29 „ „
6 to 1 for 30 or 31 „ „
7 to 1 for 32 or 33 „ „
8 to 1 for any higher number.

If the player fails to score 26 point numbers he forfeits his stake to the banker, except when he scores fewer than 11 points, when the banker pays him 4 to 1.

GAMES USING FIFTEEN OR MORE DICE

ACES

This is one of the best of the dice games. Any number may play but each player must have a dice cup and five dice. Each player puts an agreed stake into a pool and then throws his five dice and the player with the highest hand takes any seat and is the first shooter, the player throwing the second highest sits on his left and shoots second, etc. Tying players throw again. Aces count as 7.

The first shooter begins by throwing five dice. Each 1 is placed in the centre of the table; all 2's are passed to the player on his left, all 5's to the player on his right. The player continues to throw until he fails to throw a 1, a 2, or a 5, or until he has no dice left. The player on the left then begins his throw. Players with no dice are still in the game as they may receive dice from the players on either side of them.

When all the dice but one have been placed in the centre of the table the player throwing the last 1 with the last die is the winner and takes the pool.

3. GAMES WITH SPECIAL DICE

BELL AND HAMMER

Schimmel, or Bell and Hammer, came from Germany and was played in England at least as early as 1816 and as late as 1870.

FIG. 114. The five cards used in Bell and Hammer (author's collection)

Equipment

Eight cubic dice are used, each with five plain surfaces and the sixth is marked with a 1 or a 2, a 3, a 4, a 5, a 6, a Bell, or a Hammer.

There are five picture cards:

> An Inn
> A White Horse
> A Hammer
> A Bell
> A Bell and Hammer

A dicing cup, and a small ivory or wooden mallet for the auctioneer completes the set (see tailpiece, p. 176). Any number of players may take part in this fascinating game which is in three phases.

First Phase. Each player starts with 36 counters and throws the eight dice in turn, the player throwing the highest number becoming the auctioneer. The latter calls for four counters from each player to form a pool. He then offers up the five picture cards one at a time for sale, each being exchanged for counters from the successful bidder; and the proceeds are added to the pool. A player not having a card does not take part in the round; and any player being out of two successive rounds is out of the game and his remaining counters are confiscated and are added to the pool.

Second Phase. The players throw the eight dice in rotation round the table, the auctioneer throwing first.

Method of Scoring

1. If all the dice are blanks, each player pays one counter to the owner of the White Horse.
2. If the Bell, or Hammer, or Bell and Hammer turn up, the other dice being blank, the owners of the corresponding cards pay one counter to the owner of the White Horse.
3. If the Bell, or the Hammer, or the Bell and Hammer turn up with one or more numbers showing as well, the auctioneer pays this number of counters from the pool to the owner of the card.
4. If only numbers and blanks are thrown the auctioneer pays the player making the throw the number of counters from the pool equivalent to the number shown on the dice.
5. When a larger number is thrown than there are counters in the pool, the player making the throw pays the difference to Mine Host,

the holder of the Inn Card. As soon as the inn is open the third phase of the game begins.

Third Phase.

6. When any player throws all blank dice Rule 1 no longer applies but the owner of the White Horse pays 1 counter to the innkeeper.

7. If the Bell, or the Hammer, or the Bell and Hammer are thrown, the other dice being blank, the owners of these cards pay one counter to the innkeeper.

8. If a number is thrown with either the Bell, or Hammer, or Bell and Hammer, the owners of these cards must pay the inn-keeper the difference between the number thrown and the counters remaining in the pool.

9. A player wins the game by throwing the same number as the number of counters left in the pool, which he adds to his store. The winner of one game becomes the auctioneer in the next and the whole game ends when one player has won all the counters from his rivals.

FIG. 115. Three Crown and Anchor dice

CROWN AND ANCHOR

Crown and Anchor is popular in the British Navy and Fishing

FIG. 116. Exploded Crown and Anchor die to show positions of the symbols

FIG. 117. Crown and Anchor board (author's collection)

Fleet. Three special dice are used marked with a crown, an anchor, a heart, a spade, a diamond, and a club. The players sit round a board or cloth marked with the same symbols (fig. 117).

The players place their bets on the devices of their choice and the banker throws the three dice from a cup. He pays even money on singles, two to one on pairs, and three to one on three of a kind. The banker's advantage is such that eventually he will always be well in pocket and everyone else well out! The bank should, therefore, pass to each player in turn.

LIAR DICE

This game can be played with five standard dice, but is more enjoyable when using five poker dice which are marked with an Ace, King, Queen, Jack, Ten, and Nine. Fig. 119 is an exploded drawing.

FIG. 118. Five poker dice

The opening player casts the dice on to the table from a cup and hides them behind his left hand from the other players. He declares a score which may be accepted or challenged by the player on his left. If it is challenged and the throw is found to be at least as high as the declaration the challenger loses a life. If it is below the declaration the caster loses a life.

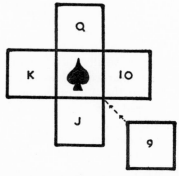

FIG. 119. Exploded drawing of poker die to show positions of symbols

If the declaration is accepted the dice, still concealed, are passed on to the next player who may retain or throw any number of dice. The number re-thrown must be stated, e.g. 'Throwing three'. He then makes his declaration which must be higher than the one he accepted and the player on his left in turn may accept the new call or challenge it.

Order of Scoring

> Five of a kind (Aces count high, e.g. above five Kings)
> A Royal Flush (the five dice in sequence, Ace high)
> A low Flush (the five dice in sequence, King high)
> Four of a kind
> Full house (three of a kind and a pair)
> Three of a kind
> Two pairs
> One pair
> Pryle

Except for the royal and low flushes, sequences do not count. A hand without a scoring combination is called a PRYLE.

If a declaration of five aces is made the next player may challenge or accept it. If he accepts he is allowed five throws of the dice to equalize. If he succeeds the caller loses a life; if not, the acceptor. Each player has three lives and when these are lost he is out of the game. The first player to lose three lives, however, is granted an extra or fourth life. This grace is known as being ON THE PARISH. The last player left in the game is the winner.

4. CHINESE DICE GAMES

Standard Chinese dice are small cubes $\frac{1}{5}$ in. to $\frac{2}{3}$ in. in size, usually made of bone or ivory and marked with incised pips from one to six which are arranged so that the sum of the opposite faces is seven. The ONE pip is uncoloured and is much larger and more deeply incised than the others which are black except the FOUR, whose pips are painted red, a relic of the dice which were imported into China from India many centuries ago. The dice are usually thrown from the hands into a porcelain bowl, the players throwing in turn in a clockwise direction.

STRUNG FLOWERS (Sz'ng luk)

Three dice are used and only four combinations score.

1. TRIPLES. Three sixes are high and three aces low (fig. 120).

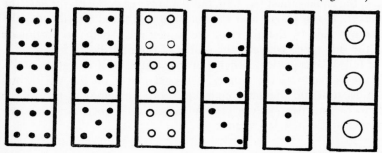

FIG. 120. Strung Flowers: The six triple throws in descending order (after Culin's *Chinese Games with Dice and Dominoes*)

2. STRUNG FLOWERS. This is a sequence of 4:5:6 and gives the game its name (fig. 121).

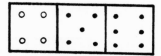

FIG. 121. The sequence of Strung Flowers (after Culin's *Chinese Games with Dice and Dominoes*)

3. TWO ALIKE. The highest score is the Two Alike Six High and the lowest is the Two Alike One High which is known as the Ace Negative (fig. 122).

The composition of the pair is immaterial.

4. THE DANCING DRAGON. This is the sequence 1:2:3 and is the lowest scoring combination (fig. 123).

Method of Play

The players throw the dice in turn and the one with the highest number of red spots becomes the banker. The other players place their stakes, usually divisible by three, on the table. The banker throws until a scoring combination appears. If he throws a Triple, Strung Flowers, or Two Alike Six High, each of the players pays him the full amount of their stakes and then the banker calls for new bets and throws the dice again.

If he throws a Dancing Dragon 1:2:3 or an Ace Negative the banker pays each player the full amount of their stakes.

If he throws Two Alike and Five, Four, Three, or Two High, he hands the dice to the player on his left. If this player makes a higher cast, the banker must pay him, but if a lower cast, the player pays the banker. If the player also throws Two Alike and an odd die, the amounts paid by the player or the banker are usually proportionate to the difference between the scores of the odd die; if it is 4 or 3, the full stake is paid; if 2 then $\frac{2}{3}$ of the stake; and if 1, $\frac{1}{3}$ of the stake. If the banker was the winner, the next player on the left throws against him and the game continues until someone out-throws the banker. The next player on the banker's left becomes the new banker and a new lap begins.

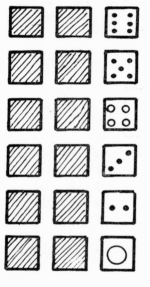

FIG. 122. Strung Flowers: Two-Alike throws in descending order (after Culin's *Chinese Games with Dice and Dominoes*)

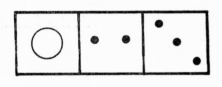

FIG. 123. Strung Flowers: The Dancing Dragon (after Culin's *Chinese Games with Dice and Dominoes*)

THROWING HEAVEN AND NINE (Chak t'in kau)

Two dice are used in this game for any number of players, and the twenty-one possible throws are divided into two series, CIVIL and MILITARY. The throws, their names, and their order of scoring are shown in fig. 124 in descending scales.

Each player throws the two dice in turn and the one with the highest number of pips becomes the banker. The banker calls for the stakes and all the other players put their bets on the table in front of them. The banker then throws and his cast determines the suit, whether civil or military, for that round. Any throw of the other suit does not count and the player must cast again until he makes a cast in the reigning suit.

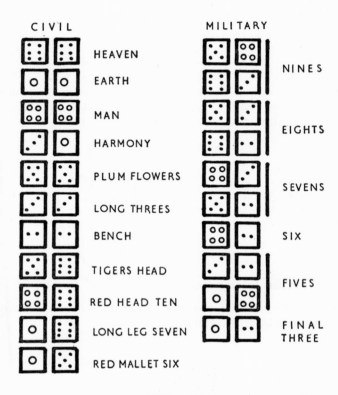

FIG. 124. Throwing Heaven and Nine: The twenty-one possible throws arranged in the Civil and Military series (after Culin's *Chinese Games with Dice and Dominoes*)

If the banker throws the highest pair of the reigning suit, that is HEAVEN of the civil or the NINES of the military, each player gives him his stake; but if he throws the lowest of the reigning suit, that is the RED MALLET SIX of the civil or the FINAL THREE of the military, the banker pays each player the amount of his stake.

L

If the banker throws any other pair than the highest or the lowest of either suit, the second player throws and is paid his stake if he throws higher than the banker, or pays the banker if he throws lower. There is no exchange if the throws are the same. The game continues until the banker is out-thrown, when he is succeeded by the second player as the new banker. When all the players have been banker in turn the game may finish or another round be started. A player may withdraw at the end of any round.

PUT AND TAKE

Each player puts an equal number of counters into a pool and then the opening player spins a six-sided teetotum and obeys the instructions on the face falling uppermost (fig. 125).

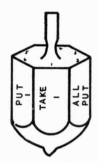

1. Take one   3. Take all   5. Take 2
2. All put   4. Put 2   6. Put 1
   (one into pool)

FIG. 125. Put and Take Spinner

The players spin the teetotum in turn, and when a player loses all his counters he retires from the game.

Antique Chinese dicing cup of ivory (author's collection)

CHAPTER SIX

Domino Games

―――◄◆◆◆◆►―――

CHINESE DOMINOES

Cubic dice were imported into China from India in the distant past; but dominoes, little tablets representing the throw of two dice, appear to have been a Chinese invention. The tiles have the same names as in the corresponding dice throws, and they are divided into the same Civil and Military series. All the tiles in the civil series are in duplicate. A domino set consists of thirty-two tiles and there

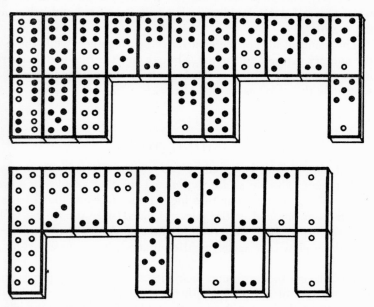

FIG. 126. Set of Chinese dominoes. The duplicate dominoes belong to the Civil series (author's collection)

are no blanks (fig. 126). It makes playing easier if the military tiles are marked with a little horizontal line in the middle though this is not Chinese custom.

Chinese dominoes are made of ivory, bone, or wood, and are known as kwat p'ai (bone tablets). They are usually longer than the European type, being about 3 in. long, $\frac{7}{8}$ in. wide and $\frac{3}{8}$ in. thick, with incised spots which are painted red or white.

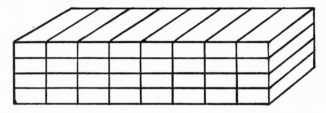

FIG. 127. A wood pile of dominoes

Most games start with the tiles stacked in a WOOD PILE (fig. 127).

The ONE and FOUR spots are marked in red, all the others are white except for the double six tile which is half red and half white (fig. 126).

The identical tiles of the civil series pair together, while those of the military pair in total counts. The 2–4 and 1–2 tiles together form the SUPREME pair which is the highest in the military series, but separately they rank as the lowest tiles.

FISHING (Tiu ü)

This simple game is played by two or three players with two sets of dominoes. The pieces are well mixed and then piled face down-wards in a wood pile four tiles high. Four stacks of four each are drawn from one end of the pile and placed face up on the table. When two play both players draw three stacks (twelve dominoes), or if three play, two stacks (eight dominoes), from the same end of the pile.

The players then examine their pieces, and the first player tries to match one of his pieces with one having the same number of spots among those turned up on the table. If he succeeds he places the matched pair face up in front of himself. Whether successful or not he draws the top domino of the stack at the end of the wood-pile from which the last stacks were drawn and tries to match it with one of those on the table. If successful, he takes the pair, but if not, he places the piece drawn with those on the table.

The second player then tries to match one of his pieces, and also draws one from the pile, and the game is continued until the pile is exhausted. A pair of double SIXES in a player's hand is laid out at once.

The two pieces composing the SUPREME, mate with each other and form an exception to the rule in this game that all pieces having the same number of spots mate with each other without reference to their belonging to the civil or military series.

If a player holds a piece in his hand identical with two pieces on the table, and the fourth piece of the same kind has not been played, he may, at his turn, pile the three pieces that are alike one on the other with the faces up, at the opposite end of the stack from which tiles are being drawn. The player who lays out the fourth piece then takes the other three.

When the last domino is drawn, the players examine those they have taken. The tiles with eight or more spots are called LARGE FISH and count two points for each spot of either colour. The tiles with less than eight spots are called MINNOWS and count one point for each red spot only. If the score of the minnows is between decades, the higher decade is counted, e.g. if a player's score in minnows is 12 he is credited with 20.

The player with the highest count becomes the winner, and is paid by each of the players for each point he has in excess of their total.

DISPUTING TENS (Tsung shap)

One set of dominoes is used in this game for two players. The tiles are piled face down, side by side, in a woodpile four high and eight long. The players divide it between them, each taking four of the stacks. The first player draws the top piece from the stack at the right of his pile and lays it face up on the table. The second player then draws a piece from his pile and lays it face up alongside the piece played by the first player. They continue to draw and place the pieces on the table at either end of the row of upturned tiles.

Rules

1. If a player puts down a tile which is a duplicate of one of the pieces at either end of the row, he takes both pieces to make a PAIR. They count ten for each spot on them at the end of the game.

2. If a player puts down a domino and its spots make a multiple of ten when added to those on the pieces at both ends of the row, or with the two tiles at either end of the row, he lifts the three pieces and at the end of the game each spot on them counts one point.

3. If there are only two pieces on the table and a player takes them, he piles them on top of each other to mark a SWEEP which counts forty. He then draws from his pile and lays out another piece.

4. If a player fails to take up a winning combination of two or three tiles his opponent may take it, then lay out a piece, and continue the game.

5. The game ends when one of the players has laid out all his pieces and the player with the highest count wins.

COLLECTING TENS (K'ap t'ai shap)

This is the favourite domino game in the Chinese gambling houses in the U.S.A. and can be played by any number from two upwards. Many sets of dominoes are used and they are carefully mixed by the players and piled face down, five pieces high, in a long woodpile down the centre of the table.

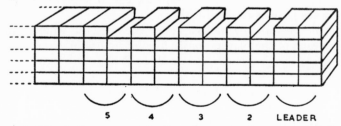

       5   **4**   **3**   **2**   **LEADER**

Fig. 128. Woodpile prepared for five players for the game of Collecting Tens

At the start of the game all the players place equal stakes in a box on the table. Five per cent. of the total is taken by the House and the rest goes to the winning player. The croupier, or one of the players, shakes four dice under a cup and counts anti-clockwise around the players starting with the player on his right, to the number thrown. This player becomes the leader.

The top piece on the third stack from one end of the pile is then removed and placed at the far end of the pile; and the top piece from each alternate stack up to one less than the number of players is also removed and placed with it; fig. 128 shows a pile prepared for a game of five players.

The leader takes the two stacks at the end containing ten pieces; the second player on his right takes the next two stacks containing nine pieces; and the remaining players each take nine pieces.

The players examine their pieces and if the leader has not drawn a winning hand he discards a piece which is placed face up on the table.

The next player on his right may take up this piece to complete a winning hand, or exchange it for a piece from his hand, which he places face up on the table. He also draws a piece from the top of the exposed stack of the woodpile. If it does not complete a winning hand he may either place it face up on the table or keep it and discard a piece from his hand.

The third player may then take one of the pieces from the table and draw one from the top of the exposed stack. The game continues until one of the players wins by collecting ten pieces consisting of a MATCHING PAIR of two identical tiles, and four DECIMAL PAIRS, the sum of the spots of each pair being ten or a multiple of ten. The piece 2-4 only counts as three in making up tens.

The winner of a game takes the contents of the stake box and a new game begins.

Collecting Tens and a game called Playing Heavens and Nines (Ta t'in kau) were the forerunners of a game which swept the western world in the 1920's and is best known as Ma-jong. Modified dominoes were used with three suits and twenty-eight special tiles.

MA-JONG

Estimates of the age of this game vary from the time of Confucius, twenty-five centuries ago, to about one hundred and fifty years. The latter is more likely as it only became popular in China about 1900. Stewart Culin, writing in 1895, was unaware how Ma-jong was played, and he described in some detail curious dominoes from Fuchau, and other sets from Shanghai and Ningpo. These sets varied in the number of the tiles and the inscriptions on them, but they belonged to games related to the now well-known Ma-jong.

There are considerable differences in the methods of playing the game in the north and the south of China, and the quality of the translations also varies considerably. No two books on the subject are in complete agreement, and if any points of dispute arise in a game, the rules in the hosts' book should be accepted as final. The account given here is taken from several sources and should be acceptable to most players.

Ma-jong was introduced into the clubs of Canton, Shanghai, and other foreign settlements in China, and sets made for foreigners had numerals added to the upper left hand corner. From the Far East the game spread to America, and then to Europe.

Equipment

The game is played with pieces of bone or ivory, backed with bamboo. Some of the most valuable sets are made of mother-of-pearl and jade, and are housed in richly carved or lacquered caskets. Cheaper modern sets of plastic materials have lowered the price though even these cost from £5 upwards. Players are advised to buy the best they can afford; a good set is a delight to handle and adds to the pleasure of the game. The price of a genuine Chinese set is high, but the 136 tiles are beautifully made with bamboo backs dovetailed into ivory or bone faces engraved and coloured. There are also 128 bone counters, two pairs of dice, a tong box, markers, and four stands for the pieces. See Plate VII opposite.

The Tiles

There are four of each kind of tile and the tiles are grouped into:

CARDINAL TILES	The Red, White, and Green Dragons.
WINDS	The East, South, West, and North Winds.
HONOUR TILES	The Ones and Nines of the three suits are honour tiles. The One of Bamboos is often represented by a rice bird.
MINOR TILES	These are the 2, 3, 4, 5, 6, 7, 8, of each of the three suits.

Many sets have eight additional tiles known as FLOWERS and SEASONS, but these are obsolete and rarely used today. See the tailpiece, p. 170. Four blank tiles serve as replacements for any lost pieces.

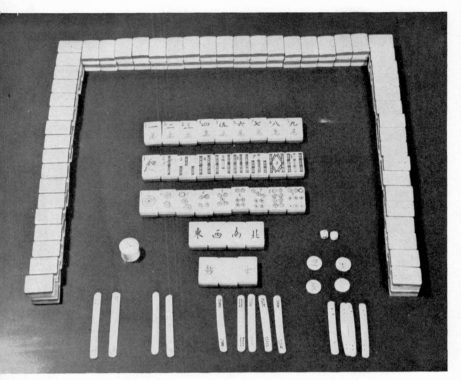

Ma-Jong set with one to nine of Characters, Bamboos and Circles, four Winds and three Dragons exposed; also Tong, markers, pair of dice, and a few bone counters (author's collection)

Lorry drivers playing Chinese Chess outside a co-operative store in
Peking, 1958 (taken by Mr. R. S. Dawson)

The Deal

As this is a vicious gambling game among the Chinese, elaborate precautions were developed to make cheating almost impossible.

1. The four players stand round the table and one of them, usually a guest, takes the two dice and throws them once. The sum of the pips is noted and the player, starting with himself, counts each player round the table and stops at the player where the count ends and puts the small round box, or tong, in front of him (fig. 129).

N   W

E   S

Fig. 129. Tong in the centre surrounded by Wind discs (from set in author's collection)

The thrower's own numbers are 1, 5, 9. After placing the tong the thrower shuffles the four round discs representing the four winds face downwards on the table and then piles them one on top of the other. He then throws the dice again, and counts out the number on the four persons standing round the table, beginning with himself. The player at the end of the count draws the top disc from the pile, and the other players take a disc in turn, beginning with the player on the right of the one who has drawn the top disc. This is in an anti-clockwise direction.

2. The person drawing East Wind takes the seat in front of the tong and drops his disc into it, device downwards. The other players then take their places from him, and each replaces his disc in the tong in the following order: South, West, and North.

W

N   S

E

This is different from the familiar geographical arrangement of the compass points.

3. The tiles are then shuffled, face downwards, by East and West. The clinking of the ivory pieces is picturesquely known as the 'Twittering of the Sparrows'. Each player then builds a wall seventeen tiles long and two high in front of himself; the completed walls, representing the walls of a city, are then pushed towards each other until they make a perfect square. Any space left at the corners is said to let in the devils of ill-luck. More realistically, it allows a possibility of cheating.

4. East then takes the dice and throws them once. The total is counted out on the walls starting with the right hand end of the wall in front of East, and where the count stops the wall is broken by lifting the two tiles up and the underneath tile is placed on top of the right hand side of the opening and the uppermost tile is placed three tiles along from the opening. These two tiles, standing up like turrets, are known as the LOOSE TILES and form with the six pairs of tiles beneath them the DEAD WALL (fig. 130).

FIG. 130. The tiles of the Dead Wall are shaded and are separated from the other tiles by moving them half a space

5. East takes the first four pieces to the left of the breach, South takes the next four, West the next four, North the next four, East the next four, and this continues until all the players have drawn twelve tiles. Each player then lifts one more tile, making thirteen in his hand except for East who takes an extra one and holds fourteen. When the end of a wall is reached pieces are lifted from the next wall, moving in a clockwise direction. Each player turns his tiles up on end or places them in a rack, and sorts his hand into the suits and special tiles.

Method of Play

If East holds nine different Honour and Cardinal tiles without a pair in his original hand he may demand a new deal. The other players, after drawing their first tile, are allowed the same privilege. East begins by discarding a piece face up in the middle of the table, and calls it out: 'Four characters' or 'Six of circles' etc. In games with advanced players the pieces are placed face downwards. The turn of play passes anti-clockwise, South following East, etc.

After East discards, and provided there are no pungs, quongs, or chows (see below), South takes a tile from the open end of the wall and adds it to his hand; and then discards a tile from his hand, etc. In drawing from the wall the end piece must always be taken, and the top piece before the bottom.

PUNG. If any of the other three players holds two tiles identical with one just discarded, he may call 'Pung!' and take it out of the pool and place it down in front of his tiles, adding the two tiles from his hand to it, to make an exposed pung or three of a kind. If the player who makes a pung is not next in turn to play, any player who has been passed loses his turn, and play continues in an anti-clockwise direction. Only the last discarded piece may be punged, quonged, or chowed, and it is available only until the next discard is placed on the table. All the other pieces lying in the middle of the table are dead and out of the game. If a player has taken a piece from the wall, and has not yet discarded and another player pungs or chows the last discard, the piece must be returned to the wall and the player misses his turn.

QUONG. Should any player have three pieces in his hand similar to a piece just discarded by another player, he may call 'Quong!' and take it from the pool, and put it in front of his tiles, face upwards, and add the three tiles from his hand to it, making an exposed quong.

If a player has an exposed pung on the table, and he picks the fourth tile off the wall, he may add it to the pung, making an exposed quong.

If a player has a pung in his hand and draws the fourth tile, he declares a concealed quong and puts the four tiles, with the first and fourth tiles face downwards, upon the table in front of himself.

If a player has a concealed quong in his hand which he has not declared, and another player goes MA-JONG before he has put his quong on the table, it only counts as a concealed pung and an odd tile. Usually it is best to put a concealed quong down as soon as it is formed, unless the player wishes to prevent his opponents knowing what suit he is collecting. Until he has drawn a loose tile to compensate for the extra tile of the quong he cannot go ma-jong.

When a player puts a quong down on the table, either exposed or concealed, he takes the loose tile from the wall furthest from the breach, and adds it to his hand, and then he discards a tile in the ordinary way. When both loose tiles have been used to provide extra pieces for quongs, the next two tiles are lifted and put on the wall to form two more loose tiles.

ROBBING A QUONG. A player needing a tile to go ma-jong may steal the fourth tile of an exposed quong from another player to do so. He may not rob a concealed quong.

CHOW. When a player discards a piece, the player next in turn may call 'Chow!' and use it to make a sequence of three consecutive numbers with two held in his hand. The three pieces are placed face up on the table before the player. A chow is a non-scoring combination, but helps towards going ma-jong. Only the player next due to play may chow a discard; and after chowing he discards in the usual way.

If two players want the same discarded tile, a player needing it to go ma-jong takes precedence; then a player requiring it for a pung or a quong; and lastly a player requiring it for a chow. If two players need it to go ma-jong the player whose turn to play comes first wins the tile and the game.

FISHING. If a player needs only one tile to go ma-jong he may declare that he is FISHING. Should any other player go ma-jong before him, his hand counts the full score of a ma-jong hand, less the bonus for going ma-jong; but having stated that he is fishing he cannot discard from his hand and begin to collect some other set or pair, even if he finds that the tile he wants is dead, or held in some other player's hand.

STANDING HAND. Should a player be fishing after his first discard in a game he may declare that he is STANDING. He must not touch or change his hand; but on completing it either with a tile drawn from the wall, or with a discard, he gets a bonus of 100 points.

DRAWN GAME. The last fourteen tiles in the wall, excluding the loose tiles, are never used, and if no one has completed his hand when this section of the wall is reached the game is drawn, and no scores are made. The tiles are re-shuffled, a fresh hand started, and the same player remains East.

THE PREVAILING WIND. Each wind, in turn, becomes the WIND OF THE ROUND. The first round is East Wind's, and continues until each player in turn has been East. South Wind's round then begins and continues until each player has been East a second time. The third round is West Wind's round and the fourth and last round is North

Wind's round. A player holding a pung or quong of the prevailing wind has his score doubled.

EAST WIND. If the player who is East in the first hand goes ma-jong he remains East in the second and any subsequent hand until he loses. Then the player who was South becomes East, and the other players change their directions also (fig. 131).

FIG. 131. Change of direction when East loses the first hand. The player who was East becomes North. The player who was South becomes the new East, etc. The players do not change their seats, but be–come different winds

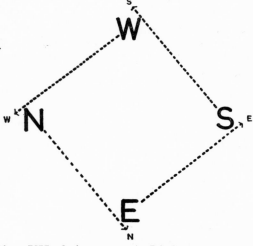

THE COUNTERS (see Plate VII, facing p. 152). Little bone sticks marked with red or black dots are used to keep the score. The number provided varies with the set, but usually each player starts with about 2,000 points, made up of:

2 markers with 10 red dots	..	value 1,000 each	2,000
2 markers with 2 red dots	..	value 200 ,,	400
10 markers with 20 black dots	..	value 20 ,,	200
10 markers with 4 black dots	..	value 4 ,,	40
			2,640

SETTLEMENT OF SCORES. At the end of each hand the player going ma-jong receives the value of his score from two of the other players and double from East. If East is the winner the other three players each pay him double his score. The three losers then settle their payments between themselves. The one with the lower score paying the one with the higher the difference between their scores; but East pays, or receives, double the difference. A loser may have a higher score than the player who went ma-jong but the winner never pays a loser.

A LIMIT. As it is possible to score a over a hundred thousand points in a single hand, it is usual to make a limit, often 1,000 points, as the maximum a player can win on a single hand from each of his opponents. East pays or receives up to double the limit.

MA-JONG or GAME. A complete hand consists of any four sets of tiles and a pair. The sets may consist of THREE OF A KIND (pungs), FOUR OF A KIND (quongs), or RUNS OF THREE (chows). The pair may be any two similar tiles. The player who goes ma-jong does not discard a piece, and thus has 14 tiles in his hand, unless he has a quong when there will be 15.

Calculation of Scores

MINOR TILES   2, 3, 4, 5, 6, 7, 8, of any suit
MAJOR TILES   1, 9, of any suit and all winds and dragons

Combination	Exposed	Concealed
A chow	0	0
A pung of minor tiles	2	4
A pung of major tiles	4	8
A quong of minor tiles	8	16
A quong of major tiles	16	32
A pair of dragons	—	2
A pair of the player's own wind	—	2

Bonus Scores applying to the winner's hand only

For going ma-jong	20
Winning piece drawn from the wall	2
Winning with the only possible piece	2
Winning with a standing hand	100

Each player works out the basic score in his hand and then this score may be doubled as below:

Doubles applying to winner's hand only

Once for hand of all chows and a non-scoring pair.
Once for winning with a loose tile.
Once for robbing a quong to go ma-jong.
Once for winning with the last tile before the hand is dead.

Doubles applying to all hands

Once for a hand of only one suit and winds or dragons (cleared).
Once for a hand of 1's and 9's with winds and/or dragons.
Once for a hand free from chows.
Three times for a hand entirely of one suit.

SPECIAL HANDS

The standard ma-jong hand is four sets and a pair as already described; but there are ten special hands which score a limit, irrespective of their ordinary scoring values.

1. A hand of all WINDS AND DRAGONS.

2. The FOUR WINDS HAND. This contains a pair of one wind, three pungs or quongs of the other winds, and any chow, pung, or quong to make ma-jong. An incomplete hand containing the four winds as described pays the winner as usual, but is paid as a limit hand by the other losers.

3. Hand of all ONES AND NINES.

4. The THREE SCHOLARS. This hand must contain at least three of each kind of dragon. An incomplete hand with these combinations also scores the limit against the other losers.

5. Concealed hand going ma-jong with no chows.

6. The THIRTEEN ODD MAJORS consisting of a one and a nine from each suit, one of each wind, one of each dragon, and a pair to any one of these thirteen tiles.

7. The CALLING NINE TILE HAND. This is made up of a pung of the ones and the nines of any suit, with a sequence of 2, 3, 4, 5, 6, 7, 8 of the same suit, and any single tile of the same suit.

8. The HAND FROM HEAVEN. This is a hand dealt to East which is complete for ma-jong.

9. EARTH'S GRACE. This is a hand going ma-jong using East's first discard.

10. EAST'S thirteenth consecutive ma-jong.

MISTAKES AND PENALTIES

If the wall is broken in the wrong place, or the tiles are drawn in the wrong order, the tiles should be reshuffled and a fresh start made.

If a player puts down an incorrect combination as a chow, pung, or quong, he must correct it before the next player discards, or his hand becomes dead.

If a player calls ma-jong incorrectly and exposes his hand completely, the hand is dead and he must pay each of the other three players double the limit; but if he finds out his mistake before exposing the whole hand he may pick up his pieces again and play on.

If a player has three sets of three exposed tiles of one suit on the table, and another player discards a piece in the same suit which enables the first player to go ma-jong, the second player must pay the winner for the other two players as well as for himself.

If a player is making a special hand, e.g. a three dragon hand, and has two sets of dragons on the table, or a hand of Ones and Nines and has three sets of Ones and Nines on the table, and another player makes a discard allowing him to go ma-jong, the latter must pay the winner for the other players as well as for himself.

When ma-jong reached America many additional rules were made and the Western game differs considerably from the Chinese form described here.

EUROPEAN DOMINOES

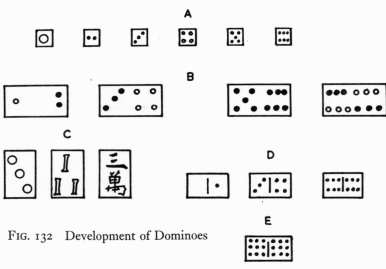

FIG. 132　Development of Dominoes

The earliest report of Dominoes in Europe comes from Italy in the fourteenth century. They may have been introduced from China by Marco Polo or some other traveller. From Italy they were taken to France, and later still to England. Strutt, writing in 1801, damned the game with faint praise: 'This is a very childish sport, imported from France a few years back, and could have nothing but the novelty to recommend it to the notice of grown persons in this country.' A hundred and fifty years later dominoes are played over most of the world, even reaching the Eskimo!

The standard Western domino set is the DOUBLE-SIX, with twenty-eight tiles. The best sets are of ivory; others are made of bone backed with ebony, plastic materials, or stained wood. The duplication of some of the tiles in the Chinese sets has disappeared and is replaced in part by the introduction of BLANK tiles. The development of dominoes is shown diagrammatically in fig. 132.

An edition of Hoyle of 1812 describes a DOUBLE-TWELVE set which is still popular in the U.S.A. today. The larger sets are essential for some of the round games, and are also used when there are more than four players. Dominoes are shuffled by mixing them face downwards on the table.

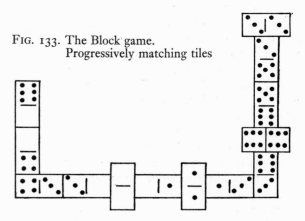

FIG. 133. The Block game.
Progressively matching tiles

GAMES USING A DOUBLE-SIX SET
THE BLOCK GAME

1. After shuffling each player draws a domino. The player with the highest double becomes the leader and the others follow in turn in a clockwise direction. If no double is drawn, the player with the domino with the most pips starts.

2. The dominoes are returned to the pool and reshuffled. If two are playing each draws seven dominoes; if there are more than two each draws five dominoes.

3. The leader plays a domino and the next player matches one end of it if possible. If he cannot do so he forfeits his turn and the next player tries. If no one can play, the game is BLOCKED and each

M

player counts the spots on the tiles still held in his hand. The player with the lowest number of spots scores the total number of spots in his opponents' hands in addition to those in his own.

4. A cribbage board (fig. 16, p. 22) is useful for scoring and the first player to reach 121 wins the game.

THE BERGEN GAME

1. The dominoes are shuffled face downwards. If there are two or three players each draws six tiles, if there are four players each draws five tiles.

2. The player holding the lowest double leads it, or if no one holds a double the lowest tile is led. Leading the lowest double is called DOUBLE HEADING and counts two points to the player. The players then match tiles, the turn moving in a clockwise direction. If a player cannot match a tile he draws one from the pool. If he is still unable to match, the turn passes to the next player. This process continues until someone can match, or there are only two dominoes left in the pool.

3. The object of the game is to make as many double headers or TRIPLE HEADERS as possible. A double header is made by matching the tile at one end of the line, so that the exposed number is the same at both ends. This counts two points.

A triple header is made by adding a double tile matching the other end of the queue, or, if there is a double tile at one end, the player plays a piece at the other end making the three exposed ends the same. A triple header counts three points.

4. A player within three points of the game only scores 2 points for a triple header, and when he is within two points of game, double or triple headers only count one point.

5. When there are three or four players game is ten points, and when there are two players it is fifteen.

6. The first player to put down his last tile calls 'DOMINO' and wins the hand, scoring two points.

7. If there are only two tiles left in the pool, and no one can match either end of the queue, the game is BLOCKED and the player with no doubles in his hand wins. If no doubles remain in any hand, the player with the lowest number of spots wins. If there is more than one double in each hand the player with the least number of double tiles wins regardless of the spot count. The winner of a blocked game scores two points.

Players tend to retain doubles as long as possible to make triple headers.

FORTY-TWO

Any number up to seven can play, though a four-handed partnership game is best. The object of the game is to win tricks, and to capture COUNTING TILES in the tricks. Each trick is worth one point; while every tile whose pips total 5 or 10 is a scoring tile and is worth the total of its pips.

1. The tiles are shuffled face down and each player draws seven. The player holding the 1-0 bids first. Each player in turn may make one bid and no more. A player may pass instead of bidding. The lowest allowable bid is 30, and each bid must be more than the previous one.

2. The highest bidder leads a tile and specifies which end is the trump suit. There are eight suits. Blanks, Doubles, and One to Six. Each player must follow suit to the lead if possible, and the tile of the suit led having the highest count wins the trick, unless a trump tile has been played. The winner of a trick leads for the next trick. When a trump is not led, the higher end of the tile determines its suit. Doubles take any trick of their kind.

3. At the end of the game one point is allowed for each trick, and the 5–5 and 6–4 tiles are worth 10 points each; the 5–0, 4–1, and 3–2 tiles are worth 5 points each, adding up to 35, and with the seven points for the tricks, the maximum score is 42.

4. If the bidding side makes more in tricks and counters than its bid, it scores the bid plus the amount of its score. If the bid, however, was 37 and the opponents make ten points, the opponents would score the bid (37) + 10 = 47 points.

BINGO

The object of this two-handed game is to win seven sets, each set consisting of 70 points.

Method of Scoring

1. All doubles score their spot value. The double blank counts 14 and is known as BINGO.

2. The 6–4 and the 3–0 score ten.

3. All tiles of the trump suit score their spot value, except the double which counts 28: e.g. when sixes are trumps the double six

is worth 28; but when sixes are not trumps the double six is only worth 12.

4. No other tiles score. The total score of a round varies according to the trump suit.

Trumps	Total Score
Blanks	143
Ones	135
Twos	138
Threes	131
Fours	134
Fives	147
Sixes	140

Method of Play

1. After shuffling the tiles one player takes a domino from the stock and the other must guess whether it is odd or even. If he guesses correctly he becomes the leader for the first trick. The domino is then returned to the stock which is reshuffled and each player draws seven pieces.

2. The second player then turns up one of the dominoes in the stock, and the higher figure becomes trumps. This tile is left face upwards. A blank counts seven.

3. The leader then plays any domino. The second player replies and he need not follow suit: the two tiles form a trick which is taken by the player of the higher domino. A trump takes anything except a higher trump or the Bingo.

4. The winner takes the trick and scores any points it may contain and then after drawing a tile from the stock he leads a domino for the next trick. His opponent also draws from the stock and then replies. The game proceeds in this way until all the dominoes have been drawn; the turned-up trump being taken by the player who has the last draw.

5. If a player has two doubles in his hand, on playing one of them he should show the other and announce DOUBLE. If he wins the trick he adds 20 to his score.

In the same way if he has three doubles in his hand, on playing one of them he calls TRIPLETS, and scores 40 if he wins the trick.

If he holds four doubles he calls DOUBLE DOUBLET and adds 50 if he wins the trick.

If he holds five doubles he calls KING, and if he wins the trick takes 60.

If he holds six doubles he calls EMPEROR and wins 70 points if the trick is won. This is one complete set towards game.

If he holds seven doubles, he calls INVINCIBLE and scores 210 points or three complete sets towards the game if he wins the trick. These combinations must be announced immediately the first double is played, otherwise they do not count.

6. When the last draw has been made the method of play changes, for the second player must follow suit if he can; if he cannot, he must play a trump if he has one; and if he can do neither he is forced to discard.

7. At any stage of the game after winning a trick a player may turn the trump on the table face down. This stops all further drawing from stock and the second player has to follow suit, or play a trump, or throw away as described above. The player who stopped the drawing contracts to score 70 points from that moment, and if he succeeds it counts one set towards game; while if his opponent has scored less than 20 points he gains two sets; and if the opponent has not taken a single trick he scores three sets.

8. If a contracting player fails to make 70 points, his opponent scores 140 points, or two sets towards game; and if the opponent had not taken a single trick before the trump was turned he wins 210 points or three sets.

9. The double blank, Bingo, takes any other piece, including a trump, and if it takes the double of trumps the one who played it scores a point. All points must be claimed as they are won, otherwise they cannot be scored. A cribbage board makes scoring easier.

DOMINO CRIB

Two, three, or four players can enjoy this game which was popular in the R.C.A.F. during the 1939–45 war. A cribbage board is used for scoring and a game consists of one circuit of 61 points or two circuits of 121 points. If the winner reaches 61 before his opponent reaches 31 in a single-circuit game, or 121 before his opponent reaches 91 in a double-circuit game, the opponent is LURCHED and the winner is credited with winning two games instead of one.

Method of Play

1. The tiles are shuffled face downwards and then each player takes six tiles.

2. After examining his tiles each player discards two from his hand, placing them face downwards on the table on the left of the dealer. These tiles form the crib.

3. After the crib has been formed, the dealer lifts a tile from the stock and turns it face upwards. This is the STARTER and it is not used during the play of the hands, but is counted with each hand, and with the crib in the final count. If the starter is a double the dealer scores two points which must be pegged before the opponent plays a tile, or the opportunity is lost.

4. The opponent places any tile from his hand face up on the table in front of himself calling its pip value. The dealer replies by playing a tile from his hand and calls the sum of the two tiles on the table. The play continues alternately, the pip value of each tile being added to the sum last called.

5. If a player can make a pip value of 15 he gains two points; the total of the tiles played must not exceed 31.

6. If, at his turn of play, a player hasn't a tile which will bring the sum to 31 or below, he calls 'GO'.

7. After GO has been called the other player plays as many tiles as he is able, announcing the sums as before, until he reaches 31, or can go no further.

8. If a player makes exactly 31 he wins two points.

9. If the score is still below 31 and neither player can play, the last to put a tile down scores one point. The other player then begins a new lap towards 31, the rules being the same as in the first lap. The players must play alternately except when one player has called GO and the other can still play one or more tiles.

10. The player playing the last tile of the hand scores one point.

11. After the tiles are played out, each player picks up his hand and counts all the points it contains, *in combination with the starter*. The dealer's opponent counts first. At the end of a close game this order is important, when first count may enable him to win before the dealer has a chance to add up his score and the crib.

12. After the dealer has pegged all the points in his hand, he turns up the crib and scores the points in it *in combination with the starter*.

Scoring Table

Any double turned up as the starter	1
Fifteen reached exactly in play	2
Playing a tile to make a pair with the previous tile played	2
Playing a third tile of the same denomination immediately after a pair, without a 31 or a pegged GO intervening	6
Playing a fourth tile of the same value after a triplet	12
Three or more tiles played in numerical rotation, though not necessarily in the sequence order, with no 31 or pegged GO intervening. For each tile of the sequence	1
Reaching exactly 31 in play	2
Being nearest to 31	1
Reaching fifteen with the last tile played	3

FIG. 134.
Domino crib:

(A) Double run of three

(B) Double run of four

(C) Triple run

(D) Quadruple run

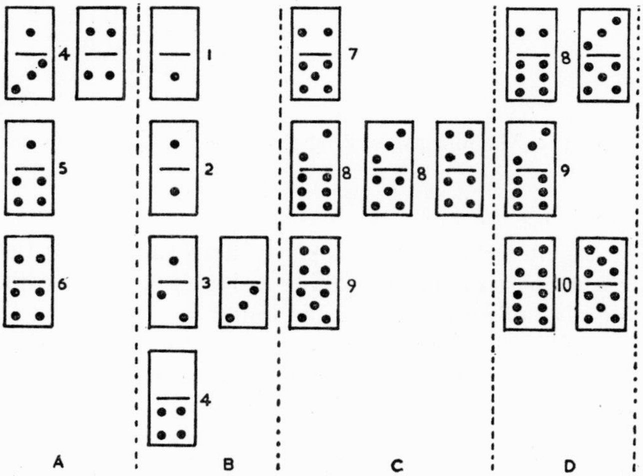

Additional Scoring at the End of a Hand

Any combination adding up to fifteen	2
Double run of three: a three-tile sequence with a pair to any one of the three tiles (fig. 134A)	8
Double run of four: a four-tile sequence with a pair to any one of the four tiles (fig. 134B)	10
Triple run: a triplet with two other tiles in sequence with it (fig. 134C)	15
Quadruple run: two pairs and a tile in sequence with both (fig. 134D)	16

GAMES USING A DOUBLE-NINE SET

THE MATADOR GAME

In this game the tiles are added to the domino queue to form sums of ten instead of in matching pairs: the sum of the two approximating tile-ends must add up to ten unless one of the special MATADOR tiles is used. A 1 is added to a 9, a 2 to an 8, etc. Only a matador may be played on to a blank and there are six of these, 9–1, 8–2, 7–3, 6–4, 5–5, and the 0–0. A matador may be played at any time (fig. 135).

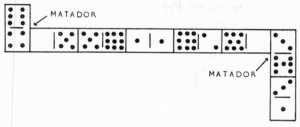

FIG. 135. Matador game. Progression by forming tens or using a matador tile

Method of Play

1. After shuffling, each player draws a domino; the player with the highest double, or failing a double, the tile with the greatest number of pips, becomes the leader.

2. The dominoes are returned to the pool and reshuffled. If there are three to six players each draws seven dominoes. If there are more, then each player only draws five.

3. The leader plays a double if he has one, if not then his highest domino. If a double 9 is led, it must be joined at either side by a 1 by the next player. If he hasn't a 1 he must play a matador or draw from the pool until he obtains a 1. If he played a 1–6, the end spots would then be 9 or 6. The next player must play a 1 to the 9, or a 4 to the 6. Play proceeds in a clockwise direction.

4. When a player cannot make the required TEN and does not wish to play a matador, or hasn't one, he must draw until he can play or until only two dominoes are left in the pool, and then if he has failed to draw a playable domino, he must play a matador if he has one.

5. When one player has drawn all but the last two dominoes from the pool, and can neither make a TEN, nor play a matador, he says,

'PASS'. If no other player can play, the game is BLOCKED and the player holding the lowest number of spots scores the spots held in his opponents' hands.

6. A player who plays his last domino cries 'OUT', and scores all the spots held in his opponents' hands.

7. A game is usually for two hundred points.

CYPRUS

The dominoes are shuffled face downwards and then the players draw their tiles.

No. of Players	No. of Dominoes
4	13
5	11
6	9
7	7
8 or 9	6
10	5

The remaining dominoes are left face downwards on the table and are not used.

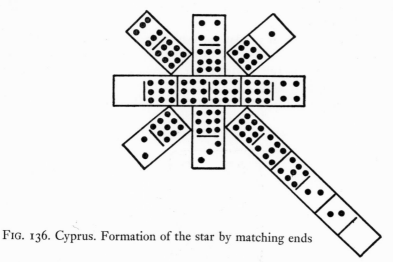

FIG. 136. Cyprus. Formation of the star by matching ends

Method of Play

1. The holder of the double 9 puts it face up on the table. If no one has the double 9 the dominoes are reshuffled and redrawn.

2. In clockwise rotation the players may play 9's to form a star, or match the ends of 9's already played (fig. 136).

3. The first player to play his last tile calls 'DOMINO' and wins the hand. He scores one point for each spot held in his opponents' hands.

4. If no player can play a 9, or match an end, the game is BLOCKED and the player with the least number of spots wins and scores the spots held in his opponents' hands. If two players have the same low count the game is drawn and no one scores.

TIDDLE-A-WINK

1. After shuffling the double-nine set the dominoes are dealt equally to all the players. Any remainder is left face down on the table and is not used.

2. The dealer then calls for the double 9 and the player holding it puts it face up on the table. If no player has it then the double 8 is called for and is played by its owner-holder.

3. A player playing a double either when leading or during the game, earns a second turn of play. Play continues in a clockwise direction, the players matching one of the open ends.

4. When a player is unable to make a match he calls 'PASS', and the next player tries.

5. The first player to play his last tile calls 'TIDDLE-A-WINK' and receives one point for each spot in his opponents' hands.

6. If no one is able to match an open end the game is BLOCKED and the player holding the lowest number of spots in his hand, or in the case of a tie, the least number of tiles, wins the game and scores a point for each spot in his opponents' hands.

7. A game is usually two hundred points.

Ma-jong Flower tile
(author's collection)

CHAPTER SEVEN

Making Boards and Pieces

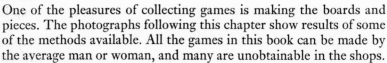

One of the pleasures of collecting games is making the boards and pieces. The photographs following this chapter show results of some of the methods available. All the games in this book can be made by the average man or woman, and many are unobtainable in the shops.

The hobby can be adapted to any length of purse: superb pieces made by the world's craftsmen are available for the wealthy connoisseur; while the handyman in his workshop can produce in formica, perspex, bone, copper, wood, or other inexpensive materials reproductions of boards only to be found in great museums; and even there often in damaged and fragmentary condition.

The ancient craftsmen inlaid wood with faience, ivory, ebony, metals, and pieces of shell or glass. Formica, acrylic sheeting, perspex, and wood veneers provide effective substitutes. If the original boards were simple, crude techniques provide satisfying reproductions; if they were elaborate, sophisticated materials and methods are readily available.

Original pieces can be obtained from friends living abroad, or from antique and curio shops: the unexpected lies just around the corner.

Collectors will find the pastime gives an insight into national character: the superstitious West Indian playing Awari and anxiously watching the evening shadows lengthen while unwelcome Djombies wait to join the game, contrasts with the blasé cosmopolitan air-traveller killing time with a game of dominoes.

METHODS OF CONSTRUCTION

POKER WORK. This is suitable for simple native boards. Lines are drawn on wood with a red-hot poker or soldering iron. The

photograph (fig. 137, facing p. 176) shows a Fighting Serpent board
made in this way with beach pebbles as counters, which could have
been made by any Amerindian.

WOOD CARVING. The fine Wari board in fig. 138 (facing p. 176)
was carved from one piece of Osese wood by a professional carver
in Old Hsuoyah, Ghana. Although made in 1957 it is in the traditional style. The stem is hollow and when the game is finished the
bung is removed, the seeds popped into the cavity, and the bung
replaced.

The holes for mancala boards are easily made by taking a round
tin lid of a suitable size and using it as a marker for the outline of
the cups; then four holes are bored sloping inwards and each cup is
hollowed out with a gouge and a mallet (fig. 139 on Plate X).

CHIP CARVING. A Ludus Latrunculorum board cut into the top of
a teak coffee table is shown in fig. 140 (on Plate X). A board for
Saxon Hnefatafl made in the same way is shown in fig. 155 (on
Plate XVIII).

INLAID WOODS. Hundreds of different woods are now imported
into England and attractive boards can be made with inlays. This
is an old technique which was much used in the Middle Ages, and
is suitable for reproductions of this period. Fig. 141 (on Plate XI)
shows a copy of fourteenth-century Tables. The background is
1 in. thick mahogany, inlaid with ranin for the light points, and with
agba for the dark. The bar was of English oak with a wild grain.
Recesses of the correct size and shape were chopped out of the background with a chisel and mallet, and the inlay pieces, some $\frac{3}{16}$ in.
thick, were fitted into them, leaving an excess standing proud. When
all the pieces had been glued in position with Britfix (which is clean
and easy to use) the surface was planed and rubbed down with
flourpaper. Two or three rubbers of white French polish followed
by beeswax and turpentine completed it.

MARQUETRY. A wide range of veneers is available and several
boards have been made by gluing shaped pieces of veneer to an
underboard of plywood at least $\frac{1}{2}$ in. thick (fig. 142 on Plate XI).
A solid underboard tends to warp a few weeks after the veneer has
been applied unless it is very thick. The application of formica is
even more likely to cause warping.

PAINT AND ENAMEL. The antique compendium of games from
western India (fig. 143 on Plate XII) is a fine example of paint-work
on wood. The upper surface is marked for Tablan, inside is a

Pallanguli board, and underneath is a Nine Men's Morris. The under surface of the lid is painted for Cows and Leopards, and two other games not mentioned in this book, Lau Kata Kati and Kaooa.

PAINTING ON MATS. The copy of an Aztec Patolli mat in fig. 144 (on Plate XII) was made by painting a bamboo mat from Hong Kong with poster paints. Costume-jewellery stones were used as counters. The originals were precious and semi-precious gems.

FORMICA. The Cows and Leopards board in fig. 145 (on Plate XIII) was made of yellow formica fastened to $\frac{3}{4}$ in. plywood with Evo-stick, and then grooved with a high-speed electric drill. Formica is also useful for making mosaic patterns. Many colours and designs are available. There is a tendency for small pieces to curl.

POTTERY. Games from Assyria, Ancient Egypt, Palestine, and Rome were scratched on tablets of clay and baked. Copies can be made at evening classes in pottery. The boards should be allowed to dry out slowly and require turning daily to prevent warping or distortion: in about three weeks they are ready for the first baking in a kiln; then they are coloured, glazed, and rebaked. If the clay is not dried out thoroughly before baking it may shatter into little pieces in the kiln.

Pottery was also used to reproduce the sandstone board found at Palenque (fig. 146 on Plate XIII).

LEATHERWORK. Some Oriental gaming boards are made of decorated leather, utilizing blind tooling, gilding, and inlay.

Method of Gilding

1. The leather is dampened.

2. The design is pressed into the leather with appropriate tools which are heated until they just hiss when touched with a damp piece of cotton wool. If they are too hot the leather is charred; if too cold the impression is unsatisfactory.

3. The blind-tooling pattern is carefully painted with a gold size made of white of egg.

4. When the size is dry, pieces of gold leaf (which is only 1/250,000 of an inch thick) are placed over the design and pressed lightly into the blind-tooling with a cotton wool pad.

5. The gilding tools are re-heated and the pattern is pressed again, the heat fixing the albumen and cementing the gold leaf to the leather.

6. The excess gold leaf is removed by rolling a ball of crude rubber over it. Rexine is a cheaper substitute for leather.

The Nine Men's Morris in fig. 147 (on Plate XIV) was made by cutting a piece of heavy cardboard into a square of 18 in., and gluing red rexine on to it. The pattern was marked out on thin tissue paper, and then pieces of gold leaf mounted on waxed paper, which is obtainable at most stationers or leather merchants, were slipped underneath and the pattern was stamped with suitable gilding tools. These should be a little cooler than when working with leather which is damp, since the rexine is dry and more liable to scorch.

BEAD WORK. The Amerindians marked buffalo or elk hide with beads, coloured dyes, or porcupine quills. Fig. 148 (on Plate XIV) shows a Zohn Ahl track of beads on leather.

EMBROIDERY. The cloth Pachisi board in fig. 149 (on Plate XV) was made in India, but it could be duplicated with coloured scraps and a little embroidery by any housewife. More ambitious projects might interest expert needlewomen.

PAPER. Chinese paper boards are fragile and are best put behind glass or perspex for protection. Copies can be made by ruling lines in Indian ink on Bristol Board or heavy paper (fig. 150 on Plate XV).

PAPER BACKED WITH LINEN. Many of the Georgian and early Victorian race games were made of paper mounted in sections on linen. Fig. 151 (on Plate XVI) shows a Royal Game of Goose made by drawing the design on a piece of paper, cutting it up and fixing it to linen with thin glue. Protective covers were made of cardboard.

METALWORK. The Pallanguli board from Travancore (1957) (fig. 152 on Plate XVII) was beaten out of a malleable white metal and chromium-plated. The metal worker may like to try his hand at tapping out a similar series of depressions in a sheet of copper, heating it occasionally to restore its ductility.

PERSPEX. Perspex sheet is excellent for inlay work and takes a high polish if buffed with jeweller's rouge. Fig. 153 (on Plate XVII) shows a reproduction of a Senat board found in Cyprus; the pieces are originals from the author's collection and were found in Egyptian tombs of the eighteenth to twenty-sixth dynasties (1570–1349 B.C. to 663–525 B.C.).

MAKING PIECES

A lathe is a great asset though not essential. The Bridges, Black and Decker, or Wolf Cub $\frac{1}{4}$ in. drill attachments are ideal.

WOODEN PIECES. These can be made of contrasting woods: teak polished with raw linseed oil, mahogany, or ebony, are excellent for dark pieces; while sycamore, boxwood, pear, or ranin are nearly white and turn well. Old lawyers'-rulers form a cheap source of ebony, while discarded bowling woods are often of lignum vitæ and are treasure trove to the turner.

Wooden pieces can be coloured most attractively with lacquer enamels which are sold in convenient small tins for about 1s. each. Humbrol art oil enamel manufactured by The Humber Oil Co. Ltd., Hull, can be recommended. It is sold in most model shops.

IVORY. Used billiard balls are sold for as little as 6d. each and are delightful for turning gaming pieces, or making dice, etc. A set of reproduction mediaeval chessmen in ivory and ebony is shown in fig. 154 (on Plate XVIII) on an unchequered board of formica.

BONE. The Vikings and Saxons used bone for their pieces and the reproduction set for Hnefatafl in fig. 155 (on Plate XVIII) was made of mutton bones. They were boiled to get rid of the tags of meat and gristle and then bleached with Domestos. The Black pieces were dyed by boiling with Black Drummer dye.

The Tibetan chess set in fig. 156 (on Plate XIX) is a somewhat gruesome example of the possibilities of this medium. The pieces are carved in human bone, probably from an executed criminal.

PERSPEX. The set of dominoes in fig. 157C (on Plate XX), made in 1958 by an old gentleman of 83, were of $\frac{1}{8}$ in. white perspex fused to $\frac{1}{4}$ in. black perspex with Tenuit adhesive. The fused sheet was then cut into the shapes, and the pips were made by filling drill-holes with cobbler's black heelball.

Six dominoes from a set made about 1850 are shown for comparison. The bone faces are fastened to the ebony backs with small brass sprigs (fig. 157D on Plate XX).

POTTERY. The beautiful reproductions in pottery of Lion and Jackal pieces for the Egyptian game of Senat were made in evening classes by a friend (fig. 158 on Plate XXI). John Flaxman designed a chess set for Wedgwood in blue and white stoneware, c. 1780.

STONES. It is surprisingly difficult to collect thirty stones of approximately the same size, shape, and colour, even on a pebble beach. A penny for every suitable stone gives great joy to the younger members of the family!

SEA-SHELLS. Cowries, used in many Indian games, can be bought quite cheaply from florists who used them for flower arrangements in bowls. Some of the sea-shells from our own shores may also be pressed into service.

SEEDS. Friends abroad may be able to send seeds used in native games; but beans, acorns, hazel nuts, and cherry stones form acceptable substitutes. The last-named are very attractive and can be stained any colour.

MARBLES. Coloured clay marbles cost about 5s. per thousand and are useful for mancala counters, Solitaire, Seega, etc.

LOTS

GAMBLING STICKS. Copies of those used by the Kiowa Indians (fig. 159 on Plate XXI) were made from ⅜ in. diameter beech dowel rod, split lengthways. Clear copal varnish was applied and when dry they were enamelled. If enamel is applied to unvarnished wood the colour edges become blurred and ragged.

The Pam-nyout were made from an old ebony ruler which was sawn lengthways and then polished.

DICE (fig. 160 on Plate XXII). These were made from ivory billiard balls. A hacksaw was used to cut them out roughly and a Bridges' sanding disc completed the shaping. The pyramidal die from Ur was reproduced in ivory with two of the points tipped with red perspex. Tenuit was used as an adhesive.

'Chinese' dice can be made from western ones by drilling larger cavities on the 1 and 4 faces and colouring them with red enamel, or filling the depression with red sealing wax.

Fig. 161 (on Plate XXIII) shows a reproduction set of equipment for the game of All-tes teg-enuk. The dice were cut with a coping saw out of a large beef bone, grooved with a high-speed drill, and painted with blue enamel. The bowl was turned from a piece of sycamore; the large tallies were made of teak, and the small tallies of a pink Brazilian hardwood.

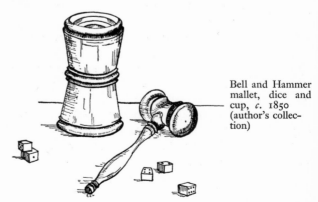

Bell and Hammer mallet, dice and cup, *c.* 1850 (author's collection)

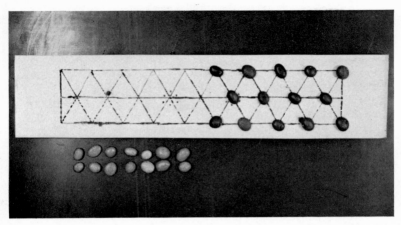

FIG. 137. *Poker work*. Board for Fighting Serpents with
beach pebbles for counters

FIG. 138. *Wood carving*. A Wari board from old Hsuoyah, Ghana
(author's collection)

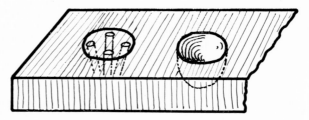

FIG. 139. Making a mancala cup

FIG. 140. *Chip carving*. A Ludus Latrunculorum board
cut into the top of a low table. The pieces of one side
are red and the other green though this does not show
in the photograph

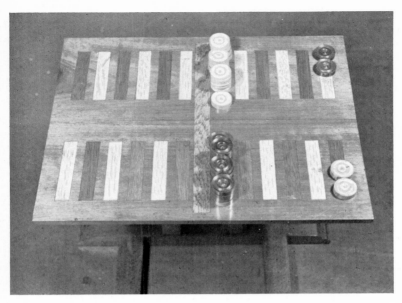

FIG. 141. *Inlaying.* A reproduction of a fourteenth-century Tables board.
Tablemen of boxwood and ebony, *c.* A.D. 1850

FIG. 142. *Marquetry.* A board for Continental draughts made
with blackwood and zebrano on $\frac{3}{4}''$ plywood

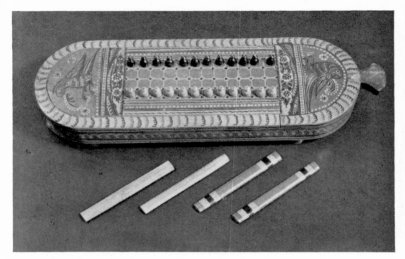

FIG. 143. *Paint work on white wood*. Antique Tablan board from western India (author's collection)

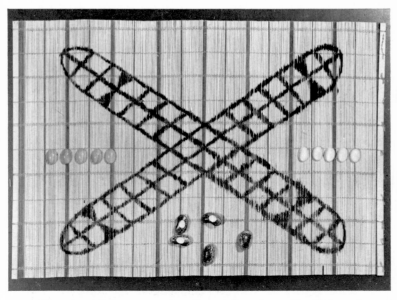

FIG. 144. *Paint on matting*. Copy of an Aztec Patolli board with pieces and beans

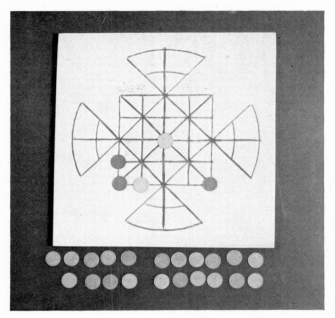

FIG. 145. *Formica on plywood*. Board for Cows and
Leopards; the cows are copper coins and the
leopards silver

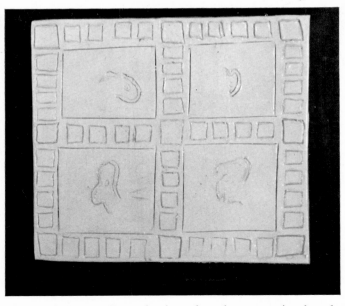

FIG. 146. *Pottery*. Reproduction of sandstone gaming board
from Palenque, Central America

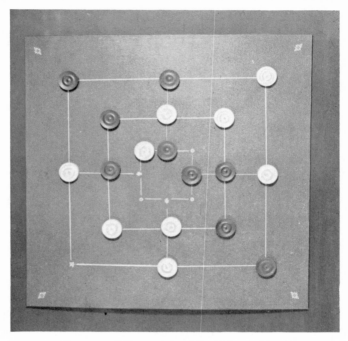

FIG. 147. *Gilt on rexine*. Nine Men's Morris

FIG. 148. *Beadwork on leather*. Zohn-ahl track
with dice-sticks and mutton-bone pieces

FIG. 150. *Paper*. Modern Chinese Chess board and wooden pieces (author's collection)

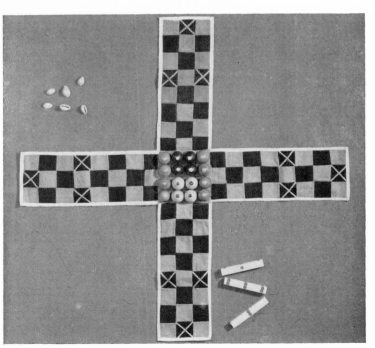

FIG. 149. *Embroidery*. An Indian Pachisi board with long dice and cowrie shells (author's collection)

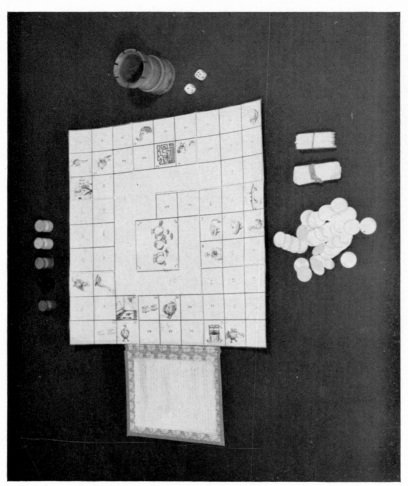

Fig. 151. *Paper backed with linen.* Reproduction of Royal Game of Goose with a wooden dicing cup, *c.* A.D. 1775. The bone counters are *c.* A.D. 1850; the dice and wooden pieces are modern

FIG. 152. *Metal work*. Modern Pallanguli board in white metal from Travancore (author's collection)

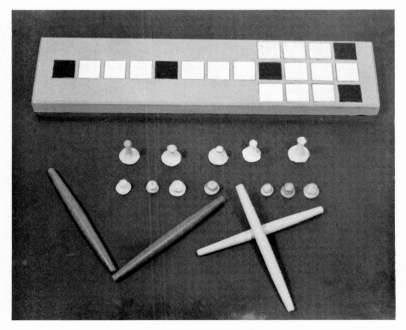

FIG. 153. *Perspex inlaid into wood*. Reproduction Senat board and dicing sticks. Original gaming pieces, *c.* 1570–525 B.C. (author's collection)

FIG. 154. *Ivory*. Reproduction Shatranj chessmen in ivory and ebony

FIG. 155. *Bone*. A reproduction Hnefatafl board of wood with
pieces made from mutton bones

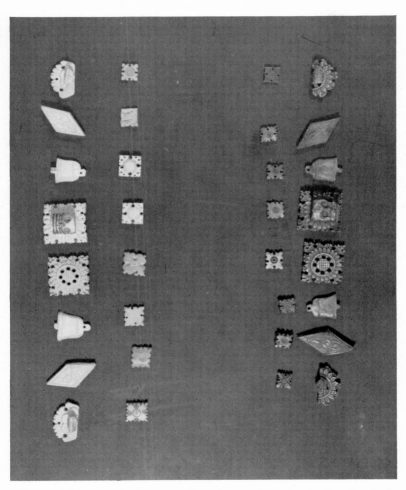

F$_{IG}$. 156. Tibetan chessmen made of human bone (author's collection)

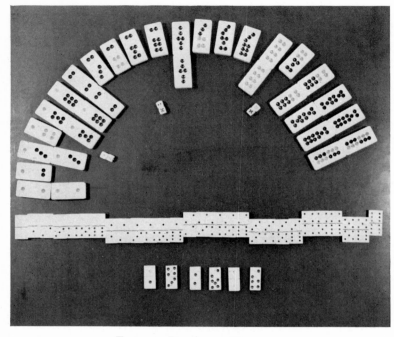

FIG. 157. Dominoes. *From top :*

(*a*) A modern set of Chinese dominoes of synthetic ivory arranged in an arc (from Hong Kong)

(*b*) Six Chinese dice arranged as if they were dominoes

(*c*) European double-six domino set made of black and white perspex

(*d*) Six pieces from an English set of bone and ebony dominoes, *c.* 1850

(Author's collection)

FIG. 158. *Pottery*. A reproduction board of the Game of Thirty Squares. Teak inlaid with formica; long die of ivory, and ten green jackals and ten blue lions of pottery

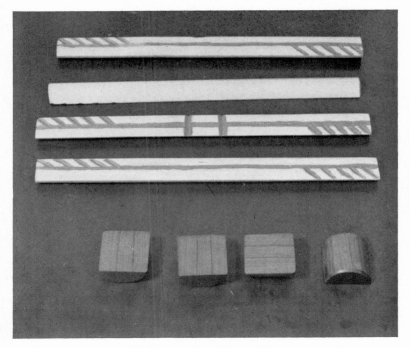

FIG. 159. Gambling sticks
Above, copies of those used by the Kiowa Indians for Zohn-ahl
Below, copies of pam-nyout for the Korean game of Nyout

FIG. 160. *Ivory*. Reproduction dice made from billiard balls. *From top :*

(*a*) English teetotum, *c.* A.D. 1800

(*b*) Large Roman fourteen-sided die, *c.* A.D. 200

(*c*) Sumerian pyramidal die, *c.* 3500 B.C.

(*d*) Long die for Shaturanga, *c.* A.D. 500

(*e*) Three long dice with pointed ends (Lucknow), *c.* A.D. 1850

(*f*) A pair of debased dice from the Gran Chaco, *c.* A.D. 1900

(*g*) Five dice from Qustul, *c.* A.D. 300

FIG. 161. *Turned wooden bowl* and equipment for All-tes teg-enuk

FIG. 162. Stone overdoor of Charles Cotton's fishing-lodge, 1674
(re-drawn from the *Complete Angler*, 1823 edition)

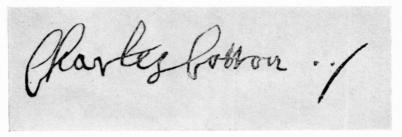

FIG. 163. Facsimile of Charles Cotton's signature in a letter to
Isaac Walton, 1675 (from the *Complete Angler*, 1823 edition)

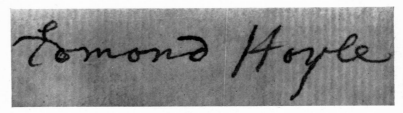

FIG. 164. Facsimile of Edmond Hoyle's signature, 1769,
when he was over ninety (author's collection)

Biographies

Date	Book	Author
A.D.		
c. 920	*Kitab Ash-Shatranj*	as-Suli
1674	*The Compleat Gamester*	Charles Cotton
1689	*De Historia Shahiludii* ⎫	Thomas Hyde
1694	*De Historia Nerdiludii* ⎭	
1743	*Short Treatise on the game of Backgammon*	Edmond Hoyle
1801	*Sports and Pastimes of the People of England*	Joseph Strutt
1860	*History of Chess*	Duncan Forbes
1892	*Games Ancient and Oriental*	Edward Falkener
1895	*Korean Games* ⎫	
1895	*Chinese Games with Dice and Dominoes* ⎬	Stewart Culin
1896	*Chess and Playing Cards* ⎭	
1905	*Chess in Iceland*	Willard Fiske
1913	*History of Chess* ⎫	H. J. R. Murray
1952	*History of Board Games other than Chess* ⎭	

Tabulated above are the books which earned their authors a place in this Appendix. Several are rare as they were 'off subject'—a term used by bibliographers for works outside a writer's usual field. Such books tend to be published in small editions, or even privately, and they are in demand both for their merit in their own subject, and also by bibliophiles collecting entire works: a small manual on seaweed, perhaps, completing the writings of a famous novelist.

AS-SULI

Abu-Bakr Muhammad ben Yahya as-Suli was descended from a Turkish prince of Jurjan, whose ancestral home was on the banks of the river Atrek at the south-eastern corner of the Caspian Sea. During the reign of al-Muktafi, Caliph of Baghdad from A.D. 902 to 908, a chess tournament was arranged between the court champion, al-Mawardi, and as-Suli. The Caliph was present and he openly favoured al-Mawardi and encouraged him during the game. At first this embarrassed and confused as-Suli, but he soon recovered his composure and defeated his opponent so conclusively

N

that there was no doubt who was the better player. The Caliph then transferred his favour from the old champion, al-Mawardi, dismissing him with a bitter pun: 'Your rose-water [maward] has turned to urine!'

The new champion's powers of improvising verse, and his attractive personality, maintained him in favour at court for three reigns. After the death of al-Muktafi, his successors, al-Muqtadir, followed by ar-Radi, gave him high positions. Ar-Radi was especially fond of him as as-Suli had been one of his tutors.

A contemporary historian, al-Mas'udi, relates that ar-Radi was once walking in the grounds of his country residence at Thurayya, and remarked on the beauty of the garden with its lawns and flowers: 'Have you ever seen anything more lovely?' The sycophants immediately began to dilate on the wonders of the garden, praising its beauty and placing it above the wonders of the world. 'You are wrong, gentlemen, the chess-skill of as-Suli is finer than all of these.'

As-Suli's reputation remained unchallenged among the Arabs for over six hundred years. His biographer ben Khalliken, who died in 1282, wrote:

'In chess he stood alone among the men of his generation. None were his equal and his play has passed into a proverb. When men wish to praise a player for his skill they say, "He plays like the Maestro as-Suli".'

Enough of his work survives in ancient manuscripts for us to assess his status as a master of Shatranj. We can see him criticizing his predecessors in a kindly fashion, though with the condescension of superior knowledge; his favourite openings are preserved, and they are based on definite principles. End games which occurred in actual play have been recorded, and there are comments on his skill in blindfold play; while occasional anecdotes underline his immense prestige.

He was the first player to try to discover the science of the game and to enunciate the underlying principles of play. His book, *Kitab Ash-Shatranj* (Book of Chess), is laid out in orderly fashion with ten standard openings; common problems in middle play; and a collection of end plays with comments. In the preface to his book he displays interest and skill in solving problems. Finally, he left behind him a pupil of outstanding merit, al-Lajlaj (the stammerer), whose memory is still respected among the Persians, Turks, and the Moghul Hindus.

As-Suli's other literary works include a history of the viziers; an unfinished history of the 'Abbasid House; an anthology of poems written by the descendants of Caliph 'Ali ben abi Talib; a history of Arabian poetry and monographs on several of the more noted poets. Many of these works are preserved in European or Istanbul libraries.

After ar-Radi's death in A.D. 940, as-Suli fell from favour through his sympathies for the 'Alids, later the Shi'ites, and he was forced to flee from Baghdad and go into hiding at Basra. He died there in poverty in A.D. 946.

CHARLES COTTON 1630–87

Cotton's story begins with the elopement of his father, Mr. Charles Cotton of Beresford Hall with Olive, the daughter of Sir John Stanhope of Elvaston in Derbyshire. Later the young swain made a reconciliatory statement saying that he did not know Sir John's daughter was under sixteen, nor that she was heiress to a considerable fortune, and that he had not carried her off at the point of a pistol.

Their only child, Charles Cotton the poet, was born on 28 April 1630 at Beresford Hall on the borders of Staffordshire and Derbyshire. The hasty, romantic marriage gradually became most unhappy and in 1647 Olive petitioned the House of Lords to enforce her husband to give her £300 a year on which to live.

Young Charles appears to have attended either Oxford or Cambridge University, but did not take a degree. He was a pupil of Ralph Rawson of Brasenose College, Oxford, and acquired a thorough knowledge of Greek, Latin, French, and Italian. As a young man he travelled in France, and probably Italy. He wrote many poems which were circulated among friends but not published until after his death.

In the summer of 1656 he married his cousin Isabella, the daughter of Sir Thomas Hutchinson of Owthorpe in Nottinghamshire. Before the marriage Cotton's father was forced to sell part of the family property to satisfy debtors, the rest was held in trust for the younger Cotton and his heirs.

Cotton was an ardent royalist and wrote several bitter satirical verses against the Roundheads. At the Restoration he published a panegyric in prose on Charles II and in 1664 his burlesque poem

'Scarronides, or the First Book of Virgil Travestie' appeared anony-mously. Six editions of this work appeared during the author's lifetime, each more gross than the last.

In 1665 Cotton was empowered by an Act of Parliament to sell part of his estates to pay his debts. About this time he was granted a Captain's commission in the Army and was posted to Ireland. The ship was nearly wrecked and the incident was described in 'The Storm', one of the poems published after his death. Some of his adventures are also recorded in 'A Voyage to Ireland in Bur-lesque'. In a letter from Ireland to a friend he wrote that 'He had grown something swab [clumsy] with drinking good ale for he loved to toss the can merrily around.' He also complained of being be-sieged by duns. After his return to England he became a Justice of the Peace for Staffordshire and continued living as a country squire and writing and translating.

In 1674 *The Compleat Gamester* was published anonymously and it was not until 1734 in the fifth edition of the book that it was acknowledged that 'the Second and Third Parts were originally written by Charles Cotton, Esq., some Years since'.

Cotton's interests were those of an educated country gentleman. He was an authority on horticulture and his cousin Cokayne com-ments on his taste in planting the grounds at Beresford. His treatise *The Planter's Manual*, 'being instruction for the raising, planting, and cultivating all sorts of fruit-trees, whether stone-fruits or pepin-fruits, with their natures and seasons' (1675), gives practical informa-tion in a plain and simple fashion.

Cotton's wife died about 1670 leaving three sons and five daughters. Some time before 1675 Cotton married Mary, the dowager countess of Ardglass, and the eldest daughter of Sir William Russell, Bt., of Strensham in Worcestershire. She had a jointure of £1,500 a year but even this addition to his income was not enough to balance Cotton's expenditure, and in 1675 he was again allowed by an Act of Parliament to sell part of his estates to settle his debts.

Cotton was an ardent angler and he contributed a treatise on fly-fishing for the second part of the fifth edition (1676) of the *Compleat Angler*, a book written by his friend, Isaac Walton. Cotton's contribution was written in ten days. In 1674 Cotton built a fishing-lodge on the banks of the river Dove. Above the door he placed a stone carved with Isaac Walton's initials 'Twisted in Cypher' with his own (fig. 162 on Plate XXIII).

In 1681 he published a descriptive poem 'The Wonders of the Peak' dedicated to the countess of Devonshire. One of the wonders was Chatsworth. The last work published in his lifetime was his translation of Montaigne's *Essays* in three volumes in 1685. This is among the masterpieces of translation into the English language and has been frequently reprinted. He started translating 'Memoirs of the Sieur de Pontis' but died of a fever before it was finished. He was buried at St. James's Picadilly on 16 February 1687. An unauthorized collection of his poems was published without his family's permission in 1689. More than two hundred years passed before they were reprinted again in 1923 by John Beresford, a member of the Beresford family.

Cotton was brilliant, but cursed with the Curse of Versatility. His poetry is good, but not the best; his prose is easy, clear, and full of energy, but even as the co-author of a work which has gone through more editions than any other in the English language, apart from Shakespeare's plays or *Pilgrim's Progress*, he is overshadowed by his friend Isaac Walton; his achievements in horticulture were notable but not outstanding; while his extravagance caused ever-recurring financial embarrassment. There is a tradition that he used to hide from creditors in a cave overlooking the Dove, in the grounds of Beresford Hall, and that one of his maidservants brought him food in his humiliating retreat.

His love of good company is perpetuated in *The Compleat Gamester* which gives a picture of the manners, habits, and pastimes of an English gentleman during the last days of the House of Stuart.

COTTON'S CHIEF WORKS

1660   Panegyric to the King's Most Excellent Majesty.

1663   The Valiant Knight or The Legend of St. Perigrine (anonymously.

1664   Scarronides, or the First Book of Virgil Travestie.

1670   A Voyage to Ireland in Burlesque.

1670   A translation of Gerard's *History of the Life of the Duke of Esperon*.

1674   A translation of *The Commentaries of De Montluc, Marshal of France*, with a dedication to his relative the Earl of Chesterfield.

*1674   *The Compleat Gamester* (anon.).

1674   *The Fair One of Tunis, or the Generous Mistress* (anon.).

1675   Burlesque upon Burlesque, or the Scoffer Scoft, being some of Lucian's dialogues, newly put into English Fustian (anon.).

1675 *The Planter's Manual.*
1676 The Second Half of the *Compleat Angler.*
1679 The Confinement. A Poem (anon.).
1681 The Wonders of the Peak. A Descriptive Poem.
1685 Translation of Montaigne's *Essays.*

Posthumously

1689 Unauthorized collection of poems.

*This work was reprinted coupled with the *Lives of the Gamesters* by Theophilus Lucas (1714) in The English Library, Routledge and Sons (1930), under the title *Games and Gamesters of the Restoration.*

THOMAS HYDE 1636–1702

Thomas Hyde was born on 29 June 1636 at Billingsley, near Bridgnorth in Shropshire. His father, Ralph, was the vicar of the parish, and gave young Thomas his first instruction in oriental languages. When he was sixteen he went to King's College, Cambridge, and became a pupil of Wheelock, the professor of Arabic. Hyde concentrated on Persian, and assisted Walton in the publication of the Persian and Syriac versions of the Polyglot Bible, transcribing the Persian translation of the Pentateuch which had been published in Hebrew characters at Constantinople into its proper alphabet. He added a Latin translation.

In 1658 when he was twenty-two he went to Queen's College, Oxford, to become a reader of Hebrew. After reading one lecture on Oriental Languages he was awarded an M.A. by order of the Chancellor of the University. In 1659 he became underkeeper of the Bodleian Library, and in 1665 was elected the chief librarian. He was made a prebendary of Salisbury Cathedral in 1666, Archdeacon of Gloucester in 1673, and a Doctor of Divinity in 1682. He succeeded Pocock as Laudian Professor of Arabic in 1691, and was Regius Professor of Arabic in 1697. In 1701 he resigned the librarianship of the Bodleian, saying that he was tired of the drudgery of a daily attendance and was also anxious to complete his work on *Difficult Places in the Scriptures.*

During the reigns of Charles II, James II, and William III, he was interpreter in oriental languages to the Court, meeting most of the envoys from those countries, which gave him an unrivalled opportunity for collecting information on oriental games without ever leaving the shores of England. This information is contained in two volumes, *De Historia Shahiludii* in 1689, and *De Historia*

Nerdiludii in 1694. In the Durham University copy the two books are bound together, and in the instructions to the binders and printers are orders to colour the fore edge of the first book and to leave the fore edge of the second book plain. This has been done.

The first 72 pages of the first book are unnumbered and contain a dedicatory Epistle to Sydney Godolphin; then a page of instructions to the publishers and bookbinders in English. Next comes a digression called 'De Shahiludo Prolegomena Curiosa' containing puzzles and diagrams, written in a curious mixture of Latin, Hebrew, and Greek, verse and prose.

The reproduction of a double page gives an idea of the extraordinary mixture of languages employed by the writer (see Plate VI, facing p. 81).

The second part of Book One is titled 'Historia Shahiludii'. In this portion he describes chess, and has a diagram of an Ashtapada board; there is also a folding chart of the layout of the Great Chess (Tamberlane's) showing the initial positions of the 28 men on each side.

The third part of 71 pages is 'Historiae Shaduludii in Tribus Scriptis Hebraicis' (Chess among the Jews). The page numbering starts again at 1; the left-hand pages contain the original Hebrew texts, and the right-hand pages Hyde's translations into Latin. The three primary works are those of R. Abraham Abenezrae; R. Bons Aben-Jachiae; and an anonymous writing called 'Deliciae Regis'.

The second Book is separated from the first by a further page in English of instructions to the printers and binders, followed by a dedication to Johannes Hampden and an introduction. These pages are unnumbered. The rest of the book of 278 pages is paginated. Pages 1 to 70 deal with backgammon, its history, pieces, and boards; the game in antiquity and the Chinese form; 70 to 101 with De Ludo Promotionis Mandarinorum—The Promotion game of the Mandarins. Next follow three sections on Alea to page 129, then Talorum to 172, Latrunculorum to 195 and Wei-ch'i to 201.

The third section of the book, headed 'Historia Triodii', contains several of the games described in the present volume; indeed any work on the subject must owe a great debt to Hyde, the first English writer on oriental games. The last three pages of the book contain a bibliography, and mentioned there is the *Compleat Gamester* (1674).

Hyde died on 18 February 1702 at his rooms in Christ Church and was buried in the church of Handborough, near Oxford. His reputation as a scholar was very high in Germany and Holland, though he was not truly appreciated in Oxford. Some idea of his energy and output is indicated by the report that at his death he was engaged on no less than thirty-one works at the same time and they were all in various stages of completion. Some sixty years later Dr. Gregory Sharp, Master of the Temple, collected and published some of them under the title *Syntagma Dissertationum et Opuscula*, in two volumes.

Hyde's *Historia Religionis Veterum Persarum* (Oxford, 1700) was his most important and celebrated work. It was the first attempt to treat the subject in a scholarly fashion, and abounds in oriental learning.

Hyde was a friend and tutor of Sir Robert Boyle, the physicist—known to every schoolboy as the inventor of Boyle's Law concerning the proportional relations between elasticity and pressure in a gas. Boyle, however, was also a generous supporter of projects for the propagation of the scriptures and he financed, partly or wholly, the printing of Indian, Irish, and Welsh Bibles, the Turkish New Testament, and the Malayan version of the Gospels and Acts—the last publication being the work of his friend, Dr. Thomas Hyde. Hyde also helped Boyle in his studies in Hebrew, Greek, Chaldee, and Syriac.

HYDE'S MAJOR PUBLICATIONS

1665   Text and Latin translation of a Persian version of an astronomical treatise, *Tabulae Stellarum Fixarum ex Observatione Ujugh Beoghi*, originally written in Arabic.

1674   Catalogus impressorum librorum Bibliothecae Bodleianae, Oxford.

1677   Malayan version of the Gospels and Acts.

1688   An account of the system of weights and measures of the Chinese in a treatise on weights and measures of the ancients by Edward Bernard.

1689   *De Historia Shahiludii* ⎱ Published together as 'De Ludis
1694   *De Historia Nerdiludii* ⎰ Orientalibus libri duo'.

1691   *Itinera Mundi*, a Latin translation, with notes, of a work by Abraham Peritsol, son of Mordecai Peritsol. This was a supplement to Abulfeda's *Geography*.

1692   An account of the famous Prince Giolo.

1700   *Historia Religionis Veterum Persarum*.

1702   *Abdollatiphi Historiae Aegypti Compendium*.

Posthumously

1712   A Treatise of Bobovius on the liturgy etc. of the Turks.

1767   Syntagma Dissertationum quas olim Hyde separatim edidit. 2 vols. 4to. This includes 'De Ludis Orientalibus'.

EDMOND HOYLE 1672–1769

'According to Hoyle' has become synonymous with the standard method of playing games. Over three hundred editions of his book have been published. Hoyle was born about 1672 and probably studied as a barrister. He became interested in the game of Whisk which in the eighteenth century was the game of the tavern and the servants' hall. About 1736 a set of gentlemen, including the first Lord Folkestone, frequented the Crown Coffee House in Bedford Row and began to study the game seriously. The vulgar 'Whisk' became the genteel 'Whist' and they formulated four fundamental rules:

1. Play from the strongest suit.
2. Study your partner's hand as much as your own.
3. Never force your partner unnecessarily.
4. Attend to the score.

Hoyle may have belonged to this coterie. It is certain that he became fascinated with the mathematics of the game about this time and in 1741 when he was over 70 began to give lessons on whist, as masters taught music or fencing. Each pupil received a set of manuscript notes; pirate copies soon appeared and to secure the copyright Hoyle published his notes in book form. The small book had a long title:

'A short treatise on the Game of Whist, containing the Laws of the Game; and also some Rules whereby a Beginner may, with due attention to them, attain to the Playing it well. Calculations for those who will Bet the Odds on any point of the score of the Game then playing and depending. Cases stated, to shew what may be effected by a good player in Critical Parts of the Game. References to cases viz. at the End of the Rule you are directed how to find them. Calculations directing with moral Certainty, how to play well any Hand or Game, by Shewing the Chances of your Partner's having 1 2 or 3 certain cards. With Variety of Cases added in the Appendix.' Printed by John Watts for the Author, London 1742.

There is only one known copy of this first edition which is now in the Bodleian Library; several of the other early editions are also preserved only in single copies. The price of the book, one guinea, encouraged piracies, the first appearing in 1743. Hoyle countered by lowering the price of his second edition (1743) to two shillings and he also certified every genuine copy with his autograph. The last edition with his signature is the fourteenth (fig. 164, facing p. 177); in the next it was replaced by a wood-block stamp.

In the earlier editions Hoyle offered to disclose the secrets of his 'Artificial Memory which does not take off your attention from your game' for a guinea. The success of his first book encouraged Hoyle to publish similar manuals on Backgammon, Piquet, Quadrille, Brag, and Chess.

An amusing skit entitled 'The Humours of Whist—A dramatic satire, as acted every day at White's and the Other Coffee-houses and Assemblies' lampooned the teacher and his pupils. The principal characters in the short comedy were Professor Whiston (Hoyle) who gave lessons on the game, and Sir Calculation Puzzle, an enthusiastic player who muddled his head with Hoyle's mathematics and always lost; together with other pupils, sharpers, and their dupes. Hoyle's many years of studying whist was dismissed with:

> Who will believe that man could e'er exist,
> Who spent near half an age in studying whist?
> Grew grey with calculation, labour hard,
> As if life's business center'd in a card?

Hoyle lived to enjoy the reward of his labours, but in the fifteenth edition of his book the well-known signature was replaced by an impression from a wood block, and in the seventeenth it was announced that 'Mr. Hoyle was dead'.

The popularity of Hoyle's teaching of Whist among ladies is referred to as early as 1743 in a Ladies' Journal; in 1753 he is called 'The Great Mr. Hoyle', but by 1755 the old maestro, then about eighty-three, had given up personal teaching. In 1769 the newspapers gave accounts of the death of the well-known public character Mr. Hoyle. A writer shortly afterwards quotes from the Parish Register of Marylebone: 'Edmund [*sic*] Hoyle, buried August 3rd 1769', adding that 'He was ninety years of age at the time of his decease.' No register or tombstone exists today. His will, dated 26 September 1761, was proved in London on 6 September 1769. No authentic portrait is known; the picture by Hogarth exhibited in 1870 at the Crystal Palace represents a Yorkshire Hoyle. Little more is known about Edmond Hoyle, Esq.

Hoyle was the first to write scientifically on whist, or indeed on any card game. His 'Short Treatise' soon became an accepted standard. His other works were:

1. *Short Treatise on the Game of Backgammon.* London, 1743.
2. *Short Treatise on the Game of Piquet, to which are added some Rules and Observations for playing well at Chess.* London, 1744.
3. *Short Treatise on the Game of Quadrille, to which is added the laws of the Game.* London, 1745.
4. *Short Treatise on the Game of Brag, containing the Laws of the Game, also Calculations, shewing the odds of winning or losing certain hands dealt.* London, 1751.
5. *An Essay towards making the Doctrine of Chances Easy to those who understand vulgar arithmetic only, to which is added, some useful tables on Annuities for Lives.* London, 1745. The book explains the method of calculating various problems in piquet, all-fours, whist, dice, lotteries and annuities.
6. *An Essay towards making the Game of Chess easily learned by those who know the moves only, without the assistance of a master.* London, 1761.

JOSEPH STRUTT 1749–1802

Joseph Strutt was born on 27 October 1749 at Springfield Mill, Chelmsford, the younger son of Thomas Strutt, a wealthy miller. A year later Thomas Strutt died leaving his widow to bring up Joseph and his elder brother, John, who later became a fashionable physician in Westminster. Joseph was educated at King Edward's School, Chelmsford, and when he was fourteen was apprenticed to the engraver, William Wynne Ryland.

In 1770, when he was twenty, he attended the Royal Academy and when he had been there only a few months was awarded one of the first silver medals. The following year he won a gold medal. In 1771 he became a student in the reading room of the British Museum —the source of most of his information for his antiquarian works. His first book was *The Regal and Ecclesiastical Antiquities of England* (1773). It contained engravings of illustrations from ancient manuscripts of kings, costumes, armour, seals, and other interesting objects.

On 16 August 1774 he married Anne, the daughter of Barwell Blower, a dyer, of Bocking, Essex, and took a house in Duke Street, Portland Place. Between 1774 and 1776 he published the three volumes of his *Manners, Customs, Arms, Habits Etc. of the People of England*; and in 1777–8 the two large quarto volumes of his *Chronicle of England*, which was profusely illustrated, and contained material from extensive original research.

In 1778 his wife died and he spent the next seven years painting pictures, nine of which were exhibited in the Royal Academy. Several of his best engravings were made during these years, using the stippled style which had been introduced from the Continent by his master Ryland.[1]

In 1785 Strutt returned to his antiquarian and literary researches, and published his *Biographical Dictionary of Engravers* in two volumes (1785–6) which has formed the basis of all succeeding works in the same field.

In 1790 he lost most of his wealth through the dishonesty of a relative; his health also failed and he left London to live very quietly at Bacon's Farm, Bramfield, in Hertfordshire. He returned to engraving and produced several of exceptional quality, including those in Bradford's edition of *Pilgrim's Progress* (1792) after designs by Stothard.

By 1795 his debts were paid and his health had improved and he returned to London and continued his researches. The *Dresses and Habits of the English People* was published in two volumes in 1796 and 1799. This was followed by *The Sports and Pastimes of the People of England* (1801), which has been frequently reprinted. Strutt was then fifty-two, and started a romance, *Queenhoo Hall*, based on an ancient manor house at Tewin, near his home at Bramfield. He planned to portray the lives and customs of fifteenth-century England, but he died at his house in Charles Street, Hatton

[1] Strutt's tutor, William Wynne Ryland, was born in 1732. He was apprenticed to Ravenet, and then to Boucher in France. Ryland introduced a stippled style of engraving from the Continent into England which imitated drawings in red chalk. Many of his engravings were of sentimental subjects based on classical themes: for example, the Judgement of Paris, printed in red. He was appointed engraver to George III at £200 a year. Eventually, he had his own print business in the Strand with a stock valued at some £10,000.

In 1783 he forged a bank bill worth several thousand pounds which was accepted and honoured by the Bank of England. Later, when suspicions arose, he disappeared. He was betrayed by a cobbler's wife who had noted the name RYLAND in a pair of boots which had been handed in for repair. He was apprehended in his hide-out in Stepney while attempting suicide with a razor. He was tried on the capital charge, found guilty, and was the last criminal to be hanged at Tyburn.

Garden, on 16 October 1802, before it was finished. He was buried in St. Andrew's Churchyard, Holborn.

The manuscript of *Queenhoo Hall* was given to Sir Walter Scott, who added an unsatisfactory ending. The book was published in 1808 in four small volumes. Two unfinished poems, 'The Test of Guilt' and 'The Bumpkin's Disaster', were published together in the same year. There is a portrait of Strutt in the National Portrait Gallery by Ozias Humphrey R.A. in crayon (No. 323).

Strutt was a pioneer in his branch of archaeology, his engravings were of high quality, and Sir Walter Scott admitted in the general preface to the later editions of the Waverley Novels that they had been inspired by Strutt's *Queenhoo Hall*.

DUNCAN FORBES 1798–1868

Duncan Forbes was born at Kinnaird in Perthshire on 28 April 1798. His parents were working-class people and emigrated to America in the spring of 1801, taking only their youngest child with them. Duncan was left behind with his grandfather in Glenfernate. He had very little schooling, and did not learn English until he was thirteen. Nevertheless, when he was seventeen he was chosen as the village schoolmaster of Stralock. Shortly afterwards he attended Kirkmichael school as a student. He entered Perth Grammar School in 1818 when he was twenty, and matriculated to the University of St. Andrews in two years, obtaining an M.A. degree in 1823. In the same year he accepted an appointment in the Calcutta Academy, but he resigned in 1826 through ill-health and returned to England, becoming an assistant to Dr. John Borthwick Gilchrist, a teacher of Hindustani.

In 1837 he was appointed Professor of Oriental Languages at King's College, London, and proved to be a successful teacher. When he retired in 1861 he was elected an honorary fellow of the college.

He was also employed from 1849 to 1855 by the Trustees of the British Museum to make a catalogue of the collection of Persian manuscripts which at that time numbered just over a thousand. While he was working on it new material was added, equalling the original collection, and Forbes's work was obsolete before it was finished, but it formed the basis for the later 'Catalogue of Persian Manuscripts'.

His tastes were very simple, even spartan. His main relaxation was playing chess. He was a member of the Royal Asiatic Society and was created an honorary LL.D. of St. Andrews University in 1847. He died on 17 August 1868.

He covered so wide a field of oriental study that his knowledge of some of the languages was rather limited, and his books contained little original thought or research, but they were clear and convenient to use and his elementary manuals were often more useful to beginners than more pretentious volumes.

Under the nom de plume of 'Fior Ghael' he opened a warm controversy in the *Gentlemen's Magazine* for May 1836 on Celtic dialects, maintaining that Welsh should not be included among them.

FORBES'S PUBLICATIONS

1828   *A New Persian Grammar* (with Sandford Arnot).

1828   *An Essay on the Origin and structure of the Hindostanne Tongue with an account of the principal elementary works on the subject.*

1830   Translation of the Persian romance, *The Adventure of Hātim Taï.*

1844   New edition of Arnot's *Grammar of the Hindustani Tongue.*

1845   *The Hindustani Manual, a pocket companion for those who visit India.*

1846   *A Grammar of the Hindustani Language in the Oriental and Roman Character.*

1846   New edition, with vocabulary, of the *Bāgh o Bahār.*

1848   *A Dictionary : Hindustani and English, to which is added a reversed Part, English and Hindustani.*

1849   *Oriental Penmanship, an Essay for facilitating the reading and writing of the Talik character.*

1852   His edition of *Tota Kahāni* in Hindustani.

1857   His edition of *Baitāl-Pachisi* in Hindi.

1860   *A History of Chess.*

1861   *A Grammar of the Bengali Language.*

1862   *The Bengali Reader . . . A New Edition.*

1863   *A Grammar of the Arabic Language.*

1864   *Arabic Reading Lessons.*

1866   *Catalogue of Oriental Manuscripts, chiefly Persian, collected within the last five-and-thirty years.*

EDWARD FALKENER 1814-96

Edward Falkener, the son of Lyon Falkener, head of the ordnance department of the Tower of London, was born in London on 18 February 1814. He was educated at a private school in Kent and then was articled to John Newman, an architect. In 1836 he became a student at the Royal Academy and in 1839 won its gold medal for a plan of a cathedral church.

In 1842 he visited all the countries of Europe except Spain and Portugal; and then continued on through Asia Minor, Syria, Palestine, Egypt, and the Greek islands. He studied the architectural remains in the places he visited, many being well off the beaten track. While in Denmark he made drawings of Fredericksberg Palace, and in 1859 when it was burned down, the King used Falkener's drawings in the restoration, and created him a Knight of the Order of Dannebrog for his services.

In 1847 Falkener was permitted to excavate the house of Marcus Lucretius at Pompeii at his own expense. A plan and a description of the house is given in his *Museum of Classical Antiquities*. Falkener practised as an architect for a few years, building some offices on St. Dunstan's Hill, London, but he spent most of his time in literary work and making drawings of restorations. Those he exhibited at the Exposition Universelle in Paris in 1855 won the Grande Médaille d'Honneur, and in 1861 the King of Prussia presented him with a gold medal for his work on classical archaeology.

In 1866, when he was fifty-two, he married Blanche Golding, gave up his private practice and retired to Wales, where he continued his studies and restorations for many years and was engaged on a treatise on the Greek houses at Pompeii when he died on 17 December 1896, leaving a widow, son, and three daughters.

Falkener had a sound knowledge of every branch of architecture and classical archaeology, and wrote on the lighting of museums and the artificial illumination of mosques and churches. Some of his illustrations appear in Fergusson's *History of Architecture* and many of his sketches were published in the Architectural Publication Society's Dictionary. He was a member of the Academy of Bologna, of the Architectural Institutes of Berlin and Rome, and was elected an honorary fellow of the Royal Institute of British Architects on 2 December 1895.

OTHER WORKS

1851– He edited the *Museum of Classical Antiquities.*

1860 *Daedalus; or the causes and principles of the excellence of Greek Sculpture.*

1862 *Ephesus and the Temple of Diana.*
Frequent contributions to the proceedings of the Royal Institute of British Architects.

1884 *Does the 'Revised Version' affect the Doctrine of the New Testament?*
Under the pseudonym of E. F. O. Thurcastle (Edward Falkener of Thurcastle).

1892 *Games, Ancient and Oriental.* This rare book is unreliable but contains interesting information. The Royal Institute of British Architects and the Newcastle Central Library each have a copy. It is not mentioned in the British Museum's catalogue.

STEWART CULIN 1858–1929

Robert Stewart Culin was born in Philadelphia on 13 July 1858, the son of John Culin. He was educated at Nazareth Hall, Pennsylvania, and then studied archaeology until 1890. In 1892 when he was thirty-four he became director of the Archaeological Museum of the University of Pennsylvania; and in 1903 he was appointed the curator in Ethnology at the Museum of the Brooklyn Institute of Arts and Sciences, a position he held until his death.

Culin was an able scientist, and a man of wide knowledge; outspoken and unorthodox in speech and habits. He was a good judge of men, pictures, books, bronzes, fans and lace, and had a flair for appreciating the valuable even when it was surrounded by rubbish. His outstanding work at the Brooklyn Institute was achieved with an outlay which would hardly have bought the equipment for a standard museum expedition.

He founded the Oriental Club in Philadelphia and was its secretary for fourteen years, and had a profound knowledge of Chinese customs and psychology; once, when he was a witness in a case involving members of a secret Chinese society, his knowledge was so extraordinary that he was thought to have been a member at some time. His friendships with young Chinese students, men who later became the leaders in the New Republic, enabled him to prophesy the overthrow of the Chinese Empire at a time when the forecast appeared absurd.

He went on several field expeditions to Japan, China, Korea, and India, setting out with his fare: a lead pencil, a set of ideas, and a smile. He came back with the same smile, more ideas, and many packing cases whose contents were used to reconstruct the very air of the visited country in the exhibition hall of the Brooklyn Museum.

When he was fifty-nine, on 11 April 1917, he married a widow, Mrs. Alice Roberts, née Mumford. She was a well-known artist who had studied in France and Spain and exhibited in salons in Paris, London, and cities of the U.S.A. Culin died on 8 April 1929.

PRINCIPAL WORKS

1887 'The Religious Ceremonies of the Chinese in the Eastern Cities of the United States' (An Essay).Privately printed, Philadelphia.

1887 'The Practice of Medicine by the Chinese of America.' *Medical and Surgical Reporter*, Philadelphia.

1891 *The Gambling Games of the Chinese in America*. Pennsylvania Univ.

1893 Exhibit of Games in the Columbian Exposition. *Journal of American Folklore*, Boston.

1894 Retrospect of the Folklore of the Columbian Exposition. *Journal of American Folklore*.

1895 *Chinese Games with Dice and Dominoes*. Smithsonian Inst., Washington.

1895 *Korean Games* (With Notes on the corresponding games of China and Japan). Pennsylvania Univ.

1896 *Mancala, the National Game of Africa*. Washington.

1896? *East Indian Fortune Telling with Dice; Syrian games with dice, tip cats etc.*

1898 *Chess and Playing Cards*. Washington. Report U.S. Nat. Museum 1896, pt.2.

1899? 'Archaeological Application of the Roentgen rays.' *Scientific American Supplement*, New York.

1899 'Hawaiian Games.' *American Anthropologist*, n.s., i. 1899.

1903 'America the Cradle of Asia?' *Harper's Monthly*, New York, March 1903.

1907 *Games of the North American Indians*. Smithsonian Inst.

On the eve of forwarding the manuscript of this book to the publishers the Department of Primitive Art of the Brooklyn Museum kindly provided the additional list of Culin's works given below. They were unknown to the author and have not been consulted.

1916 'Bibliography of Japan.' *Brooklyn Museum Quarterly*.

1918 'Christian Relics in Japan.' *B.M.Q.*

1919 'Ceremonial Diversions in Japan.' *Asia*.

1920 'Japanese Game of Sugoroku.' *B.M.Q.*

1920 'Across Siberia in the Dragon Year of 1796.' *Asia*.

1924 'Beiderwand.' *B.M.Q.*

1924 'Creation in Art.' *B.M.Q.*
1924 'Game of Ma-jong, its origin and significance.' *B.M.Q.*
1924 'Amir Hamzah.' *B.M.Q.*
1925 'Japanese Game of Battle Dore and Shuttlecock.' *B.M.Q.*
1925 'Burri-burri Gitcho—Japanese swinging bat game.' *B.M.Q.*
1925 'The Art of the Chinese.' *International Studio.*

WILLARD FISKE 1831–1904

Daniel Willard Fiske, of puritan stock, was born on 11 November 1831 at Ellisburg, New York. He went to school at Cazenovia Seminary, and then to Hamilton College, but he left in his second year to study Scandinavian languages in Copenhagen and at the University of Uppsala in Sweden. When he returned to New York in 1852 he spoke fluent French, German, Danish, Swedish, and Icelandic, and could read classical Icelandic and interpret runic characters. He joined the staff of the Astor Library until 1859. In 1860 he became the General Secretary of the American Geographical Society. From 1857 to 1860 he was also co-editor with Paul Morphy of the newly-founded *American Chess Monthly*. In 1861 he was appointed attaché to the United States Legation in Vienna for two years, and while there he learned Russian, Italian, and Roumanian. In spite of his excellent ear for languages he had no musical appreciation, to his own considerable regret. When he returned to America he joined the 'Syracuse Daily Journal' for two years and then became a bookseller in Syracuse. In 1868 he was appointed professor and librarian of North-European Languages at Cornell University.

In 1880 after several years' friendship, Professor Fiske married, in Berlin, Miss Jennie McGraw, the wealthy daughter of a lumberman millionaire, and they began a protracted honeymoon travelling through Europe and Egypt in search of better health for the bride. Unfortunately, they were unsuccessful and she died the following year. At Fiske's direction flowers were placed on her tomb for the next twenty-three years on the fourteenth day of every month in commemoration of their wedding.

Jennie left a large part of her fortune to Cornell University for extensions to the library, but when it appeared that the money was to be misappropriated for other purposes, Fiske brought a legal action against the University Trustees and won his case, the legacy becoming part of his estate.

Two years after his wife's death he left Cornell and settled in Italy. In 1883 he rented the villa Forini in the eastern quarter of Florence. Mark Twain (Samuel Clemens) and his wife were near neighbours and friends. In 1892 Fiske bought the villa Landor, between Florence and Fiesole, and carried out extensive alterations. The villa dated back to the days of Boccaccio, and it is claimed that it was the scene of the famous Decameron.

Fiske spent his time in study and writing and he had his own private printing press. He was an ardent bibliophile and made no less than four separate great collections of books. His libraries of Dante, Petrarch, Icelandic literature, and the Rhaeto-Romance languages were each among the finest in the world. Two examples of his collecting methods give an insight into his character.

When visiting a village church in Iceland he noted an early Icelandic bible and offered to buy it from the elders. They were perturbed at the thought of exchanging a holy book for money and Fiske fell in with their scruples. He offered to exchange the book for a church organ, and the offer was accepted until one member asked who would play it. Fiske then offered to provide the organ, and to send the vicar's son to Reykjavik for lessons. The bible was added to Fiske's collection!

Late in the summer of 1891 Fiske was unwell and went to the baths of Tarasp in the lower Engadine. One afternoon he walked to the village of Schulz and saw some books written in Rhaeto-Romance. This language is a survival of the speech used by Roman settlers in 16 B.C. who were later entirely cut off from Italy by German-speaking tribes, and their language developed independently of the romance languages elsewhere. It is confined to the higher recesses of the valley of the Inn and along the steeply-sloping sides of the upper Rhine. Fiske entered the shop and bought twenty small volumes, mainly school books; the same evening he wrote to Leipzig for a Rhaeto-Romance bibliography and a dictionary. For the next few weeks he attended the baths in the morning and in the afternoons slipped off with a friend into the surrounding villages and went from door to door buying Rhaeto-Romance books. Women came with dusty volumes in their aprons, boys and girls lugged baskets and satchels full of books. The two Americans sat at a table and checked off the volumes against their bibliography, Dr. Boehmer's *Verzeichniss Rätoromanischer Litteratur*, and then bought what they required. They spent the evenings in collating and cataloguing the purchases and packing them up to send to London for binding.

They wrote to the booksellers of Innsbrück, Trento, Udine, and Gorizia and bought the cream of their Rhaeto-Romance literature. Later they went to St. Moritz and explored the villages of the upper Engadine in the same way and then to Chur to repeat the process once again.

Fiske was a man of boundless enthusiasm. He campaigned for the reformation of the Egyptian alphabet, worked for the advancement of Icelandic culture, and belonged to many learned societies including the American National Institute of Arts and Letters; he was an honorary member of the National Icelandic Literary Society, and a corresponding member of the Royal Society of Northern Antiquities, Copenhagen. He was honoured by King Humbert I of Italy in 1892, and by King Christian X of Denmark in 1902, for his literary achievements. His writings were varied and numerous, and included some excellent verse.

He died in Germany in 1904, when seventy-two, and in spite of his quarrel with the trustees of Cornell, left more than half a million dollars to the University library, thus fulfilling his wife's wishes, together with three of his magnificent collections of books; the fourth, of Icelandic literature, was given to the people of Iceland. His will was long and complicated, but he provided for his adopted son, once a destitute Italian lad, and left a sum of money to be spent annually on books and literature for one of the outlying Icelandic communities. He was buried by his wife's side in a memorial chapel built by the trustees of Cornell in the grounds of the University.

Chess in Iceland was published in Florence a year after his death. It is an extraordinary book, full of information on many subjects, including chess. It is disjointed and repetitive. Fiske apologizes for this confusion in his introduction: '. . . but I am too tired to sort things out—I will leave it to others to do that for me. . . .'

H. J. R. MURRAY 1868–1955

The greatest of the chess historians was born on 24 June 1868 in Peckham Rye, London, the eldest of eleven children. His father was Sir James A. H. Murray, the editor-in-chief of the Oxford English Dictionary. Harold went to school at Mill Hill and won an exhibition in mathematics to Balliol College, Oxford. He graduated in

1890 with a First in mathematics and became an assistant master at Queen's College, Taunton, and then at the Carlisle Grammar School. He became headmaster of Ormskirk Grammar School, Lancashire, in 1896, and on 4 January 1897 he married Miss Kate Maitland Crosthwaite, the eldest daughter of his former headmaster at Carlisle.

In 1901 he was appointed by the Board of Education as an Inspector of Schools and in 1916 he became a Divisional Inspector. On retirement in 1928 he was made a member of the Consultative Committee of the Board of Education. He was responsible for drafting large sections of the reports on The Primary School (1931); Infant Nursery Schools (1933); and the Spens Report on Secondary Education (1938). He also served as a member of the War Graves Education Committee (1929-37) which was concerned with the education of children of gardeners and other English staff in the cemeteries in France. He was a member of the Midhurst Rural District Council from 1931-55 and Chairman of the Housing Committee, 1938-48.

In 1897, with the encouragement of Baron von der Lasa, Murray began a monumental research into the development of chess from its obscure Indian origin to the modern European game. He collected and collated material from hundreds of sources, sifting the wheat from the chaff. He obtained help from scholars of living and dead languages, and himself learned Arabic which enabled him to unravel the chess writings of al-Lajlaj, a Mohammedan chess player of the tenth century A.D. J. C. White of Cleveland, Ohio, and J. W. Rimington Wilson in England put their magnificent collections of manuscripts and rare books at his disposal and in 1913 Murray published his incomparable 900-page *History of Chess*, well illustrated and with scores of diagrams. It received world-wide appreciation. Unfortunately it is now out of print.

In 1952 when he was eighty-four his second book, *A History of Board Games other than Chess*, was published. It was full of scholarship and learning and formed a valuable check-list for future works, but it lacked popular appeal and brought only a moderate reward to its distinguished creator.

Murray loved young children and played delightful imaginative games with them. He was also interested in string games (cat's cradles) and, when bored in company, he had the disconcerting habit of practising them by going through the motions, sometimes to the consternation of strangers! He wrote poetry and studied the psychology of dreams, writing down some of his own which were highly entertaining. He was a shy and modest man and avoided the limelight. His outstanding trait was his tremendous power of concentration: he would sit sunk in some mathematical problem throughout a beautiful summer's day, oblivious of the weather. His wife declared that he wrote the *History of Chess* with his three children playing round his study and quite unaware of their noise. Cooking, too, was wasted on him. He would become absorbed in *The Times* crossword, a daily pleasure, and never notice what he was eating.

When he died in 1955 at the age of eighty-six he was working on a history of Heyshott, the village of his retirement.

MURRAY'S WORKS

1913   *History of Chess.*
1952   *History of Board Games other than Chess.*
1954   An article on chess in *Things* edited by Geoffrey Grigson.

UNPUBLISHED

A Shorter History of Chess (in the press).
The Dilaram Arrangement.
The Dilaram Position in European Chess.
A History of Draughts (two versions).
A History of Heyshott (unfinished).
The Early History of the Knight's Tour (bibliographical).
The Knight's Problem (1942).
Magic Knight's Tours. A Mathematical Recreation (1951).
The Classification of Knight's Tours.

Rajah from
Indian chess set
(from Hyde's
*De Ludis
Orientalibus*)

Shāh.

Conclusion

When asked 'Which is the best game?' how does one reply? The short list below contains strong contenders for the title but the reader is left to make his own award.

BACKGAMMON

CONTINENTAL DRAUGHTS

INTERNATIONAL CHESS

LIAR DICE

MAH-JONG

NINE MEN'S MORRIS

PACHISI

WARI

WEI-CH'I

Pompeian Wall-painting

Index

Games described in detail in the text, and the main reference to them, are in bold type ; references to illustrations are in italics

Abenezrae, A., Rabbi, 183
Aben-Jachiae, B., Rabbi, 183
Ace Negative, 144
Aces, 137–8
Aces in the Pot, 128
Ad Elta Stelpur, 37
Adhesives: Britfix, 172; Evo-stick, 173;
　Tenuit, 175
Adindan, 28
Agathias, 34
Agra, 9
Ahl stone, 4
Akbar, Mogul emperor, 9
Ak-hor, 26, 27, *fig. 21*
Akkad, 22
al-Beruni, 54, 58
Alea, 35, 183
Alexanderplatz, 64
Alfonso X, 36, *fig. 48*
Allahabad, 9
al-Lajlaj, 178, 197
All-tes teg-enuk, 125–7, *figs. 111, 112, 161*
al-Mas'udi, 178
al-Mawardi, 177, 178
al-Muktafi, 177, 178
al-Muqtadir, 178
Alquerque, 36, **47–48,** 71, *figs. 38, 39*
America, 3, 43, 64, 65, 72, 89, 130, 133,
　150, 152, 160, 161, 189, 192, 194
American 90th Infantry Division, 64
Amerindian games, 3, 4, 7, 48, 50, 89, 123,
　125–7, 172, 174
Andalus, 58
Angle (Chinese chess), 68
Arabia, 113
Arabs, 12, 27, 43, 47, 123
Armitage, Robinson J., 80, *Pl. V*
Army, Gen. Patton's Third, 64
ar-Radi, 178, 179
Aschaffenburg, 36
Ashanti, 115
Ashtapada, 51, 183, *figs. 43, 45*
as-Sarakhsi, 58
as-Suli, 58, **177–9**
Assyria, 22
Aswan, 28
Athelstan, King, 80
Austin, R. G., 31, 34, 84
Automatic doubling (Backgammon), 46
Awari, 119–21
Axon, W. E. A., 61
Ayabite dynasty, 58

Aztecs, 6, 173

Babylon, 22, 42
Backgammon, 23, 37, 38, **42–46,** 95, 186,
　fig. 37, 46, 146 (tailpieces)
Baganda, 121
Baggara, 12
Baghdad, 58, 179
Ba-Ila peoples, 121, *fig. 108*
Ball, billiard, 176, *fig. 160*
Ballana, 28
Balliol College, Oxford, 196
Bambra-ka-thul, 58, *fig. 47*
Baqt, 26
Bar, the (Backgammon), 43, 45
Barbudi, 128–9
Bare King, 60
Basra, 58, 179
Bassus, S., 84
Beadwork, 174, *fig. 148*
Bear off (Backgammon), 44
Becq de Fourquière, L., 34, 85
Bell and Hammer, 138–40, *fig. 114, 176*
　(tailpiece)
Bellasis, A. F., 58
Benihasan, 26, 27, *fig. 22*
ben Khalliken, 178
Beresford Hall, Staffordshire, 179, 181
Beresford, John, 181
Bergen Game, 162–3
Berlin, 64
Bhavishya Purana, 52
Bible, Polyglot, 182
Bingo, 163–5
Bishop, 63
Bland, N., 61
Blemyes people, 28
Blocked game, 161, 162, 169, 170
Block Game, 161–2, *fig. 133*
Blot, 41, 45
Boccaccio, 195
Boehmer, Dr., 195
Bone, 70, 175
Bowles and Son, booksellers, 15
Bowl Game, 125–7, *figs. 111, 112*
Boyle, Sir Robert, 184
Brag, 186
Bramfield, 188
Brandenburg, Elector-Prince Frederick
　William of, 62
Britain, games in, 35, 43, 76, 80, 84, 92, 93,
　96, 123, 124, 125, 138, 152

Bruges, 60
Buck Dice, 134
Buck: big, 134; little, 134
Building an Empire, 55
Burma, 65
Bush Negroes, 120
Bustamente, C. M., 7
Buzurjmihr, 57
Byzantine court, 57, 58

Cairo, 27
Calcutta Academy, 189
Calling Nine Hand, 159
Camp (Halma), 98
Cannon, 66–68
Canterbury, 92
Canton, 152
Capita aut Navim, 125
Cardinal tiles, 152, 154
Carlisle, 197
Carnarvon, Lord, 20
Carter, H., 20
Carving, 172, *figs. 138, 140, 155*
Caspian Sea, 177
Caster, 94, 130, 131
Cat, 69
Caxton, Wm., 60, 61
Cazenovia Seminary, 194
Cessolis, Jacobus de, 60
Ceylon, 47, 51, 81, 93, 113, *fig. 69*
Chak t'in kau, **144–6**
Chance point, 130
Chariots, 66, 67
Char-koni, 9, 11
Charlemagne, emperor, 58
Charles II, King, 182
Chasing the Girls, 37–38, *fig. 31*
Chaucer, G., 130
Chausar, 12
Check, 68; Perpetual, 60
Checkers, 72
Checkmate, 60, 68
Chelmsford, 187
Cheshire, F., 106
Chess, 95, 183, 186; Circular, 61, **62,** *fig. 49*; Chinese, **66–68,** *figs. 54, 55, 150, Pl. VIII*; Courier, **62–65,** *figs. 50, 56*; Great Chess, 61, 183; International, **65,** *Pl. IV*; Medieval, 43, *fig. 154*; Shatranj, **57–60,** *fig. 154*; Shaturanga, **51–57**; Tibetan, 70, 90 (*tailpiece*), *fig. 156*
Chess Players, The, **64–65,** *Pl. III*
Chester, 86
Chesters, 84, *fig. 73*
Chichen Itza, 3
China, 42, 65, 92, 99, 147, 151, 152, 192
Chinese Chess, 66–68, *figs. 54, 55, 150, Pl. VIII*
Chisolo, 121–2, *fig. 108*
Chow, 156, 158

Christian X, king of Denmark, 196
Chrosroes I, king of Persia, 57
Chur, 196
Cicero, M. T., 32, 35
Circular Chess, 61, 62, *fig. 49*
Citadels, 62
Civil series, 144–5, 147, *figs. 124, 126*
Claudius, emperor, 33
Codex, *see* Manuscripts
Collecting Tens, 150–1, *fig. 128*
Commodus, emperor, 32
Comparetti, D., 30
Concourse of Shipping, 55
Confucius, 92, 109, 151
Copenhagen, 194
Corner-rattler, 38
Cotton, Charles, 40, 177, **179–82,** *figs. 162, 163*
— Charles (his father), 179
— Isabella (first wife), 179
— Mary (second wife), 180
— Olive (his mother), 179
Cotton manuscript, 59, *fig. 48*
Counters, 157
Courier Chess, 62–65
Cow, 81, 113
Cows and Leopards, 51, 81–82, 173, *figs. 69, 145*
Crabs, 130
Craps, 130, 133
Cr Bri Chualann, 93
Crib, 166
Cribbage, 22, 162, 165, *fig. 16*
Crockford, Wm., 131–3
Cross and Circle games, 1, 6, 8
Crosthwaite, Kate M., 197
Crown and Anchor, 140–1, *figs. 115, 116, 117*
Crown Coffee House, 185
Crowning, 71
Crusades, 58
Culin, R. Stewart, 1, 4, 5, 49, 50, 98, 123, 126, 143, 144, 145, 151, 177, **192–4**
— John, 192
Cunliffe, Lord, 61
Custodian capture, 78, 81, 82, 83, 97, *figs. 71, 85*
Cyprus, 25, 174, *fig. 19*
Cyprus, 169–70, *fig. 136*

Dahomey, 119
Dakarkari people, 95
Damascus, 57
Dame, 71
Dancing Dragon, 143, *fig. 123*
Dante, 195
Dara, 95–96 *fig. 82*
Dead Mass, 103
Dead Wall, 154, *fig. 130*
Decimal pair, 151

Decision: one shot, 129; two shot, 129
'Deliciae Regis', 183
Denbighshire, 31, *fig. 26*
Denmark, 79, 191, 194, 196, *figs. 66, 81*
Dice, **123–5**:
 Bell and Hammer, 139; Chinese, 142, 176, *146 (tailpiece)*, *fig. 157*; cowrie shells, 9, 18, 175, *fig. 9*; Crown and Anchor, 141, *figs. 115, 116, 117*; cubic, 12, 29, 94, 147, *figs. 23, 47, 109, 160*; Dodecahedron, *fig. 160*; Egyptian, 123; Etruscan, 123; grotesque German and Roman, 124, *fig. 110*; Liar, 141, *figs. 118, 119*; long, 10, 25, *figs. 9, 13, 45, 158, 160*; Maiden Castle, 123; pyramidal, 23–4, 123, *figs. 17, 160*; Rome, 123; seeds, 17, 89, 175, *figs. 7, 75, 144*; sticks, 2, 4, 5, 12, 87, 176, *figs. 2, 6, 74, 143, 153, 159*; Sumer, 23–4, 123; Teetotum, *fig. 160*; to make, 176
Dice-box, 29
Disputing Tens, 149–50
Dog, 69
Dominicans, 61
Domino Crib, 165–7, *fig. 134*
Dominoes, Chinese, 147–60, *figs. 126, 127, 128, 132, 157*; European, 160–70, *figs. 132, 133, 134*
Dönhoffstrasse, 64
Double Doublet, 164
Double Heading, 162
Double Twelve, 161
Doubles, 46, 158, 164
Doublet, 39, 45
Dragons, 152, 159
Draughtsman, 72, *fig. 58*
Drawn game, 56, 60, 156
Draughts:
 Continental or Polish, 75, *figs. 61, 142*; Diagonal, **73,** *fig. 59*; English, **71–72,** 75, *figs. 57, 58*; Italian, 73; Losing Game, 72–73; Turkish, 73, *fig. 60*
Drop Dead, 135
Duran, D., 6, 7
Du Chaillu, 79, *figs. 66, 81*
Durai, Mrs. H. G., 122
Dux, 86

Earth's Grace, 159
East's Thirteenth Consecutive Ma-jong, 159
Edward III, King, 125
Edward IV, King, 76
Egypt: Ancient, 20, 21, 22, 25, 26, 28, 29, 47, 57, 58, 86, 87, 92, 112, 123; modern, 28, 82, 87, 111
Elephant, 52, 54, 56, 59, 66, 67, 69, 70
Ellisburg, New York, 194
El-quirkat, 47
Embroidery, 174, *fig. 149*

Emery, W. B., 28, 29
Emperor, 165
Engadine, 195
England, *see* Britain
Enkomi, Cyprus, 25, *fig. 19*
En prise, 48
Ernakulam, 113
Esharhaddon, king of Assyria, 22
Eskimo, 161
Etruscan die, 123, *fig. 109*
Exoniensis, Codex, 35

Fader, 128–9
Falkener, E., 27, 107, 177, **191–2**
Fallas, 41
Faro, 131, 133
Fayles, 41, *fig. 35*
Fellaheen, 82, 86, 123
Fences, 105, *fig. 100*
Fers, 71
Fierges, 71
Fighting Serpents, 50, 172, *figs. 41, 137*
Final Three, 145
Firdausi, 57
First Hand, 106
Fish, Large, 149
Fishing, 148–9
Fishing, 156
Fiske, D. W., 42, 77, 92, 177, **194–6**
Five Field Kono, 98, *fig. 86*
Fitzgerald, R. T. D., 95, *fig. 82*
Flaxman, J., 175
Flowers, 152
Flush: Royal, 142; Low, 142
Forbes, D., 52, 57, 61, 177, **189–90**
Formica, 173, *fig. 145*
Fortification, 107, 108
Fortress, 66
Forty-two, 163
Four Winds Hand, 159
Fox, 76
Fox and Geese, 76–77, 109, *figs. 62, 63, 103*
France, 38, 43, 58, 64, 71, 75, 92, 160
Frederick William, Elector-Prince of Brandenburg, 62
Fredericksberg, 191
Freystafl, 77
Fritillus, 29, 32, *fig. 24*
Full-house, 135
Fuchau, 151
Fyn, 79

Gambia, 119
Gammon, 43
Geese, 76
Gemara (Babylonian Talmud), 42
General (Chinese chess), 66, 67, 68
Gentlemen's Magazine, 190
George IV, King, 131

Germani, 123
Germany, 43, 62, 63, 64, 124, 138
Ghana, 114, 172
Ghazna, 54
Gilcrist, Dr. J. B., 189
Gilding, 173-4
Glenfernate, 189
Gloucester, 92
Go, 166
Go-bang, 96, *fig. 83*
Godolphin, S., 183
Goh, 106
Gokstad ship, 93, *figs. 66, 81*
Golding, Blanche, 191
Goldsmith, O., 16
Gomara, 6, 174
Goose, Royal Game of, 14-16, *fig. 150,*
    Pl. I
Gorizia, 196
Grand Forçat, Le, 75
Grande Acedrez, 36
Gravenburg, W., 63
Greece, 57
Gronow, Capt. R. H., 131
Guiana, 119
Gusman, P., 33
Gye, 132

Hadrian's Wall, 84
Haidarabad, 58
Hala-tafl, 76
Halberstadt, 62
Halma, 98-99, *fig. 87*
Hamilton College, 194
Hampden, J., 183
Hand from Heaven, 159
Handicap (Wei ch'i), 108, 109, *fig. 102*
Hasami Shogi, 97-98, *figs. 84, 85*
Hatshepsut, Queen, 26, *fig. 20*
Hatton Garden, 188
Haus der Kunst, Munich, 65
Hazard, 124, 130-3
Heads and Tails, 125
Heaven, 145
Heraclius, emperor, 57
Herskovits, M. J., 120, *fig. 107*
Hesy, tomb of, 14
Heyshott, 198
High Jump, 83, 84, 86, *figs. 71, 72*
Hillelson, S., 13
Himly, K., 42
Hising, 124
Hitler, Adolf, 64
Hnefatafl, 77, 79-81, 93, 172, 175, *figs.*
    66, 67, 68, 155, Pl. V
Hnefi, 80, *fig. 67A*
Hogarth, Wm., 187
Holt, Denbighshire, 31, *fig. 26*
Honan, 109
Honour tiles, 152, 154

Hornaskella, 38
Horse, 53, 67
Horsemen, 66, 67
Hoyle, E., 131, 161, 177, 185-7, *fig. 164*
Huff, 48, 72
Humbert I, king of Italy, 196
Humphrey, O., 189
Hun Tsun Sii, 42
Hunns, 80, *fig. 67B*
Hyde, Thomas, 51, 92, 177, 182-5, *198*
    (tailpiece), Pl. VI
— Ralph, 182
Hyena, 12-14, 123, *fig. 11*
Hyrcania, 54

Iceland, 37, 76, 80, 195, 196
I-go, 96, 97, *fig. 83; see* Wei ch'i
'Il più col più, 73
Impasse, 104, *fig. 98*
Inciti, 35
India, 9, 17, 42, 51, 54, 57, 58, 65, 87, 113,
    147, 189, 192
Indian Dice, 135-6
Inlay, 172
Inn, 140
Invincible, 165
Innsbrück, 196
Ireland, *see* Britain
Irene, empress, 58
Iron Age, 79
Isidore of Seville, 35
Italy, 43, 73, 92, 94, 123, 160, 195, 196
Ivory, 28, 175, *fig. 154*

James II, King, 182
Japan, 42, 66, 96, 97, 99, 105, 109, 192
Jester, 63
Jeu Forcé, 71, 75; Plaisant, 71
Jito, empress, 42
Jobson, R., 119
Jonson, Ben, 41
Jonsson, Finnur, 76
Joy-leap, 63
Jump, short, 71
Jungle Game, 68-70, *fig. 56*

Kaooa, 173
K'ap t'ai shap, 150-1
Karnak, 112
Kekchi Indians, 89
Khiva, 54
Khusru Parviz, king of Persia, 57
Khwarizm, 54
Kibi, Lord, 109
Kill, 81
King, 59, 62, 70, 71, 72, 75, 77, 78, 165;
    bare, 60
King's College, London, 189
Kinnaird, Perthshire, 189
Kiowa Indians, 4, 176

Knight, 63
Kolowis Awithlaknannai, 49–50
Konakis, 77, 78
Konungahella, 124
Korea, 1, 123, 192
Kramer, Agnes, 89
Kurna, 47, 92, 93, 112, figs. 38, 78, 80
Kwat p'ai, 148

Ladies' Journal, 186
Lake dwellings, 93
Lampridius, A., 32
Lanciani, R., 30, 31, 125
Landor, villa, 195
Lane, E. W., 82, 87, 111
Lansquenet, 132
Lapland, 77, 79, figs. 64, 65
Lasa, T. von der, 94, 197
Lathe, 174, fig. 161
Latrunculi, 33
Lau kata kati, 173
Laws of Manu, 56
Le Havre, 64
Leatherwork, 173, fig. 148
Lebanon, 43
Leipzig, 63, 195
Leofric, 35
Leopards, 81
Leyden, Lucas v., 64, fig. 50, Pl. III
Liar Dice, 141–2, figs. 118, 119
Li'b el Merafib, 12
Libraries: St. Lorenzo del Escorial,
    Madrid, 36; King's College, Newcastle
    on Tyne, 183; Astor, New York, 194;
    Bodleian, Oxford, 182, 186; Victor
    Emmanuel, Rome, 94
Limit, 158
Linnaeus, C., 77, 79, figs. 64, 65
Lion, 69, 70
Londesborough, Lord, 125
London, 61, 92, 131–3, 186, 188, 189, 191,
    196
Loose tiles, 154
Lucretius, M., 191
Ludo, 12, fig. 10
Ludus Duodecim Scriptorum, 30–34,
    figs. 25, 26, 27
Ludus Latrunculorum, 82, 84–87, 172,
    183, figs. 73, 141
Luk tsut k'i, 92
Lurched, 165
Luxor, 113

Macao, 132
Macrobius, A. T., 86
Macuilxochitl, 6
Madrid, 36
Mahadathika Maha-Naga, 93
Maharajah and the Sepoys, 65, fig. 53
Maiden Castle, 123

Main point, 130
Maine, 125
Maize Highway, 89
Ma-Jong, 151–60, 170 (tailpiece), figs.
    129, 130, 131, 132, Pl. VII
Major tiles, 158
Making a point, 45
Mancala games:
    Awari, 119–21, fig. 107
    Chisolo, 121–2, fig. 108
    Mankala'h, 111–13, figs. 104, 105
    Pallanguli, 113–14, 122 (tailpiece), fig.
        152
    Wari, 114–19, fig. 106
    making a cup, 172, fig. 139
Mandarin, 66, 67
Mankala'h, 111–13, figs. 104, 105
Mansura, 58
Manuscripts: Alfonsine, 39, 41, 43, 47, 94,
    fig. 48; Athelstan, 80; Civis Bononiae,
    94; Codex Exoniensis, 35; Cotton, 59;
    North Italian Academies, 94; Persian,
    61
Marelles, 77
Marin, G., 82
Marquetry, 172, fig. 142
Martial, M. V. M., 92
Martinetti, 134, fig. 113
Marylebone, 186
Matador, 168–9, fig. 135
Matching pair, 151
Maurice, emperor, 57
Mayas, 3, 89, figs. 3, 4
McGraw, Jennie, 194
Mecca, 57
Medina, 57
Megiddo, 20, 21, fig. 14
Memphis, 112
Merels, see Morris
Merker's saltmine, 64
Mesopotamia, 23
Metal-work, 174, fig. 152
Mexico, 6, 7, 128
Mihintale, Ceylon, 93
Military series, 144–5, 147, figs. 124, 126
Mill, 94
Mill Hill, 196
Mine Host, 139
Minnows, 149
Minor tiles, 152, 158
Mississippi, 133
Montezuma, 6
Moors, 47
Morphy, P., 194
Morris, see Three, Six and Nine Men's
    Morris
Mouskat, P., 71
Muhammad, 113
Munich: Art Exposition, 36; Haus der
    Kunst, 65

Murray, H. J. R., 22, 62, 80, 100, 101, 177, 196–8
— Sir James H. H., 196
Muscovite, 77, 78
Museums: Blackgate, Newcastle-on-Tyne, 84; British, 26, 57, 58, 187, 189, *fig. 20*; Brooklyn Institute, 192, 193; Cairo, 27, *fig. 21*; Chesters, Northumberland, 84; Kaiser Friedrich, Berlin, 64; Nat. Museum of Wales, 31, *fig. 26*; University of Pennsylvania, 192
Myrine, 34
Mysore, 87

Nard, 27, 42, 43
Nathan ben Jechiel, 42
National Gallery of Art, Washington, 65
Naushirawan, 57
Nazareth Hall, Pennsylvania, 192
Negro's Game, 133
Nerdshir, 42
Nero, emperor, 32, 125
Neutralization (Wei ch'i), 107
New Mexico, 48
New Orleans, 133
Newgate Prison, 15
Newman, J., 191
Nicks, 130
Nigeria, 95, 119
Nine Men's Morris, 79, 93–95, 173, 174, *figs. 66, 80, 81, 147*
Nines, 145
Ningpo, 151
Noddy, 22
Norway, 93, 124
Norwich, 92
Notabae people, 28
Noughts and Crosses, 91, *fig. 76*
Nubia, 28, 29
Nui Seng-ju, 68
Nyout, 1–3, 123, *figs. 1, 2, 159*

Oklahoma, 4
Olaf, king of Norway, 124
Olaf, king of Sweden, 124
Old Hsuoyah, 172
On the Parish, 142
Ones and Nines (Ma-jong), 159
Ordinarii, 35
Oriental Club, 192
Ormskirk, 197
Osese wood, 114, 172
Over the Top, 127
Ovid, P. O. N., 33, 84, 92
Oxford, 80, 184

Pachisi, 9–12, 174, *figs. 8, 9, 149*
Paint work, 172, 173, 175, *figs. 143, 144*
Palenque, 3, *figs. 3, 146*
Palestine, 20, 21

Palestrina, 30, *fig. 25*
Palm Tree Game, 20–22, *figs. 13, 14, 15*
Pallanguli, 113–14, 173, 174, *122 (tail-piece), fig. 152*
Pam-nyout, 2
Panther, 69
Paper boards, 174, *figs. 150, 151*
Paris, 75, 191
Parker, H., 47, 81
Pass, 169, 170
Passamaquoddy Indians, 125
Patolli, 6–8, *figs. 7, 144*
Pawn, 53, 59, 63; privileged, 56; promotion of, 55
Perpetual attack, 100, 104, *fig. 99*; check, 60; positions, 108
Persia, 42, 57
Perspex, 174, 175, *figs. 153, 157*
Petrarch, 195
Petrie, F., 14, 111, 112, *fig. 105*
Philadelphia, 192
Pieces: bone, 175, *figs. 155, 156, 157*; cowrie shells, 175, *fig. 149*; ebony, 175, *fig. 154*; faience, *fig. 153*; ivory, 175, *fig. 154*; marbles, 176; perspex, 175, *fig. 157*; pottery, 175, *fig. 158*; sea-shells, 175; seeds, 176, *figs. 138, 152*; wood, 174–5, *figs. 52, 140, 141, 142, 143, 147, 149, 150, 151, Pl. IIb*
Pig, 128
Piquet, 186
Plaisant, 71
Playing Heavens and Nines, 151
Point Number, 134
Points, 43; making, 45; game, 46
Poker work, 171, *fig. 137*
Poland, 74, 75
Polo, Marco, 160
Pompeii, 33, 86, 191, *199 (afterpiece), figs. 28, 29*
Pottery, 173, 175, *figs. 146, 158*
Prevailing Wind, 156
Priest of the Bow, 49
Prime Minister, 59
Pryle, 142
Puff, 43
Puluc, 89–90, *fig. 75*
Pung, 155, 158
Put and Take, 146, *fig. 125*
Pyrgus, 32, *fig. 24*

Quadrille, 186
Queen, 63
Quinn, J. P., 133
Quirkat, 47
Quong, 155, 158; robbing a, 156
Qustul, 28, 29, 31, *fig. 23*

Raichi, 78
Rajah, 51, 52, 54, 55

Rashepses, 26
Rat, 69, 70
Rattray, R. S., 115, *fig. 106*
Rawson, R., 179
Red Mallet Six, 145
Regaining a throne, 54
Reindeer, 78
Reversi, 75-75
Rexine, 173, *fig. 147*
Reykjavik, 195
Rhaeto-Romance language, 195
Rhodesia, Northern, 121
Richborough, 84
Rimington-Wilson, J. W., 197
River (Chinese chess), 66
Roberts, Alice, 193
Roka, 56
Roman soldiers, 28, 29, 31, *fig. 160*
Rome, 15, 32, 92, 94, 123, *fig. 27*
Rook, 63
Royal Academy, 187, 188, 191
Royal Asiatic Society, 190
Rubbish Holes, 114
Ruhk, 59
Ruiz, A., 3
Ruppert, K., 3
Russell, Lt.-Col., 64
Ryland, W. W., 187, 188 n.

Sagas, 77, 80
Sage, 63
Sahagun, Fr. Bernardino de, 6
Sahe, 5
St. Andrews University, 189, 190
St. Kitts, 120, *fig. 107*
St. Lorenzo del Escorial, Madrid, 36
St. Moritz, 196
Sakkarah, 26
Saladin, 58
Salisbury, 92
Sanskrit, 56
Sapper, K. von, 89
Saracens, 58
Saramacca, 120, *fig. 107*
Sargon, king of Assyria, 22
Saturnalia, 35
Scandinavia, 75, 77
Scarne, J., 134, *fig. 113*
Schimmel, 138-40
Schulz, 195
Scotland, *see* Britain
Scott, Sir W., 189
Screen (Chinese chess), 68
Seasons, 152
Seega, 82-84, 85, 86, *fig. 70*
Seizing a throne, 54
Senat, 25, 26, 174, *figs. 19, 153*
Selenus, G., 63
Sennacherib, king of Assyria, 22
Sequences, 136-7

Seville, 35
Shanghai, 151, 152
Sharp, Dr. G., 184
Shatranj, 57-60, 62, 65, 66, 178, *figs. 47, 48, Pl. IIb*
Shaturanga, 51-57, *figs. 44, 45, 46, 47, 160, Pl. IIa*
Shepherd, J., 14-15
Ship, 53, 55, 56, *fig. 46*
Ship, Captain, Mate and Crew, 136
Shipping, concourse of, 55
Shooter, 128-9
Short jump, 71
Siang K'i, 66-68
Sicily, 43
Silko, king of the Notabae, 28
Six Men's Morris, 92, *fig. 79*
Sixe-Ace, 39-41, *figs. 33, 34*
Sixteen Soldiers, 50-51, *fig. 42*
Slain (Puluc), 90
Soldiers (Chinese chess), 68
Solitaire, 109-10, *fig. 103*
Somali people, 82, 84, 86, *fig. 71, 72*
Spain, 35, 43, 47, 58
Spens Report, 197
Spoil Five, 96
Stack, 90, 148
Stalemate, 68; strangled, 60
Standing hand, 156
Starter, 166
Stralock, 189
Strangled stalemate, 60
Ströbeck, 62, 63
Stone Warriors, 48-49, *fig. 40*
Strung Flowers, 143-4, *figs. 120, 121, 122, 123*
Strutt, J., 61, 160, 177, **187-9**
Suckling, Sir J., 22
Sudan, 12, 28
Suetonius, G., 33
Sultan (race horse), 131
Sumer, 22, 123, *frontispiece, figs. 15, 17, 18, 160*
Sumerian Game, 23-25
Sung period, 42
Sunoroko, 42
Supreme pair, 148, 149
Swahili, 121
Swedes, 77, 78
Syracuse, 194
Syria, 57, 58
Sz'ng luk, 143-4

Tab, 87, 123
Taba, 13
Ta'biyat, 60
Tablan, 87-89, 172, *figs. 74, 143*
Tablas de Alcedrez, 36
Tablas reales, 43
Table, inner, 43, 45; outer, 43

208 INDEX

Tablemen, 71, *46 (tailpiece)*, *fig. 141*
Tables, 36, 37, 43, *figs. 36, 141*
Tablut, 77–79, *figs. 64, 65*
Tabula, 33, **34–35**, 86, *fig. 30*
Tacitus, C., 123
Tafl, **75–81**
Talmud, 42
Talorum, 183
Tamberlane, 61, 183
Tamil, 20, 113
Tarasp, 195
Tattersall's, 131
Taunton, 197
Tavole reale, 43
Teetotum, 146, *fig. 160*
Thaayam, **17–20**, 51, *fig. 12*
Thebes, 20, 21, 22, 112, *fig. 13*
Thillai-nayagam, Dr., 20
Thirteen Odd Majors, 159
Thirty-Six, 127
Thirty Squares, Game of, **26–28**, *figs. 20, 158*
Three Men's Morris, **91–92**, *figs. 77, 78*
Three Scholars, 159
Throne, 54
Throwing Heaven and Nine, **144–6**, *fig. 124*
Thurayya, 178
Tibetan chess, 70, 175, *90 (tailpiece)*, *fig. 156*
Tiger, 69, 70
Tiles, blank, 161; cardinal, 152, 154; counting, 163; flower, 152, *170 (tailpiece)*; honour, 152, 154; loose, 154; major, 158; minor, 152, 158
Timgad, 32, *fig. 27*
Tiu ü, 148–9
Todas Tablas, 43
Togoland, 119
Tong, 153, *fig. 129*
Torquemada, Juan de, 6
Tourne-case, **38–39**, *fig. 32*
Tower of London, 191
Trajan, emperor, 86
Trap, 69, 70
Travancore-Cochin, 113, 174, *fig. 152*
Trento, 196
Tric-trac, 43
Trimalchio, 92
Triple Heading, 162
Triplets, 164
Troy, 93
T'shu-p'u, 42
Tsung shap, 149–50
Tuichi, 78
Turkey, 73
Tutankhamen, 26
Twain, Mark, 195
Twenty-six, 137

Twittering of the Sparrows, 154
Tyburn, 15
Tze, 100–1, *110 (tailpiece)*

Ude (chef), 132
Udine, 196
Universities: Cornell, 194, 196; Durham, 183; Oxford, 182, 186, 196; Pennsylvania, 192; St. Andrews, 189, 190; Uppsala, 194
Uppsala, 194
Ur, 21, 23, 25, *frontispiece*, *figs. 15, 17, 18*

Vagi, 35
Varnish, 176
Varro, M. T., 84
Vesuvius, 33
Victim, 60
Viking, 79, 93
Voluntary Doubling, 46

Wadi es Sebua, 28
Wales, *see* Britain
Walton, I., 180, *fig. 162*
War Horse, 59
Wari, **114–19**, 172, *figs. 106, 137*
Washington, 65
Wei-ch'i, 68, 96, 97, **99–109**, 183, *110 (tailpiece)*, *figs. 83, 84, 88, 89, 90, 91, 92, 93, 94, 95, 96, 97, 98, 99, 100, 101, 102*
Wei dynasty, 42
Wellington, Duke of, 132
West Indies, 119
Westminster Abbey, 92
Wheelock, Prof., 182
White, A. S., 91
— J. C., 197
White Horse, 139
Whitehouse, F. R. B., 15
Whisk, 185
Whist, 185
Wiesbaden, 64
Wild, J., 15
William III, King, 182
Wimose, 79, 80, *fig. 66*
Wind discs, 153, *fig. 129*
Wind of the Round, 156
Winds, 152, 153, 156–7, 159, *fig. 131*
Wolf, 69
Woolley, Sir Leonard, 21, 23
Wolverhampton, 15
Woodperry, Oxfordshire, 80, *fig. 67*
Woodpile, 148, 149, *figs. 127, 128*
Wright, T., 124, *fig. 110*

Yucatan, 3

Zeno, emperor, 33, 34, 35, *fig. 30*
Zohn Ahl, **4–5**, 174, *figs. 5, 6, 148, 159*
Zuni Indians, 48, 49

Printed in Great Britain by Western Printing Services Limited Bristol

30102

794
B41

Date Due

1/12/64			
APR 5 '77			
MAY 6 '80			
NOV 25 1980			
OCT 18 1983			
JAN 6 00			

NYACK MISSIONARY COLLEGE
Nyack, New York